"*Michael is one of Africa's foremost evangelists and prophets. I fully commend his thoughtful offering to fellow travellers.*"

– Moss Ntlha, General Secretary of The Evangelical Alliance of South Africa

"*I wonder how this author could dig so deep. Surely, God, the Holy Spirit has given these insights.*"

– Professor B. E. Vijayam, founder of Carmel University, Hyderabad

"*What endears me to him more than anything is his passion for the Lord Jesus Christ.*"

– Angus Buchan, author of *Faith Like Potatoes*

"*I've learned that prayer involves listening as much as talking, aligning us with what God wants done in the world more than what we want God to do for us. Michael Cassidy's life models that principle.*"

– Philip Yancey, author of *What's So Amazing About Grace?*

"*Michael Cassidy has lived a life of Christian nobility, and numberless people are in the embrace of Christ's love because of his faithful efforts. Don't pick up* The Church Jesus Prayed For *if you are looking for quick fixes, shallow inspirations, simple formulas. Its reading will not be completed in a two hour plane flight. No, the book is the scholarship of a lifetime, and it comes from a man who has lived out what he has written. Cassidy is an author you can trust.*"

– Gordon MacDonald, Chancellor, Denver Seminary

"*I don't know anybody as qualified to write with such mor   d biblical authority. Michael's vision and courage were kev mobilizing the church in South Africa to challenge a most evil and divisive systems in the world, namel the product of a lifetime of dynamic leadership. hope for our broken world at a time when w*"

– S. Douglas Birdsall, Executive Chair World Evangelization

"*Michael Cassidy has put his heart, soul and .   what might end up as a landmark study of John 17, arguably the g   t, deepest and most mysterious chapter in the whole Bible... I warmly commend this terrific book.*"

– Lord Carey, Archbishop of Canterbury 1991–2002

"For more than 50 years I have observed Michael's amazing achievements in evangelism, feeding the hungry, subverting apartheid, leading African Enterprise and bringing reconciliation throughout the continent of Africa. He is one of the spiritual giants of our day, and it is all sustained by prayer. This is a lasting contribution to the renewal of the church into what Jesus longed for it to be. It is profound but full of illuminating stories. It is a book to buy and to give away. Don't miss it. It will be a classic for generations still to come."

– Canon Dr Michael Green, Oxford

"Michael Cassidy brilliantly unpacks the wonders and mysteries of Jesus' prayer in John 17 and opens our eyes to what the church is truly meant to be. This is Cassidy at his best: his theological analysis is incisive, his wisdom penetrating and his stories deeply illuminating. This is the writing of a true elder statesman of the faith and an absolute must-read."

– Rebecca Manley Pippert, Salt Shaker Ministries

"Throughout the world, the church has often forgotten that she is called to model the very Trinitarian nature of God characterised by Truth, Holiness and loving Unity. Michael Cassidy has wrestled with precisely the same issues, especially in the context of South Africa. His exposition of John 17 is therefore a sharp reminder to Christians to get back to basics, so that the world may know the wonder of the Gospel and believe."

– Bishop Hwa Yung, The Methodist Church in Malaysia

"I have known Michael and worked under his great ministry many times. His practical faith, deep knowledge of Jesus, his willingness to expend his life for the Gospel, and his many years of walking with Christ are all reflected in his work here on the High Priestly Prayer of Jesus. This volume is a blessing waiting to be poured out like the oil of anointing. May God breathe on this book."

– Most Revd Henry Orombi, Archbishop of Uganda

"In this book Michael cuts through the doubts and hesitations that often descend on us when in despair about the uncertain witness of the church. He points us to the amazing gift that the church continues to be – because Christ deems it so."

– Revd Dr Mvume Dandala, former Presiding Bishop of the Methodist Church of Southern Africa, and former General Secretary of the All-Africa Conference of Churches

THE CHURCH
JESUS
PRAYED FOR

A personal journey into John 17

Michael Cassidy

MONARCH
BOOKS

Oxford, UK & Grand Rapids, Michigan, USA

Published by Monarch Books
an imprint of
Lion Hudson plc
Wilkinson House, Jordan Hill Road,
Oxford OX2 8DR, England
www.lionhudson.com/monarch
monarch@lionhudson.com

ISBN 978 0 85721 330 3
e-ISBN 978 0 85721 380 8

First edition 2012

A catalogue record for this book is available from the British Library

Printed and bound in the UK, October 2012, LH27.

For my Christian friends, both old and young,
most supremely Carol, my best of friends
– but also others in my family,
in the work of African Enterprise,
especially my late mentor Calvin Cook,
plus many I'm privileged to know in the church across
Africa,
and around the world,
– all of whom long and labour to see the advent of
The Church Jesus Prayed For

Also by Michael Cassidy:

Where Are You Taking The World Anyway?
Prisoners of Hope
I Will Heal Their Land (ed)
Facing The New Challenges (ed)
A Passion For Preaching
Together in one Place
Thinking Things Through
In Deep In India
Bursting the Wineskins
Chasing the Wind
The Passing Summer
The Politics of Love
A Witness For Ever
Window On The Word
The Relationship Tangle
Christianity For the Open-Minded
Getting to the Heart of things
What on Earth Are You Thinking for Heaven's Sake?
So, You Want To Get Married?

Contents

About African Enterprise and Michael Cassidy

African Enterprise (AE) was founded by Michael Cassidy in 1961. It is a non-racial, interdenominational and Pan African ministry sprung from African soil which firmly believes Africa will become the fulcrum of world mission some time in the twenty-first century. AE's aim of "Evangelising the cities of Africa through word and deed in partnership with the church" is contributing, via citywide evangelistic campaigns, to spiritual renewal and the transformed lives of thousands who have been brought to personal faith in Jesus Christ.

However AE seeks also to demonstrate the love of Christ in powerful, tangible ways. In addition to preaching the gospel, AE's peacemaking work has been ongoing in formerly violence-wracked countries such as Rwanda, Burundi and (Congo) DRC since the mid-1990s. Thousands of widows and orphans of the 1994 Rwandan genocide have been assisted and ministered to. Prostitutes and street children are discipled and given job training in Ghana, while Foxfire youth evangelists in Kenya, South Africa, and Zimbabwe impact the lives of countless young people, equipping them – among other things – to live according to biblical sexual standards, thus enabling them to avoid the ravages of the HIV / AIDS epidemic.

Among the more remarkable contributions of AE were its pre election endeavours in South Africa in 1994, when AE founder Michael Cassidy played a crucial backstage role in bringing in the Kenyan diplomat, Dr Washington Okumu, who – with others – facilitated the political breakthrough which averted near-certain civil war.

African Enterprise has sought, in the spirit of John 17, to be a unifying force among Christians by spearheading the largest Christian interdenominational leadership gatherings in Africa over the last generation: at the South African Congress on Mission and Evangelism in Durban (1973); the Pan African Christian Leadership Assembly in Nairobi (1976 and 1994); the South African Christian Leadership Assembly in Pretoria (1979 and 2003); and the National Initiative for the Reformation of South Africa (NIRSA) in 2008. Michael also led and chaired the Marriage Alliance of South Africa.

AE has ten teams based around Africa in South Africa, Zimbabwe, Malawi, Tanzania, Uganda, Kenya, Rwanda, (Congo) DRC, Ghana, and Ethiopia, as well as a number of support offices around the world.

Michael Cassidy is a Christian leader, an internationally respected evangelist, the author of many books, and the founder of African Enterprise. In 2012 he was made the Honorary Chairman of the Lausanne Movement for World Evangelization, succeeding the late John Stott. He was educated at Michaelhouse, the University of Cambridge, and Fuller Theological Seminary and holds an honorary doctorate from Azusa Pacific University. He was also made the Distinguished Alumnus of Fuller Seminary for 2012. He and his wife Carol have three married children and eight grandchildren, and live in Pietermaritzburg, South Africa.

Foreword

Michael Cassidy has been writing this book for fifty years. For a long time he did not know he was writing it. He was in fact living out the theme of the book – he was living John 17. John 17 contains Jesus' prayer for his church and it is this that Michael had embraced as the basic text for his life. He lived it for thirty-seven years before he even started writing. Then thirteen years ago he put pen to paper and has now completed what you now hold in your hands: *The Church Jesus Prayed For*.

I am not acquainted with anyone more qualified or with better credentials for writing a book on the church and Jesus and prayer. African Enterprise, the evangelistic mission that Michael founded and has given leadership to, has provided a major Christian voice throughout the continent of Africa, developing communities of Christians among the many African countries who have been making a difficult transition from colonialism to independence. It is hard to imagine a more difficult environment in which to establish a mature Christian witness than in Africa with its many languages, and so many tribal and spiritual elements – many inimical to the Christian gospel. But African Enterprise has been tireless, persistent, and imaginative in gathering thousands of men and women, primarily in the larger African cities, into "the church Jesus prayed for".

At the same time, Michael, as a citizen of South Africa, was living in a nation that was crippled by apartheid. This political legislation divided the population into black and white and resulted in enormous oppression and suffering.

But apartheid was also firmly entrenched in the church, with many Christians in consequence worshipping in segregated congregations. As a result, Michael, alongside others in the South African church, worked diligently and quietly behind the scenes for many years, mediating gatherings of leaders from black and white factions of the church and government until apartheid eventually crumbled thus allowing the church Jesus prayed for to eventually be free to work at becoming "completely one" (John 17:31).

Michael Cassidy's influence was not confined to Africa; in fact it penetrated the world church. Michael and I, for instance, first became acquainted when together we led a week-long gathering of the Presbyterian Church in Ireland, a church that had struggled for decades with the "Troubles" of post 1963. I heard and admired the gentle and gracious way he made present and possible the church Jesus prayed for among Christians who had been for so long pressurised by divisive leaders.

A couple of years later Michael and his wife Carol spent a few days with me and my wife, Jan, at our home in Montana. That was when I first learned of Michael's intention to write a book on John 17; this long prayer of Jesus that he had been participating in for so many years in his preaching and teaching and travel. As he left he asked us to pray for him in the writing of this book.

That was thirteen years ago. From time to time, throughout these thirteen years, I would remember Michael's request and pray for him and this book. As I did this I would say, "Lord Jesus, it's time to join Michael in the 'John Seventeen Prayer Meeting'." The more I did that the more I have come to realise how important and timely the "John Seventeen Prayer Meeting" is for the church worldwide and for the political culture in which we live today. I have also been inviting others to join me.

Two things stand out in this completed exposition of *The Church Jesus Prayed For*. The first is tone: gentleness; ease; compassion; dignity; and respect permeate these pages. This is unusual. The prevailing climate in so many quarters is accusation and complaint. "I love Jesus but I hate the church" has achieved mantra status in many areas. Well, Jesus certainly didn't hate the church.

And then there is this: praying for the church involves us in many interlocking acts and understandings, theological insights, and biblical contexts. Becoming and praying in the church Jesus prayed for involves an immersion in a highly intricate and complex communion of saints and sinners and all the operations of the Trinity. Everything contributes to the being of everything else, enabling everything to be what it distinctively is. Every person has to do with every other person. There are never one or two things that will accomplish Jesus' prayer. There is no "solution" offered here, no over-simplification provided. All (whether they know it or not) are involved, whether in submission or in resistance to the Holy Spirit. A new generation of baptised sinners enters the ranks of church every thirty years or so and calls forth new acts of obedience and faith and worship. Ten marks of the church Jesus prayed for are identified, but we cannot pick out two or three and specialise in them – they are all happening at the same time. The reality of church is highly complex and cannot be hurried or coerced. Attentiveness and patience are required.

But in this masterful exposition, written out of a lifetime of faithful living in and serving the church, there is no idealism, no romanticism, nothing naïve. No. In Chapter 1, Michael tells us that "another reality was constantly running through my soul and that was a deep sense of perplexity that generally speaking I couldn't see around me (by and large) the church Jesus prayed for, though isolated congregations here and there approximated."

It is understandable that many survey this sorry track record and decide to leave the room where Jesus is praying and take matters into their own hands. Some Christians, impatient with what they perceive as the inefficiency of Jesus' prayer, attempt to solve the problem by coercion, imposing unity and truth by an authority depersonalised into an institution. Any person or congregation who refuses to conform is excluded: anathematised, excommunicated, or shunned. Church is depersonalised and prayer is stifled.

Other Christians who are also impatient with Jesus' prayer solve the problem by reducing the scale of church to what can be managed by gathering men and women of like mind and spirit and then split off, reducing church to something more like an exclusive club. The repetitive urgency with which Jesus prays that we be one just as He is one with the Father, exposes this reduction as something more like an act of defiance, defying Jesus in the cause of Jesus. But such defiance doesn't prevent Jesus' prayer from finally doing its work – slowly, incrementally, marvellously.

When we stay in the room with Jesus as He prays for us, we will eventually acquire a readiness to embrace all who are baptised as brothers and sisters. It may be slow in coming, but the prayer Jesus prayed for His church will have its way with us. Jesus is our master in prayer; He is also our companion in prayer. He says to us "I'll pray for you..." – and does it. His promise to pray for us is not lost or overlooked in a vast heavenly clutter of petitions and intercessions, confessions and thanksgivings, ascending in a cloud of incense to His altar. It defeats our imagination to understand how this takes place, but we have it on good authority that it does.

In this masterful, comprehensive, and timely book Michael Cassidy keeps Jesus' prayer for His church current, contemporary, local, and personal. We are immersed in a Jesus-relational prayer in which we are included – every one of us.

Eugene H. Peterson
Professor Emeritus of Spiritual Theology
Regent College, Vancouver, BC

Preface

This preface has a story because it has two parts: a "then" part, and a "now" part. Both parts were written during "solitude" retreats. The "then" part was written thirteen years ago on the West Coast of Canada. The date and place, says the sign-off at the end, was "March 1999, Jabulani Cabin, Sunshine Valley, British Columbia".

The "now" part is January 2012, in Shambala Cottage, owned by my son-in-law and daughter, Gary and Debbie Kirsten, on the Breede River in the Western Cape, South Africa. Both are brilliant places of solitude and quiet, the one midst mighty mountains, the other on a restful riverbank. And the God of heaven and earth and of mountains and rivers owns and presences Himself in both places. That is very special.

So, the "then" part.

*** ***

I pen these words from the silent solitude of a wood cabin in the Coastal Mountains east of Vancouver, Canada. My dear friends and colleagues in African Enterprise, David and Lesley Richardson, have loaned me this piece of paradise for some days of retreat and quiet and for seeking the Lord's face for myself and for this book. Total silence reigns outside. The ground is covered with that purity of whiteness which only freshly fallen snow can bring. A log fire burns and the only sounds are those of the licking of flames and crackling wood. Outside it is several inhospitable degrees below zero. Inside I am warm and cosy.

The name of this cabin is "Jabulani" – Zulu for "rejoice" or "sing for joy". And I do rejoice. In fact this afternoon I walked and talked and rejoiced before the Lord as I stomped over snow and ice in the blessing of being alive and well. I rejoiced in and thanked God sequentially and chronologically for all He had done for me these last sixty-three years in giving me marvellous parents, a wonderful wife, a precious family, grand friends, amazing work colleagues, and an astonishing richness of experiences and Christian ministry across the years. I rejoiced too, and blessed Him, for those who first put me on the road to faith and finally led me to Christian commitment.

As it happened, I also asked the Lord to touch my heart afresh with His love for the church of Jesus Christ and all who are in it, in spite of the many weaknesses and failings in both institution and individuals. For while there is so much that is both lovable and laudable in so many in the church, there is also much that is both damning and deplorable. Not only do I see this dichotomy in others, but more depressing personally is the fact that I also see it and know it most acutely in myself. Yes, I see the enemy in the church. And it is I.

That's why when I got back to Jabulani Cabin this evening I first listened to a worship tape for an hour to fix my soul on the Lord and His holiness and majesty. Then I spent a long time searching and seeing so many wicked ways in my own heart. Then I confessed them sequentially to God, claiming His forgiveness and cleansing.

How else but with worship and confession could one start to write a book on the Christian church, first as it is – and then as it is meant to be, according to the prayer Jesus prayed in St John's Gospel, chapter 17?

*** ***

That was then. At which point I went on to narrate how I got interested in this John 17 chapter – material which I have now put into Chapter 1 of the book.

In fact at that point (1999), I went on to write about half of the book as first visualised. But it wasn't really coming together satisfactorily. And I got discouraged, as well as over-busy and unduly preoccupied with other pressures and challenges in our ministry. So the book went into cold storage for some ten years before a mix of conscience and the Lord's Spirit, I think – and hope – prompted me to get it out and underway again in a major rework.

The final fruit you now have before you. If truth be told, I feel OK about the delay, because what has now come forth is in my view a better product – hopefully more mature and more deeply considered.

Now as I sit here at "Dad's Writing Desk" (as Debbie calls it) in Shambala Cottage, I look out on pristine South African riverine and the breathtaking beauty of the Breede River, two-and-a-half hours north of Cape Town.

The early evening sky is bathing the river in pink and the mountainous bank and outcrop opposite has a warm, orange glow.

It's an ideal place to do some final topping and tailing, plus adjustments here and there, with a few last minute additions.

For sure, it has been an adventure grappling with this most major, arguably most important and certainly most mysterious of chapters in all the Bible. I am acutely conscious of only having touched the hem of its garment. I imagine in another lifetime and upon another shore I will reach a fuller understanding.

But if in the meantime what I here set forth can in even modest measure challenge the Lord's people in many places to strive in new ways after the church Jesus prayed for, I will feel well rewarded, and will surely say a *Jabulani* or two. Most assuredly does this tired old planet need this church Jesus prayed for as maybe never before.

As to how the book may be read, studied, or used in groups, please note the suggestions that follow this preface.

Inevitably, there are more people to thank than I can

possibly enumerate adequately. But pride of place must go to my indefatigable and amazing secretary Brenda Harrison, whose vast typing labours and endless patience with my seemingly endless edits must earn her numerous feathers in caps, jewels in crown, and mention in despatches. Then my editorial assistant, Megan Whatley, and executive assistant David Rees have put in sterling labours of note. Thank you, you are both serious stars. And, Megan, I especially bless you, dear one, for your huge labours on the bibliography and index. My late and most esteemed mentor over fifty-one years, Calvin Cook, counselled me all along the way, prayed fervently for the finalising of the text and gave such wise encouragement when I most needed it. How I miss his counsel and friendship! I hope that in heaven he is happy with the final product. I also had a lovely team of editors who in November 2011 went over the volume page by page, secured hard-fought cutting (I hate murdering my darlings!) and challenged me to think through better on assorted chapters. Heading this list are my long-time friends Philip le Feuvre and Hugh Wetmore whose theological acumen saved me again and again from bad slips or poor thinking. Others in that editorial team were Peter Veysie, Paul Culwick, Nellis du Preez, Lunga Dlungwana, Linda Grant, and Darien Khlentzos, the latter having done an amazing job in converting many of my RSV quotations to NRSV, which numbers of friends finally thought would be more feasible. Thank you, brother. My sister Olave Snelling and former colleague Abiel Thipanyane made useful suggestions for the chapter on Protection from Evil Supernaturalism.

I also in 2010 had a group of about fifty friends come to AE for a conference on the John 17 chapter and they were both long-suffering and gracious enough to let me teach and lecture through the chapters while they gave creative critiques plus a bucket-load of good suggestions.

Nor must I forget those I listed at the end of the preface of 1999, so many of whom gave major counsel or provided me during that sabbatical with havens and shelter where I could read, study, think, and write. I think of Frank Brock, then President of Covenant College (Lookout Mountain, Tennessee), Don Page, then President of Trinity Western University (Langley, British Columbia), Jim Houston, then at Regent College (Vancouver, BC), Graham Cray, then Principal of Ridley College (Cambridge), and Alister McGrath, then Principal at Wycliffe College (Oxford). Eugene Peterson, in our stay with him and Jan at Lake Flathead, Montana in February 2009, always had wise words and such warm encouragement and was also wonderfully affirmative about the volume from the very inception of the idea. And I also bless him with all my heart for his warm and gracious foreword to the book. Thank you, dear friend. David and Lesley Richardson lent Jabulani Cabin, and Gary and Debbie Kirsten lent Shambala Cottage. Such blessings. Thank you, guys. Canadian intern Lori Hargreaves and my former PA, the late Yvonne Whitton, dug out material from dozens of commentaries. And my secretary back then, the splendid Colleen Smith, put in huge labours on my very first draft manuscripts. I am thankful to Derryn Hurry, who also helped me in times gone by with a couple of my other books, for thoughts and insights given me along the way. I must not forget the SA Board of African Enterprise who sanctioned that 1999 sabbatical and the Canadian AE Board and David Richardson who made my stay in British Columbia not only possible, but also so pleasurable and restorative.

Special gratitude must also go to Monarch Books, and most especially Tony Collins who graciously believed in this volume and then steered it so capably through all the publishing processes. I am so thankful also to Miranda Lever and Jenny Ward for their meticulous and very professional work on all the final details of the final text. A huge task.

Most certainly are there numbers of people left out to whom I owe gratitude for encouragement and help. Please forgive my amnesia for any such omissions.

But I can't and won't leave out my beloved Carol who, in this writing venture as in others, always stands back of me with prayerful support and astonishing patience. At times she must want to cast these writing ventures to outer darkness, but she refrains and just keeps the encouragement going. Thank you, darling.

It's now dark over the Breede River and time for me to terminate this preface and entrust this volume to the Lord's tender care. May He prosper what reflects His mind and Spirit and forgive all places of error, of which I suspect there are a good many.

Michael Cassidy
Dad's Writing Desk,
Shambala Cottage,
Lemoentuin,
Breede River,
Western Cape
January 2012

Using the book in groups

My suggestions for using this book in groups would be along these lines:

1. First of all, let each member of the group individually, and privately, read the first five chapters beforehand to get the setting, key ideas, outline, and flow of the prayer. Maybe each person could even photocopy for ease of reference a couple of the diagrams outlining the chronology of events and the prayer's major headings.

2. Then as the group assembles, start in on Chapter 6 ("Truth"), the first of the ten marks that Jesus prayed for, with this, as with the others, having been read privately ahead of time by each group member before the group session.

3. Then take the mark to be studied (such as truth, joy, or mission) and discuss in the groups how each person, initially at least, feels they or their church would score out of ten. Honestly. I mean honestly. Ten is full marks. Nine is brilliant. Five is poor. Three is dreadful. If, for example, struggling with truth is only average in you and your congregation, then score yourself five. Likewise, if you have no real mission(s) programme, or no serious grappling with protection from evil supernaturalism, then score yourself or yourselves zero and begin doing something about it. And so on.

   At the end of the study course it will be instructive to work up your or your church's overall percentage score. Then ask – where from here? How can I or we fix this? How can we become more truly like the church that Jesus prayed for?

If we are not that, then courageous honesty must acknowledge it, bring forth repentance, and work on change.

4. While the group reads the chapter ahead of time, the leader can draw forth out of his or her own ingenuity several key discussion questions. For example:

- How did this chapter speak to you?
- What points brought a particular challenge?
- How does our home group, church, congregation or para-church organisation measure up against this particular mark? (e.g. Truth? Holiness? Mission? Prayer? Love? Unity?)
- What could be done to change this? Or improve things?
- What could or should each of us do to make practical progress, for example, in:
  » Prayer?
  » Joy?
  » Mission and witness?
  » Facing evil supernaturalism?
  » And so on.

5. End up praying together about how the mark under discussion can more fully be embraced by each individual and each congregation.

6. Homework: The group leader then reminds the group that each individual should read the next chapter (next mark) ahead of time and be ready to discuss it when the group meets again.

Chapter 1

A Thirty-five-year Itch

The Story of the Birthing of an Idea

"As for my next book, I am going to hold myself from writing it till I have it impending in me: grown heavy in my mind like a ripe pear: pendant, grand, asking to be cut or it will fall."

Virginia Woolf

"Now write what you see…"

Revelation 1:19

This book comes from the convergence of three impulses:

- *Firstly* a thirty-five-year-old itch to write a reflection on John 17 and the church Jesus prayed for;
- *Secondly* to explore my perplexity in not often seeing the church Jesus prayed for around me;
- *Thirdly* the urging from a number of friends to tell the story of my own persevering experience to see the church Jesus prayed for become more of a reality in this tired and troubled old world.

Impulse 1: A thirty-five-year itch

In 1974, the epoch-making International Congress on World Evangelization took place in Lausanne, Switzerland. One year later, the Continuation Committee met in Mexico City and formed the Lausanne Committee for World Evangelization (LCWE). Bishop Jack Dain of Sydney, Australia, was our chairman, and evangelical leaders from a score of countries were present. John Stott took us through our Bible studies each day and one of his themes was that of John 17. In his lucid and inimitable expository style he explored four marks that Jesus prayed would characterise the church – namely truth, holiness, mission, and unity.

I had of course read this chapter of John's Gospel many times in my life, but that day it lit up for me as never before and I came spontaneously to conclude with the great bishop, J. C. Ryle, that this chapter "is the most remarkable in the Bible. It stands alone. And there is nothing like it."[1]

As I began to explore the chapter further and to preach or lecture on it I saw and appreciated more and more why others had reached similar conclusions to Ryle.

The Reformer Martin Luther once wrote of the chapter: "It is so deep, so rich, so wide, no one can fathom it."[2]

Philip Melanchthon, another of the Reformers, said in his last lecture before his death: "There is no voice which has ever been heard, either in heaven or on earth, more exalted, more holy, more fruitful, more sublime, than this prayer offered up by the Son to God Himself."[3]

John Brown, in *An Exposition of Our Lord's Intercessory Prayer*, put it this way: "The seventeenth chapter of the Gospel of John is, without doubt, the most remarkable portion of the most remarkable book in the world."[4]Archbishop William Temple once reflected that "it is perhaps the most sacred passage even in the four Gospels".[5]

John Stott himself wrote:

> *John 17, without doubt, is one of the profoundest chapters of the Bible. Whole books have been written to expound it. There are depths here we will never fathom; all we can do is paddle in the shallows. Here are heights we cannot scale; we can only climb the foothills. Nevertheless, we must persevere. For if the upper-room discourse (John 13–16) is the temple of Scripture, John 17 is its inner sanctuary or holy of holies. Here we are*

introduced into the presence, mind and heart of God.
We are permitted to eavesdrop, as the Son communes
with the Father. We need to take off our shoes, since this
is holy ground.[6]

But the fascination with this chapter is not simply a preoccupation of the past. A friend of mine said she had googled John 17 and found 25 million references!

For myself I began to see that everything to do with the church's life is here in this text – its authority, its characteristics, its lifestyle, its mission, its inner dynamics, plus both its heavenly and its earthly purpose. Nothing seems to be missing.

Beyond that there seemed to me to be special poignancy in the fact that here we were seeing Jesus not as public instructor or teacher, *but as private intercessor.* Here was our Lord not instructing the disciples, but pouring out His heart to the Father for what He wanted the church to be and do. Here were, and are, the longings of His heart, the anguished desire of His soul. This continues to strike me as something very special.

From then on the idea began to live with me that I would like one day, when ready to do so, to write a reflection on this chapter and my interaction with it. So I left it all to germinate a few more years. In fact for three and a half decades!

Impulse 2: Real perplexity about the reality of the church compared to the prayer

Anyway, during this time another reality was constantly running through my soul, and that was a deep sense of perplexity that generally speaking I couldn't see around me (by and large) the church Jesus prayed for, though, isolated congregations here and there approximated.

Why was this? Slowly the conviction took shape: both the people of precept and the people of practice in the church, in fact all of us, fall short for just this reason – that we constantly miss the delicate balance of imperatives present in John 17, the High Priestly Prayer of Jesus.

Suddenly it was clear. One could not just write idealistically and theoretically about what Jesus prayed for in all its positive glory and ignore the negative fact that the church in reality seemed light years from the patterns our Lord longed for. Somehow there seemed something slightly dishonest about that. Should one not therefore grapple with the reality of, and reasons for, this discrepancy?

I also recognised that my experience and ministry had given me exposure across a pretty wide landscape to the different facets of the church universal in many parts of the world, albeit from a layman's vantage point. This meant of course that I would be limited to the extent that I had never had experience of the mysterious inner workings of things like church synods and assemblies, and I had never been a big shot like a canon, archdeacon, or bishop; none of these offices (as it happens) having ever fallen remotely within the realm of my own aspirations.

POTENTIAL MOMENTS OF GLORY

Actually once or twice in my life I have missed potential moments of episcopal glory – once when, though a layman, I was asked to let my name go forward as an episcopal nominee for a South African diocese that, in desperation, was scraping the bottom of the barrel to find candidates for their new bishop! Knowing they had lost their mind I was determined not to lose mine and after overnight prayer politely declined. No doubt it was a mighty deliverance for the diocese concerned.

The other time was when in some fit of folly I was nominated from the floor to be archbishop, if you please, of another city, this time overseas – the first layman, I was told, to be nominated for an archbishopric since the twelfth century or something like that! It seems my nomination lasted all of ninety seconds before sanity was restored to the gathering as I was cast to archiepiscopal outer darkness. Oh, well, you can't win 'em all!

So by two mighty divine interventions I remained a layman with a layman's limitations. Or maybe advantages!

But might one not nevertheless explore meaningfully how the discrepancy between the church Jesus prayed for and the reality around us was the consequence not of poor praying by Jesus, but of poor theological, moral, and missiological obedience by the church?

The fact is that every Christian should be faced daily with the distinction between the ideal and the real in terms of the church's nature, life, and character. Thus theologian P. T. Forsyth could write "the church of Christ is the greatest and finest product of human history... the greatest thing in the universe".[7]

On the other hand, Thomas Arnold, once Professor of History at Oxford, affirmed, "The church as it now stands no human power can save... When I think of the church, I could sit down and pine and die."[8]

Then Philip Yancey, writing in his book, *Disappointment with God*, says that in reality the contrary problem is God's disappointment with us. "The church's obvious defects would seem to be the greatest cost to God."[9]

ORDINARY

When contemplating the church, Dorothy Sayers concluded that, "In an awesome act of self-denial, God entrusted His reputation to ordinary people."[10]

Actually that word "ordinary" played a great part in my own call. Not long after my conversion at university in October 1955 I was introduced to John Pollock's inspiring little classic, *The Cambridge Seven*, about seven young Cambridge graduates who went out to do missionary work in China. On the last page of that book Pollock says: "This is the story of *ordinary* men, and thus may be repeated" (my italics).[11]

I fell on that word "ordinary" like a beggar pouncing on

a morsel of bread and said: "Lord, oh, I thank you! Because if it's 'ordinary' people you can use, then I as one of the more ordinary around can qualify." And there and then I offered myself for Christian service.

So midst all the failings of the church we celebrate that God can use *even* us – the most ordinary of the ordinary, and perhaps birth the extraordinary.

It's an interesting and antiphonal interplay of notions. The real and the ideal. The dream and the nightmare. The mountaintop and the valley. The very ordinary and the extraordinary.

So why not explore these and share how or why? No doubt I am not alone with my perplexities. All of that was "idea" and "Impulse 2".

Oh yes! One other thing. I felt such an exploration could create a sort of thermometer by which churches and individuals could take their temperature and see how well or unwell they were!

A POWERFUL QUESTION

I also came to realise that I couldn't and shouldn't write on the church with judgment, because I was subject to the same judgment.

In January 1999 Carol and I had been with Eugene and Jan Peterson of *The Message* fame at their lovely lakeside home on Lake Flathead in Montana. Eugene said to me one afternoon while out hiking in the hills: "Will your book be a rebuke and challenge to the church?"

"Eugene, I am in no position to rebuke anyone," I replied, "but I do hope the book will challenge the church. However what I *can* say is that Jesus' prayer for the church in John seventeen *has* deeply challenged me. Beyond that it has in fact also deeply rebuked me personally in terms of my own shallowness of faith and shabbiness of witness."

In fact once when studying this chapter I found myself almost in tears and crying out in my heart, "Lord, Jesus, if you still pray this prayer, as I imagine you do as the Great Intercessor, then please pray it again for me RIGHT NOW. And not just today but every day."

Yes! – that's probably the need for all of us reading these pages.

Impulse 3: I have a story to tell

Impulse three focused in on the part about telling a story. This came from several quarters.

Following Mexico City's 1975 hosting of the LCWE, and with it the amazing group of leaders from every continent, Jesus' prayer continued to grip my spirit and imagination. Then in 1978 – during the so-called "Rhodesian Bush War" when the Church of Rhodesia (now Zimbabwe) was rent asunder by divisions as to whether one was pro Ian Smith (and the white government) or pro the Freedom Fighters and the black Liberation struggle – I took this chapter as the basis for a series of five well-received lectures.

My interest in the chapter thereafter deepened and I used it at other times and in other places.

Thus for "The Sadleir Memorial Lecture" series I was invited to deliver in October 1991 at Wycliffe Theological College in Toronto, Canada, I chose John 17 for my theme. Being in a theological environment I was of course ever so keen to be ever so theological and ever so impressive! – you know, trotting out little bits of Hebrew or Greek here or there or riding in with the fearsome trio of Barth, Brunner, and Buber! And if that didn't impress then toss in a touch of Tertullian, Tyndale, and Tillich!

But to my considerable interest, alarm, and surprise, the audience (consisting of theologians both budding and budded) pleaded with me after the first lecture to tell more stories: "We want to hear more stories of your experiences in Africa with the principles coming out of the High Priestly Prayer. We've loved the few stories you've told. Tell us more."

That set me thinking. Keep it reasonably simple. Tell the stories.

Then there was my friend Tom Houston – then Executive Director of the LCWE. During a phone conversation with him in the UK in October 1992 he asked me if I was doing any more writing. I told him of the John 17 possibility.

"Great idea, Mike. But tell the stories," said Tom simply, abruptly, and unprimed. "And tell yours."

So I decided to write and to try and put down something of my adventure with this chapter. Yes, I would seek to share the story of my love affair with this poignant prayer – of my perplexity that most of the time I do not see around me the answer to it, but also of my persevering determination to try and make just a little bit of a contribution to the answer coming in – "one day"!

Thus it was that I decided that if I ever did write a book on this extraordinary prayer of Jesus, I would ground and contextualise it in real-life situations by mixing in stories, personal experiences, and the anecdotal along with the chapter's more obviously theological material.

My prayer for the book then – as now – is that its reflections will indeed challenge, bless, encourage, and yes, if need be here and there, rebuke – as it has done to this author – all who might take up its pages to read. Especially the thinking layperson. And the average pastor.

*** ***

A quiet read

So then, let's quietly, deliberately and prayerfully read the prayer that is found in John 17 – twice. First in the NRSV and second in Eugene Peterson's translation, *The Message*.

NEW REVISED STANDARD VERSION

(1) After Jesus had spoken these words, he looked up to heaven and said, "Father, the hour has come; glorify

your Son so that the Son may glorify you, (2) since you have given him authority over all people, to give eternal life to all whom you have given him. (3) And this is eternal life, that they may know you, the only true God, and Jesus Christ whom you have sent. (4) I glorified you on earth by finishing the work that you gave me to do. (5) So now, Father, glorify me in your own presence with the glory that I had in your presence before the world existed.

(6) "I have made your name known to those whom you gave me from the world. They were yours, and you gave them to me, and they have kept your word. (7) Now they know that everything you have given me is from you; (8) for the words that you gave to me I have given to them, and they have received them and know in truth that I came from you; and they have believed that you sent me. (9) I am asking on their behalf; I am not asking on behalf of the world, but on behalf of those whom you gave me, because they are yours. (10) All mine are yours, and yours are mine; and I have been glorified in them. (11) And now I am no longer in the world, but they are in the world, and I am coming to you. Holy Father, protect them in your name that you have given me, so that they may be one, as we are one. (12) While I was with them, I protected them in your name that you have given me. I guarded them, and not one of them was lost except the one destined to be lost, so that the scripture might be fulfilled. (13) But now I am coming to you, and I speak these things in the world so that they may have my joy made complete in themselves. (14) I have given them your word, and the world has hated them because they do not belong to the world, just as I do not belong to the world. (15) I am not asking you to take them out of the world, but I ask you to protect them from the evil one. (16) They do not belong to the world, just as I do not belong to the world. (17) Sanctify them in the truth; your word is truth. (18)

As you have sent me into the world, so I have sent them into the world. (19) And for their sakes I sanctify myself, so that they also may be sanctified in truth.

(20) "I ask not only on behalf of these, but also on behalf of those who will believe in me through their word, (21) that they may all be one. As you, Father, are in me and I am in you, may they also be in us, so that the world may believe that you have sent me. (22) The glory that you have given me I have given them, so that they may be one, as we are one, (23) I in them and you in me, that they may become completely one, so that the world may know that you have sent me and have loved them even as you have loved me. (24) Father, I desire that those also, whom you have given me, may be with me where I am, to see my glory, which you have given me because you loved me before the foundation of the world.

(25) "Righteous Father, the world does not know you, but I know you; and these know that you have sent me. (26) I made your name known to them, and I will make it known, so that the love with which you have loved me may be in them, and I in them."

THE MESSAGE

(1) Jesus said these things: Then raising his eyes in prayer, he said: "Father, it's time. Display the bright splendor of your Son so the Son in turn may show your bright splendor. (2) You put him in charge of everything human so he might give real and eternal life to all in his charge. (3) And this is the real and eternal life: That they know you, The one and only true God, And Jesus Christ, whom you sent. (4) I glorified you on earth By completing down to the last detail What you assigned me to do. (5) And now, Father, glorify me with your very own splendor, the very splendor I had in your presence

Before there was a world.

*(6) "I spelled out your character in detail To the men
and women you gave me. They were yours in the first
place; Then you gave them to me, And they have now
done what you said. (7) They know now, beyond the
shadow of a doubt, That everything you gave me is
firsthand from you, (8) For the message you gave me, I
gave them; And they took it, and were convinced That
I came from you. They believed that you sent me. (9)
I pray for them. I'm not praying for the God-rejecting
world But for those you gave me, For they are yours
by right. (10) Everything mine is yours, and yours mine.
And my life is on display in them. (11) For I'm no longer
going to be visible in the world; They'll continue in the
world While I return to you. Holy Father, guard them as
they pursue this life That you conferred as a gift through
me, So they can be of one heart and mind (12) As we
are one heart and mind. As long as I was with them, I
guarded them in the pursuit of the life you gave through
me; I even posted a night watch. And not one of them
got away, Except for the rebel bent on destruction (the
exception that proved the rule of Scripture).*

*(13) "Now I'm returning to you. I'm saying these
things in the world's hearing So my people can
experience My joy completed in them. (14) I gave them
your word; The godless world hated them because of
it, Because they didn't join the world's ways, (15) Just
as I didn't join the world's ways. I'm not asking that you
take them out of the world but that you guard them from
the Evil One. (16) They are no more defined by the world
Than I am defined by the world. (17) Make them holy –
consecrated – with the truth; Your word is consecrating
truth. (18) In the same way that you gave me a mission
in the world, I give them a mission in the world. (19) I'm
consecrating myself for their sakes so they'll be truth-
consecrated in their mission.*

(20) "I'm praying not only for them But also for

*those who will believe in me Because of them and their
witness about me. (21) The goal is for all of them to
become one heart and mind – Just as you, Father, are
in me and I in you, So they might be one heart and mind
with us. Then the world might believe that you, in fact,
sent me. (22) The same glory you gave me, I gave them,
So they'll be as unified and together as we are – (23)
I in them and you in me. Then they'll be mature in this
oneness, And give the godless world evidence That
you've sent me and loved them in the same way you've
loved me.*

*(24) "Father, I want those you gave me To be with
me, right where I am, So they can see my glory, the
splendor you gave me, Having loved me Long before
there ever was a world. (25) Righteous Father, the world
has never known you, but I have known you, and, these
disciples know that you sent me on this mission. (26) I
have made your very being known to them – who you
are and what you do – and continue to make it known,
so that your love for me might be in them exactly as I am
in them."*

*** ***

Well, there you are! The prayer Jesus prayed. And the church
Jesus prayed for.

I end this introductory story with a personal and deeply
felt prayer from a hymnwriter of yesteryear, William C. Dix:

*Intercessor, Friend of Sinners,
Earth's Redeemer, plead for me
Where the songs of all the sinless
Sweep across the Crystal Sea.*

Chapter 2

The Prayer's Basic Outline and Key Ideas

"The last thing that we find in writing a book is to know what we must put first."

Blaise Pascal

"Most communicators agree that orderly arrangement is necessary... So... whether our approach is visual or logical, we still have to organise our thoughts into some structure if they are to be communicable."

John Stott[1]

As we come to the prayer itself we are inevitably going to feel very daunted, so that we tremble to paddle even in its shallows, let alone seek to plumb its depths. But it's worth a try. For the treasures here are life-transforming personally and revolutionary for the church corporately if taken sufficiently seriously.

Small wonder then, let us repeat, that this prayer has been showered with praise. I mentioned a few superlatives at the beginning of our first chapter.

To be sure it is a place where we can anchor our lives.

On his deathbed the Scottish Reformer John Knox was asked by his wife: "Where do you want me to read?" Knox responded: "Read where I first put my anchor down – in the seventeenth chapter of John."[2]

Just before being executed in the reign of Henry VIII, John Fisher, Bishop of Rochester, asked that this prayer be read to him before he faced his gruesome death.

Yes, here we are in waters unfathomable and unequalled for scope in all the Scriptures.

Let's see anyway if we can get to the prayer's headlines.

The general outline and key ideas

Many have said a neat outline is impossible. However, the reality is that at one level there is in fact a very broad and generally accepted outline in the following terms.

1. Our Lord prays (John 17)

2. Our Lord prays for *Himself* (1–5)

3. Our Lord prays for *His immediate circle of disciples* (6–19)

4. Our Lord prays for *the church that will subsequently come into existence through their testimony* (20–26).

Our problem

However, our problem comes in that the many and various concepts raised even in Jesus' prayer for Himself, let alone in His prayer for the immediate disciples, have application or overlap with similar or identical ones of subsequent centuries that relate to the church.

For example, "the eternal life" which comes through "knowing the one true God" (as referred to in His prayer for Himself), is as applicable to both the immediate apostolic group as it is the church that would later be born through their witness.

So too the joy of Jesus (verse 13) and protection from the evil one (verse 15) which He prays for the apostolic group can hardly be confined to them and not to the church of subsequent centuries.

Likewise we could never say that the *love* He wants in the church of subsequent centuries was not a critical qualification required for the first disciples.

A mass of overlapping ideas

So there is a mass of overlap that renders the normal broad outline of John 17 only modestly serviceable. That's why I prefer to seek and see the marks Jesus prays for in His church embedded like an assortment of jewels, whose sparkles go up and down and round about, in a three-tiered crown of this three-part prayer:

Truth, holiness, joy
Protection, mission, prayerfulness
Unity, love, power, glory

Together they form a kind of prism of variegated colours bringing glory to the prayer, even as those same marks transferred not in isolation but in cluster from the prayer to reality in the church would bring a glory evident not only to us who are within the church but also to a watching world.

So what are the key ideas that recur with special frequency?

1. FATHER

The term "Father" appears *five* times in the High Priestly Prayer. It is indeed the very first word of the prayer when Jesus lifts up His eyes to heaven and says, "Father" (Latin *"Pater"*,

Aramaic *"Abba")*, the modern equivalent of which would be "Daddy". This is a word that speaks of the profoundest intimacy, relatedness, and connectedness. This concept of God as Father is applied to God in the Gospels more than double the number of times found in the remaining books of the New Testament. In fact in the Gospel of John alone it occurs 107 times.

Our Lord saw Himself standing in an intimate and unparalleled relationship with God as Father and He Himself as the pre-existent, eternal Son who was equal with the Father and became incarnate for the fulfilment of the divine purposes of salvation. And of course as prayer is to be made to God only, so it is our duty, privilege and indeed, prayer, to see Him as a Father and indeed to call Him *"Our Father"*. On the basis of both our redemption and our adoption (Galatians 4:5–6) we can call out *"Abba*, Father". And if God indeed is our Father then we have a freedom of access to Him, a basis of enormous confidence in Him, and the celebration of great expectations from Him. We note also in the prayer that Jesus calls His Father both *"Holy Father"* (verse 11) and *"Righteous Father"* (verse 25).

Yes, what a lovely word is this word Father! And there can probably be no greater or more ecstatic moment for any man than when his baby son or daughter says "Dada!" or "Daddy!"

Yes, the one with whom we have to do and to whom we pray is Father and all the finest and highest attributes of the best of human fathers are multiplied beyond infinity into the Father heart of our heavenly Father.

2. GLORY

"Glory" occurs *eight* times in the prayer. Indeed, the divine is not about anything if it is not about glory; glory being both the honour due to God and His radiant character and moral beauty shining through. Thus for example, Jesus can say, "I have been *glorified* in them" (verse 10). "The *glory* that you have given me I have given them" (verse 22). Then He says: "Father, I desire that they also… may be with me where I am, to see my *glory*" (verse 24).

We remember that in his prologue John writes:

> *In the beginning was the Word, and the Word was with God, and the Word was God… And the Word became flesh and lived among us, and we have seen his glory, the glory as of a father's only son, full of grace and truth.*
>
> **John 1:1, 14**

So even in a preliminary way we register right from the beginning the central importance of this reality – namely the glory of God.

3. GIVE/GIVING/GIVEN

This idea occurs no less than *seventeen* times in the prayer and seventy-six times in the Gospel of John. Within the Trinity and from the Trinity, all is *giving*. Giving from the Father to the Son, from the Son to the Father, and from the Son to the disciples, from the disciples to each other, and finally from the church to the world through the Holy Spirit. Yes, all is giving. God and the New Testament are all about giving. Some characteristic verses from the prayer are:

- Verse 2: "since you have given him authority over all people, to give eternal life to all whom you have **given** him."

- Verse 4: "…by finishing the work that you **gave** me to do."

- Verse 6a: "I have made your name known to those whom you **gave** me from the world…" When a disciple is given by God the Father to Jesus the Son, it means that the Spirit of God so moves in the heart of that potential disciple as to make him or her respond to the appeal of Jesus. This is what one might call the *prevenient* grace of God and what the Reformers were referring to in measure when they spoke about the doctrine of *illumination,* this referring to the illuminating work of the Holy Spirit in the openhearted seeker that causes him or her to understand the gospel and respond to Jesus.

- Verse 6b: "They were yours, and you *gave* them to me..."
- Verse 7: "Now they know that everything you have *given* me is from you..."

For me at conversion, one of the really major revelations was that salvation was a *gift.* Says the Apostle: "The wages of sin is death, but the free *gift* of God is eternal life" (Romans 6:23). Says our Lord: "I *give* them eternal life" (John 10:28).

Prior to my own conversion, my whole understanding of the Christian faith was about trying to be good and doing things that would impress God, thereby making me acceptable to Him. When I heard that salvation was a free gift to be received by grace through faith, the truth seemed awesome beyond words. Imagine the excitement when I first read Ephesians 2:8–10:

> For by grace you have been saved through faith, and this is not your own doing; it is the gift of God – not the result of works, so that no one may boast. For we are what he has made us, created in Christ Jesus for good works, which God prepared beforehand to be our way of life.

It was unimaginably liberating – as Martin Luther and the Reformers and myriads of others down the ages have found – to grasp that we are not saved *by* works but *for* works and that works are not the root of our salvation but the fruit of it.

There must be a catch in it

I remember many years later in ministry sharing this truth in a lunchhour meeting for business people. I had explained that salvation, forgiveness, and eternal life were all part of a free gift of God that we reach out to receive by grace through faith. Afterwards, an old family friend, Taffy Walters, came up to me and said: "Michael, I just can't really believe this; there must be a catch."

"There is no catch, Taffy," I insisted. "Everything to do with our God, including how He gives salvation, is a *gift* which we are required to receive by faith and with gratitude."

Years later when I was at the bedside of the now dying Taffy, who had by this time long since received the message I had given him, he looked up into my face and with a twinkle in his now weakening eyes said: "Michael, I am so glad there is no catch." He had received the free gift, praise God.

So then if it was and is in the very nature of God to be giving freely, no wonder the Lord Jesus spoke to His Father as the great giver with Himself as the Son and Saviour being the one who has authority to *"give* eternal life to all" … who have been *"given* to Him" (verse 2).

4. KNOW/KNOWING/KNOWN

This idea occurs *nine* times in the prayer. The realm of the divine and of the Spirit is about *knowing.* It is about *knowing relationally* in fellowship and about *knowing intellectually* with the mind. The latter speaks of knowledge that is certain and sure, about the cognitive and not just the speculative. The former speaks about interpersonal and relational knowing. So there is a knowing about facts and truth. Then there is knowing relationally. The *knowing* of the High Priestly Prayer is thus both propositional and personal.

Some examples are as follows:

Verse 3: "And this is eternal life, that *they may know you,* the only true God, and Jesus Christ whom you have sent" (relational knowing).

Verse 7: "Now *they know* that everything you have given me is from you" (propositional knowing).

Verse 8: "for the words that you gave to me I have given to

them, and they have received them and *know in truth* that I came from you" (propositional knowing).

Verse 23: "I in them and you in me, that they may become completely one, so that the world may *know* that you have sent me and have loved them even as you have loved me" (propositional knowing).

Verse 25a: "Righteous Father, *the world does not know you*" (relational knowing).

Verse 25b: "but *I know you*" (relational knowing).

Interestingly enough it was this question of *knowing* which created the spiritually instructive crisis for me on 23 October 1955 when, after going to Communion together, my friend Robbie Footner put the question to me up there in his little bedsit: "Michael, do you mind if I ask you something? Do you *know* Christ?" I was absolutely thrown by this question, "Well, Robbie, I go to church and all that and read my Bible."

"But that is not what I asked," said Robbie rather firmly. "I am asking whether you *know* Christ in a personal way."

I think Robbie sensed at that moment that I was completely bamboozled and out of my depth. He then explained that there is a difference between knowing *about* the Queen of England and knowing her personally. This flummoxed me totally.

Have you surrendered to Christ?

Robbie then decided to pursue another line of approach and asked me equally firmly: "Michael, have you ever surrendered your life to Christ?" Now on that issue there could be no confusion. Who basically and fundamentally was running my life? Was it I, or was it Christ? Who was on the throne of my heart determining how I would spend my days on earth?

At that point I had to acknowledge that I had done the bulk of what my religious life up to that point seemed to require of me. I had been baptised, gone to Sunday school and church, been confirmed, gone regularly to Communion, given some little bits of money now and then, even read my Bible and said my prayers, but I knew profoundly and in my innermost being that I had never surrendered my life to Christ and maybe it was in consequence of that that I had never come to know Him. Robbie was quite clear on the New Testament definition of eternal life as found in our Lord's High Priestly Prayer here at John 17:3: "And this is eternal life, that *they may know you*, the only true God, and Jesus Christ whom you have sent..." There it was. To know the Father and Jesus Christ whom He had sent.

Wow! There it was – the possibility of knowing God the Father on the basis of surrendering to God the Son. I knelt down with Robbie beside his bed, received Christ as my Saviour, surrendered to Him as my Lord, and opened the door of my heart and asked Him to come in as personal friend. And that was that. By late afternoon that day I knew something had happened of overwhelming consequence for my life, I had come to *know* God in Christ.

5. TRUE/TRUTH

This occurs *five* times explicitly and another *four or five times at least* implicitly (verses 7, 8c, 14a, 25c, for example). The Christian faith generally, and Jesus specifically, are concerned about the truth, and what is true or not true. There is no escaping this, not even in a postmodern world totally sceptical of truth claims or the veracity of so-called metanarratives such as the Bible. Chapter 6 will be dedicated to this matter, so I only touch on the subject here. But the fact is that there is no "good news" if the news is not true!

Nossir! If it is not factually, truly, and historically true as something that actually happened, as against something that did not happen, then we must pack up shop, call it a day on the Christian faith, and eat, drink, and be merry for tomorrow we die.

But our Lord would not have it so and He could therefore say:

Verse 3: "And this is eternal life, that they may know you, the *only true God.*"

Verse 8c: "and know *in truth* that I came from you."

Verse 17a: "Sanctify them in the *truth*".

Verse 17b: "your Word is *truth.*"

Verse 19: "I sanctify myself, so that they also may be sanctified *in truth.*"

Of course, the fact is that in spite of the modern world's professed scepticism about truth and truth claims, most people nevertheless have a fairly deep concern about the issue of truth on endless assorted matters in politics, medicine, or aerodynamics. No one wants to fly with an aerodynamically broad-minded pilot!

It is clear that Jesus here in this prayer understood truth as that which coheres with the facts and realities of life as they are. The postmodern indifference to truth and making it relative will have a hard time with Jesus in this John 17 prayer.

6. THE WORLD

This is one of the most dominant notions in the prayer. It occurs no less than *eighteen* times with three different meanings.

- The first meaning is that of the planet and physical universe.
- The second is that of the human family inhabiting the planet.
- The third is that of society organised in its thought and behaviour without or against God.

We can see examples of this in the following:

Verse 5: "the glory that I had in your presence before *the world* existed." Clearly here the reference is to planet Earth.

Verse 6: "those whom you gave me from *the world*." Here the reference is clearly to the human community.

Verse 9: "I am not asking on behalf of *the world*." The human community again.

Verse 11: "I am no longer in the world, but they are in *the world*." Once more this is the human community.

Verse 13: "I speak these things in *the world*." The reference here is both to the planet and to the human community.

Verse 14a: "The *world* has hated them", i.e. people on the planet and in Israel at that time have hated the disciples.

Verse 14b: "because they do not belong to *the world*". Here clearly the word refers to a system of thinking hostile to the gospel and of which the disciples with their spiritual commitments cannot be a part.

Verse 14c: "just as I do not belong to *the world*". Jesus is here declaring that He has neither part nor lot with this system, nor with this evil and non-spiritual way of thinking.

So we need to register here afresh that our modern society thinks of the world only in two senses, namely that of planet Earth, as for example when we see global warming as "a threat *to the world*". And then secondly as the human community, for example, when we are listening to the *world* news which tells us what's happening in the international community.

But Jesus and the Bible very clearly and strongly see a third sense here of the world as a system of thinking hostile to Himself and to the gospel. In other words, the way the average human around us thinks and acts should not be the way we as the Lord's people think and act. Nor must we be surprised when we find that often we as Christians experience hostility or even hatred from the world around us. But we are not to be unduly alarmed because before that hostility and hatred had been directed at us, they were directed at our Lord.

To be sure I can testify, and maybe some of you reading

this volume can do likewise, that I have at times encountered hostility from people who do not know me personally at all, but who do know that I am a Christian and a preacher of the Christian gospel. And that alone is enough to get their backs up, their negative juices going, and their hostility operative. Thus it ever was.

William Barclay succinctly puts it this way: "In John's Gospel, the world stands for human society organising itself without God."[3] Very clear also is American theologian David Wells's fine definition: "This third basic sense of *kosmos* refers to fallen humanity, en masse, to the collective expression of every society's refusal to bow before God, receive His truth, to obey His commandments or to believe in His Christ."[4]

7. KEEP/KEPT (I.E. PROTECT)

There are five instances in the prayer of this notion, and used in the two senses, firstly of *obedience* and secondly of *protection*. Here they are:

Verse 6: "they have *kept* Your word". Here the word obviously speaks of spiritual, moral and theological *obedience*.

Verse 11: "Holy Father, *protect [keep] them* in your name". The meaning here is: *"Protect them so that they maintain the divine character."*

Verse 12a: *"I protected [kept] them* in your name." Here the meaning is that He has prevented them from departing morally and spiritually from the divine character. He has kept their behaviour godly.

Verse 12b: "I guarded [*kept*, watched over] them." Again the sense is of moral protection.

Verse 15: *"protect [keep] them* from the evil one". This time the prayer is for protection from evil supernaturalism and most specifically Satan himself.

William Barclay makes his comments in these terms, "Jesus prayed that God would keep and protect His disciples from the attacks of the evil one. The Bible is not a speculative book. It does not discuss the origin of evil; but it is quite certain that in this world there is a power of evil which is in opposition to the power of God, the power which seeks to lure people out of the right way and into the wrong way."[5]

Clearly our Lord knows only too well that His followers will be under the direct attacks of Satan himself and they need spiritual protection.

*** ***

All that we have said at this point underlines that in the Christian life, obedience is key ("they have kept thy word"; John 17:6, KJV) and protection from Satan is vital. As we are protected from Satan so too are we enabled to be spiritually obedient.

Committing ourselves to obedience means we won't fall into the trap of the little girl who had being trying to memorise Psalm 23 for her Sunday school teacher, with the first verse starting out "The Lord is my Shepherd I shall not want." The little girl didn't get it quite right and recited: "The Lord is my Shepherd I can do what I want." "No, darling, you can't!"

One might add here that as our Lord prays that we be protected from the evil one, so we should take on board that this is a vital prayer to pray over one's children, one's family, one's colleagues, one's pastor and church leaders, and oneself. "Lord, keep them, and all of us, from the evil one. And keep us obedient to You."

8. THE NAME (CHARACTER) OF THE FATHER (I.E. HOLINESS, SANCTIFICATION, SET APARTNESS)

As *"Your Name"* refers to the character of godliness, or holiness of God, I put these together with "sanctify" (Greek *hagiazo*) meaning "make holy", or set apart, or consecrated.

Examples of this in the text are:

Verse 6: "I have made your *name [character]* known to those whom you gave me from the world."

Verse 11: "I protect[ed] them in your *name [character]*."

Verse 26: "I made your name known to them, and I will make it known." Here our Lord is not only saying that He has revealed the Father's character to His disciples, as much as they could understand at that point, but that there was more to come which He would make known in due time.

These dimensions of the prayer underline most powerfully the importance of what we might call "the character issue". There is little point in our being able to preach or verbally witness well if our characters do not line up with our verbal profession.

I remember back some years ago there were those serious moral and spiritual tumbles of certain televangelists in the United States. These of course created much scandal and much questioning of Christian integrity and seriousness across America. *Time* magazine then carried an article entitled "And Then There Was Billy". The article spoke of the immense integrity, exemplary moral and spiritual behaviour, and track record of Billy Graham. That was very special. I wrote to Billy Graham a note at that time saying how much I thanked the Lord for his spiritual example, his moral faithfulness, and his financial integrity.

Yes, we are all called to manifest the character of Christ as best we are able.

9. I–YOU: YOURS–MINE

Another startling notion all the way through the prayer is the intimate interplay and relationality of Father and Son in the constant alternating in equality between Jesus and the Father as the "I–You", "Mine–Yours" conversation unfolds. Striking examples among a host come as follows:

Verse 1: "glorify your Son so that the Son may glorify you."

Verse 4: "I glorified you on earth by finishing the work that you gave me to do."

Verse 6b: "They were yours, and you gave them to me."

Verse 10: "All mine are yours, and yours are mine."

Verse 23: "I in them and you in me, that they may become completely one."

Here now we see intimacy, reciprocity, relationality, communication and fellowship of a nature beyond human imagining. Everything the Son does is with and through the Father in the Holy Spirit. This is the Trinitarian, tri-une God in conversation and action.

Ten marks Jesus wants to characterise the church

From these key ideas, as presented above, there seem to me to emerge here ten marks which our Lord wants to characterise His church. These are:

Truth – as coherence with the relational and factual realities of God and His world

Holiness – as human character conforming in measure to the divine

Joy – as being Jesus Himself and given from His heart to those who love and obey Him

Protection – as deliverance from both the power of evil supernaturalism and the ways of the world

Mission – as Christian labours carried out in the manner in which Jesus fulfilled His own

Prayer/Prayerfulness – as constant communication with and dependence on the Father

Unity – as exists within the Trinity and to be striven for and maintained by Jesus' disciples

Love – as the active and bonding emotion between the Persons of the Godhead and the supreme requirement of us, His disciples

Power – as released in us by the Son through the Holy Spirit

Glory – as reflective of the radiant character and multi-coloured dimensions of God shining through.

Two poles

I believe that as we see these prayed-for marks we have to grasp something very critical. There really are, in many ways, two poles to this prayer with truth and holiness at one end and unity and love at the other. All else unravels and is set between these two poles, like points along a long horizontal line.

Now for something critically important. Achieving the holding together of these two poles is incredibly difficult and, in human strength and capacity alone, impossible. I would say this cannot be done without one being thrust into the way of the Cross. If that line with the ten points along it from one pole to the other is a horizontal tree trunk, then it needs another vertical tree trunk down through its centre making the vision and way of the Cross inescapable.

I believe exclusively focusing on truth and holiness is easy, in fact even satisfying in a fleshly way. To be a mighty champion for truth and to crusade against all error and wrong behaviour can seem heroic and courageous. But endless churches have been split and broken by such crusades when those who carry them out do not bear in mind and keep in purview the demands of love and unity. Without the Cross-like Holy Spirit demand to be a person of love and unity, the crusader for truth and holiness operates more and more in the flesh and in the dynamics of divisiveness, alienation, and party-spirit (labelled by Paul along with *dissension* as a work of the flesh in Galatians 5:19).

Thus can congregations, organisations, even denominations be split asunder and rent in pieces by such brothers and sisters.

Unbiblical tolerance

On the other hand, and by contrast, are those who do not stress truth, biblical faithfulness, the gospel of salvation and conversion, holiness, orthodox Christian behaviour and morals, traditional heterosexual marriage, etc., but rather major into the demands of the other pole of the prayer in terms of love, unity, and understanding tolerance. All one has to do is love and tolerate everyone, accept every viewpoint uncritically, and sanction behaviour which is Christianly eccentric or even immoral. For these folk issues of biblical faithfulness, Christian salvation and holy behaviour are not issues of great importance, because the demands of love must trump those of soteriological, exegetical, moral, or behavioural truth.

The love and unity exponents can thus likewise betray the faith by not being willing to bite the bullet of theological truth or biblically orthodox moral and marital behaviour.

Reactions to our Lord's ministry

It has often struck me about the person and ministry of our Lord Jesus Himself that while He was only understood as a person of love, all went well for Him. But as soon as He and His claims and His demands relating to truth, salvation, and behaviour were really understood, people started to want to crucify Him. In fact, it is probably true to say of Him that He only enjoyed universal acclaim for the first half of the very first public sermon He ever preached: "All spoke well of him and were amazed at the gracious words that came from his mouth" (Luke 4:22). But by verses 28–29, "When they heard this, all in the synagogue were filled with rage. They got up, drove him out of the town, and led him to the brow of the hill on which their town was built, so that they might hurl him off the cliff." I guess most of us would have pretty well packed up the ministry if people wanted to kill us before the end of our first public sermon!

So my thesis is that when we seek to bring together both poles of the prayer, on the one hand the prayer for truth and holiness, and on the other hand the prayer for love and unity, plus everything in between, then we are really in trouble. And we will find ourselves crying out for the help of the Holy Spirit as we discover there to be no escape from walking the way of the Cross if we are to hold both ends of the prayer and everything in between in tension and in personal commitment.

Not surprisingly Jesus' own commitments on all these fronts led Him to Calvary. And as we commit ourselves to the totality of this prayer, we will find ourselves required to

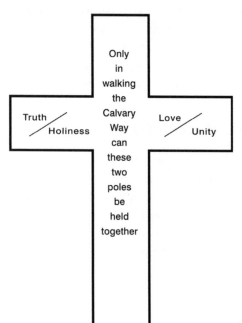

take up our Cross and follow Him. For the way is not easy. It requires in fact walking the Calvary Road.

This is why the apostle Paul's challenge has to settle in the centre of our souls – "speak the truth in love" (Ephesians 4:15). That is the posture required of us as we speak. But it is also the same posture to be held as we behave and work out our faith. Thus faith has to "work through love" (Galatians 5:6) and "the truth" has to be "obeyed" (Galatians 5:7). Orthodoxy and orthopraxis belong together. Faithfulness is required both to the word of truth and the way of love. Likewise, unity can never be at the expense of truth, nor our passion for truth promulgated without serious attempts also to walk in the ways of love, unity and fellowship.

In both my view and my experience, this is a tough ask.

I repeat. It is also one that calls us to Calvary.

Only that way can we begin to become "the church Jesus prayed for".

Chapter 3

The Context of the Prayer

"When Jesus had spoken **these words,** he lifted
up his eyes to heaven and said, 'Father...'"

John 17:1

In terms of of the context of the prayer, I remember well
an experience I had in early 1991. It occurred during that
aforementioned sabbatical when I went to David and Lesley
Richardson's little cabin, Jabulani, in the Rockies. I was setting
myself aside for some days of quiet, retreat, prayer, seeking
the Lord, and thinking about this book. Agreeing with Maria's
song in *The Sound of Music*, I thought, "Let's start at the very
beginning, a very good place to start ..." So naturally that
took me to verse one of John 17.

I had only read six words when I had a light-bulb moment.
It came as I read: "When Jesus had spoken *these words*, he lifted
up his eyes to heaven and said 'Father'..." "Now, what have
we got here?" I thought.

Clearly this opening verse says that Jesus' High Priestly
Prayer was set firmly in the context of the words He had
just spoken to the trembling disciples in His Final Discourse
in chapters 14–16, which of course followed on from the
momentous Upper Room experience in chapter 13.

Yes, here was the context. And if the High Priestly Prayer
followed these words then the content of *these words* needs to be
explored to give vital clues as to the meaning of what it is that
Jesus would pray to the heavenly Father in His prayer.

And of course the question of context is always critical

when seeking to understand the meaning of any utterance of any sort.

So we must underline the order of things in the previous four chapters. So there is:

- the *heart-stopping encounter* the disciples had had with Jesus in the Upper Room (John 13) when the Saviour had washed their feet in the ultimate demonstration of humble servanthood
- then came His majestic and *Final Discourse*
- then the *Prayer*
- then of course the *Cross.*

1. Practice, principle and precept

So the order is firstly **action and demonstration** in the Upper Room, secondly **teaching and exhortation** in the discourse, thirdly **prayer and supplication** to the heavenly Father, and finally **action and demonstration** again in the full drama of Calvary.

So one could say that the order is:

- practice
- precept
- prayer
- and then practice again.

NOW TRY TO GET THE PICTURE

Jesus' earthly ministry is coming to a climactic end. His disciples are feeling – as so many of us at times have felt – bewildered and frightened.

He has told them He is going away.

The coming of the Spirit in His place to indwell them is only remotely grasped, if at all.

The thought of capital punishment around the corner for this friend of friends on whom they had pinned all hopes seemed unimaginable.

In reality all else had been done. What else could be left to do now but to pray? He had spoken from the Father to them. Now He must speak to the Father *for* them and *about* them. Yes, the prayer was about the teaching He had just given them, and of necessity it flowed from that teaching.

WE ALL KNOW THE FEELING

How many times have so many of us mere mortals, when leaving our families or friends, felt the moment called for nothing other than petitions of prayer, words of worship, or cries from the heart for care and protection over those we are leaving behind?

How much more the Son of God leaving behind the huddled and panting little flock of fragile friends who had been with Him day and night for three years and to whom He was now entrusting, midst all their weakness, the sacred cause of taking the "good news" of forgiveness and salvation to the ends of the earth.

They had seen His amazing and mystifying actions, felt His watered hands upon their feet, heard His final and heart-stopping words of teaching and instruction, and must now – with trembling hearts – listen in for their lifelong encouragement and edification, and for ours, on His prayer both for Himself and for them. They were in effect hearing:

- a family prayer
- a parting prayer
- a preparatory prayer
- a specimen prayer.

They were in effect truly hearing "The Lord's Prayer", as opposed to the "Our Father Who Art in Heaven" prayer, which is not the Lord's prayer but rather the disciples' prayer. What we are looking at here is of course the Lord's Prayer and there is nothing like it that has ever been prayed anywhere by anyone. For here we have one member of the Trinity talking to another and we are being given the privilege of listening in.

2. The place?

We are in fact left uncertain as to where exactly the prayer took place. However, I incline to the view that they had left the Upper Room, as conveyed by John 14:31: "Rise, let us be on our way", but had not yet crossed the Kidron stream which only happened after the High Priestly Prayer had been prayed (18:1). So perhaps they were in a quiet vineyard near the brook called Kidron. John 17:1, saying that Jesus lifted His eyes towards heaven, suggests they were outside and looking up into the sky rather than at the ceiling of a room or building.

The overall picture probably looked something like this:

	CONTENTS AND HAPPENINGS	PLACE
13	The Last Supper; washing of the disciples' feet; departure of Judas; announcement of Jesus' own departure; command to love; prediction of Peter's denial.	Upper Room
14	Words of comfort; promise of the Spirit; further announcement of Jesus' departure; promise of peace.	Still in Upper Room
14:31	"Arise, let us go from here."	They rise to leave

15	The allegory of the vine; the command to love repeated; warnings of the world's hatred; further promise of the Spirit.	Along the way to Kidron, either in Temple precincts or a nearby vineyard, or beside the brook, Kidron.
16	Further references to Jesus' departure and the promise of the Spirit and His ministry and illuminating work; Jesus' farewell, prediction of sorrow being turned into joy; final words of comfort and explanation in which "because" is used twelve times.	
17:1	"When Jesus had spoken these words, he lifted up his eyes to heaven."	Somewhere outside, perhaps beside Kidron, looking to heaven, rather than the ceiling of the Upper Room
17	The High Priestly Prayer of Jesus i. For Himself (verses 1–5) ii. His immediate disciples (verses 6–19) iii. The later church (verses 19–26)	
18:1	"After Jesus had spoken these words, he went out … across the Kidron valley..."	Across Kidron and the valley to Gethsemane, House of Caiaphas, and Praetorium
18	Gethsemane; prayer, disciples sleep; Jesus' arrest, trials before Jewish authorities and Pilate.	
19	The Cross	Golgotha

20	The resurrection and first appearances	Jerusalem
21	Final teaching	Galilee (Sea of Tiberias)

Now in order to get an idea of the probable footprints of Jesus during his last days, just cast your eyes over the following diagram:

FOOTPRINTS OF JESUS DURING HIS LAST DAYS

(Jerusalem at the time of the Crucifixion)

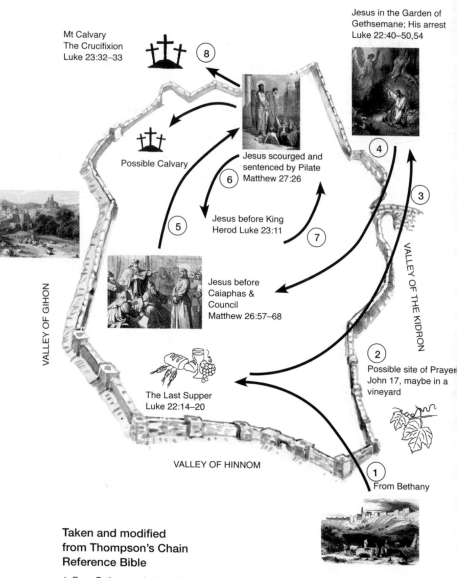

Jesus in the Garden of
Gethsemane; His arrest
Luke 22:40–50,54

Mt Calvary
The Crucifixion
Luke 23:32–33

Possible Calvary

Jesus scourged and
sentenced by Pilate
Matthew 27:26

Jesus before King
Herod Luke 23:11

Jesus before
Caiaphas &
Council
Matthew 26:57–68

VALLEY OF THE KIDRON

VALLEY OF GIHON

Possible site of Prayer
John 17, maybe in a
vineyard

The Last Supper
Luke 22:14–20

VALLEY OF HINNOM

From Bethany

**Taken and modified
from Thompson's Chain
Reference Bible**

1. From Bethany to the Last Supper
2. From the Last Supper to site of
   John 17 Prayer
3. Crossing Kidron post Prayer
4. From Gethsemane to Caiaphas

5. From Caiaphas to Pilate
6. From Pilate to Herod
7. From Herod to Pilate
8. From Pilate to Calvary

With our Lord's mission almost accomplished, and His face now set more resolutely than ever to the Cross of Calvary, the victory from the divine side is already won (13:31; 15:33). From the human side, the full realisation of this victory was yet to be grasped and experienced (14:30; 16:22; 14:18–19).

3. The purpose of the Final Discourse and prayer

While the geographic context and location remain modestly uncertain, there is, however, nothing doubtful about what exactly Jesus' purpose is now, and what the Saviour is doing here. He is preparing His (by now trembling) disciples for His imminent departure.

They are tumbling hesitatingly but surely to the fact that somehow He is leaving them, yet not leaving them; going away physically, yet promising to remain spiritually. No doubt this is all too much for them to absorb satisfactorily. Their heads must have been spinning, their hearts churning, their wills weakening.

THEY NEEDED TO UNDERSTAND GOD AS TRINITY

And of course their minds must have been deeply confused when they heard about God as Trinity. They had been given the most mind-stretching teaching (chapters 14–16) about this Trinitarian, Tri-une God – who is all unity, yet distinct as Father, Son, and the now promised Holy Spirit.

Yes, on the hills of Galilee they had known God *above them* in the brilliant night sky. Then they had known God *around them* in His creation. Then in Jesus, albeit falteringly, they had discerned God *with them*. Now they had been promised God *within them* by one called the Holy Spirit – the Comforter, the Counsellor, the Spirit of Truth (for example, John 14:15–17; 14:26; 16:7, 13).

Thus it was God *experienced* as Trinity that led the church to *understand* Him as Trinity, and then formulate Him thereafter as Trinity with the Trinitarian formula of theological description as we now know so well.

THEY NEEDED TO UNDERSTAND THE MEANINGS OF FELLOWSHIP, FRUITFULNESS, TRUTH, AND JOY

Jesus must now reassure His disciples of the wobbly knees and failing hearts that although He is now departing, nevertheless all that is necessary to equip and empower them for the task ahead without His physical presence has been set in place. And in this regard they will not be left "orphaned" (14:18). How come? Because He, Jesus, would be with them in the Person of the Holy Spirit.

Though hatred from the world (as a negative and erroneous system of thinking and behaving, as we have just seen) (15:18–23), plus tribulation, persecution (16:32–33) and difficulty await them, nevertheless they are not to be afraid, for as He has overcome this world system and its hostile thinking, so will they (16:33). Fellowship and intimacy with Himself and with the Father through the Holy Spirit will be theirs (14:20–23).

4. There were other headline teachings to grasp

In that Final Discourse there were a number of other headlines that the Lord wanted them to register, including:

- **Prayer** will give them access to the prayer-answering Father and to Jesus the Son through the Holy Spirit (14:13–14; 15:7). The New King James language is lovely at this point: "And whatever you ask in My name, that I will do, that the Father may be glorified in the Son. If you ask anything in My name, I will do it." Then John 15:7: "If you abide in Me, and My words abide in you, you will ask what you desire, and it shall be done for you."

- **Joy**, like Jesus' own joy in obedience which He will pray to be in His disciples (17:13), will flood their souls as they live obedient lives (15:11), see answers to prayer (16:24) and live in resurrection celebration (16:26).

- **Peace**, which the apostle Paul says "passes all

understanding" (Philippians 4:6–7) will also garrison the spirits of the disciples as they come to understand His victory over the systems, thought, and behaviour patterns of the world: "I have said this to you, so that in me you may have peace. In the world you face persecution. But take courage; I have conquered the world!" (16:33). And what a mighty blessing to the human spirit is that peace of God passing all understanding.

- **The Person and work of the Holy Spirit.** More than all of that, this incredible One called *the Holy Spirit* will lead them on not only into some truth, but into "all truth" (16:13), at least all the truth necessary for a lost humanity to know and find His salvation. This Counsellor, this Holy Spirit, this "Spirit of Truth" (16:13) will further explicate to them the full significance of Jesus Christ. Indeed, says Jesus, "All that the Father has is mine. For this reason I said that he will take what is mine and declare it to you" (16:15). *A fullness of revelation will reach them.* And supernaturally by the Spirit, they will have perfect recall of everything He has taught them (14:26), obviously so that it may all be reliably inscripturated.

5. What is the point of it all?

The disciples must also have been asking themselves, in some measure at least, what is the point of it all? The answer from our Lord is: *mission carried out in love.*

They must get on out there to the world, which He is "leaving" (16:28), but which they must reach out to and tell about the interconnectedness of Father to Son, Son to Father, and both to Holy Spirit (14:25–31). Above all they must keep on loving each other (13:34; 15:17) because this will be the distinctive thing which will impress and convince the world (13:36) of something supernatural being on the go.

THE DISCIPLES BAMBOOZLED!

That the disciples remained somewhat bamboozled and befuddled by all this is suggested in the remark of relief they all utter when Jesus finally says very simply, and almost monosyllabically: "I came from the Father and entered the world; now I am leaving the world and going back to the Father" (16:28, NIV).

"Oh," they all say heaving a sigh of final and comprehending relief, "now you are speaking *clearly* and without figures of speech" (16:29, NIV). To them, poor things, everything up to that point must have seemed to have been "figures of speech"; riddles, metaphors, allegories, picture-talk. Anything but reality and fact! Now it seemed the clouds were lifting and comprehension was dawning.

THEN THE DISCIPLES ARE SHATTERED

However, their brief moment of relief and comprehension is then shattered by Jesus' parting shot!

His word (John 16:31–33) effectively is this: "You guys are in for such a rough ride just round the corner that your present and seemingly unshakeable togetherness is going to be shattered very shortly. You're going to scatter all over the place, and what's more, abandon me. Big time! And huge trouble is going to come at you from that hostile world-system. Anyway, not to worry. I won't be alone, in spite of your leaving me alone, as the Father will be with me. I'm telling you this so that 'in me you may have peace'" (verse 33a).

Jesus continues that they must "Cheer up, because this world-system, so opposed to me and which will also be opposed to you, I have in reality overcome" (verse 33b).

By this point the renewed appearance of expressionless eyes, blank stares and again uncomprehending demeanour of the disciples must have announced in the clearest possible terms to the Saviour that there was now nothing left to do for this little band of lost lads than pray for them!

Likewise for those of us who are preachers, the moment often comes at the end of a talk or sermon when we know the constraint not only to pray to the "Father" (17:1) and "the one true God" (17:3) but to sum up in the prayer the main contents of what has been shared and taught in one's talk. And this is exactly what Jesus does now.

SO HE PRAYS

As Jesus prays, the prayer for Himself, as the Man of Heaven, is *intercessory.*

But for His friends it is *exhortational*, containing words of comfort and encouragement. And all the threads of everything that has happened and been said from the Last Supper to the Last Sayings will be summarised now in this Last Supplication.

In fact the prayer really summarises all that has gone before in the Fourth Gospel. This simple reality explains why the main keys to understanding the prayer in chapter 17 lie in comprehending what has contextually preceded it, both more distantly and more immediately.

Another vital interpretive clue here is to register that our Lord is –

6. Connecting the church of subsequent centuries to the disciples in the first century

This is where we in the here and now are being prayed for. So it is that Jesus now connects the church of subsequent centuries into all He has just prayed for the disciples of the first century and vice versa. All His disciples of the past and the future are now caught up in the totality of the prayer as He prays not "for *these* only, but also for *those* who will believe in me through their word" (verse 20), so that the new and deeply prayed for unity is of both "these" and "those", "that they may *all* be one" (verse 21).

Thus the church of today is to manifest a unity with the apostolic church of yesterday (verse 22) in life, glory, truth, godliness, joy, mission, and love. This is the true so-called "apostolic succession". It is not some automatic, historical, ceremonial or organisational linking by the church and denominations of today to the church of the apostles, but a *spiritual* linking in truth, godliness, mission and love.

The real linkage is via these prayed-for qualities. Without these the world simply will find the whole so-called gospel story unbelievable. The credibility gap will be total.

How essential therefore to pray for such a unity of *these* of the first century with *those* of subsequent centuries "so that the world may believe" (verse 21), and beyond that (in factual, true, and sure terms) "know that you have sent me" (verse 23).

That's what Jesus really wants – that this world, which "God so loved… that he gave his only Son" (John 3:16) should *believe and know* that this is all true. Really true. Fact not fancy. History not mythology. True not false.

7. The deepest utterance ever

It is probably by now finally and at last dawning on the disciples, and they are ready to acknowledge it, that they have just eavesdropped, as it were, the deepest utterance our universe had ever heard. This utterance is now over. And the acts of love, atoning sacrifice, resurrection power, and Pentecostal outpouring of the Spirit, by which the universe would forever change gear, are about to happen.

And the whole universe is indeed on tiptoe. History cannot wait. It must now all proceed. "After Jesus had spoken these words, he went out with his disciples across the Kidron valley…" (18:1) to meet His final destiny on the other side of that little stream.

He is crossing His Rubicon.

HIS FACE NOW SET

With our Lord's mission almost accomplished, and His face now set irrevocably to the Cross of Calvary, *the victory from the divine side is already won* (13:31; 15:33).

From the human side, the full realisation of this victory was yet to be grasped and experienced (14:30; 16:22; 14:18–19).

THE DISCIPLES FINALLY REGISTER

But for the disciples they must surely have been beginning by now to register that they were being caught up in the central drama of all human history.

And they had overheard a prayer the likes of which had never before, or since, been heard on planet Earth. It would take both them and all who would follow them all their days to come to terms not only with what they had heard, but also with the shocking claims, assumptions, identity and petitions of the intercessor Himself.

And that of course is something with which we have to come to terms too. It is for each of us the challenge of a lifetime and sets the context and content of this book. It leads aptly into the next chapter where Jesus' world view or frame of reference is unpacked. And that inevitably means that our own worldview will be challenged.

Chapter 4

Jesus' World View (I)

Heaven and the Father

"A worldview… is a set of presuppositions (assumptions which may be true, partially true, or entirely false) which we hold (consciously or subconsciously, consistently or inconsistently) about the basic make-up of our world… for any of us to be fully conscious intellectually we should not only be able to detect the worldviews of others but be aware of our own – why it is ours, and why in the light of so many options, we think it is true."

James W. Sire, _The Universe Next Door_[1]

"Jesus… lifted up his eyes to heaven and said: 'Father…'"

The apostle John, John 17:1

"Then I saw a new heaven and a new earth; for the first heaven and the first earth had passed away…"

The apostle John, Revelation 21:1

As I got into this prayer, it wasn't long before I realised that its opening words throw us in the deep end of issues we might subsume under the category of "World View". In other words, we find ourselves face to face with how Jesus saw the world and the nature of the reality around Him. This happens in verse one as it records: "When Jesus had spoken those things, he lifted his eyes to heaven and said: 'Father…'"

As noted above, the American author James W. Sire has said: "A worldview is a set of presuppositions (assumptions which may be true, partially true, or entirely false) which we hold (consciously or subconsciously, consistently or inconsistently) about the basic make-up of our world."[2] Jean Paul Sartre's worldview was that "Every existing thing is born without reason, prolongs itself out of weakness and dies by chance."[3]

Then there is E. F. Cioran, one of the French atheistic and existentialist philosophers, who said: "Mankind is a race of convulsionaries living at the centre of a comic farce." One of Shakespeare's most famous characters, Macbeth was of the opinion that "Life's but... a tale told by an idiot, full of sound and fury, signifying nothing."[4]

Other views of the world we could take a look at include those of the late and celebrated astrophysicist, Carl Sagan: "The cosmos is all that is or ever was or ever will be."[5] In other words, he is saying that our planet is an accidental and inexplicable speck in the great enveloping dark of the cosmos. Or take the celebrated, and some would say, notorious Richard Dawkins: "We are survival machines... blindly programmed to preserve the selfish molecules known as genes. Our genes made us. We animals exist for our preservation and are nothing more than throwaway survival machines."[6]

In addition, he says:

In a universe of blind physical forces and genetic replication, some people are going to get hurt and other people are going to get lucky and you won't find any rhyme or reason in it, nor any justice. The universe we observe has precisely the properties we should expect if there is at bottom no design, no purpose, no evil and no good, nothing but blind pitiless indifference...[7]

A child working on his own world view prayed: "Dear God, I am American. What are you? Love, Robert."

An alternative religious world view holds to the notion of

reincarnation, that after living our lives here on earth we come back as some other creature or person. Thus reincarnation is the process whereby some entity – the soul, the self, or the consciousness – departs from our bodies upon death and is reborn as another form of life. In India, for example, the final goal of several of the different religions there is to escape from the cycle of reincarnation into a state of peace and spiritual fulfilment called "nirvana".

Of course there is also the popular lampooning of "pie in the sky". But suppose there is indeed pie in the sky! Might we not be pretty stupid to ignore it? And then miss it!

A world view quite clearly therefore speaks about our take on the world and how we perceive reality. The importance of this is that these things dictate how we react and how we respond to the circumstances and people around us.

1. So how is our world view formed?

A world view is formed first by our *perceptions*. In other words, it is formed by what our eyes see. Looking at a cloud formation, someone may say they see a man's face. Someone else says they see nothing but indications of rain!

Secondly, our world view is formed, and perception comes by, *what we are taught*. Our elders have taught us certain things. Certainly, through the process of having our culture taught and explained to us, we are – to a certain extent – indoctrinated to have the same world view as other members of our society.

Thirdly, our world view *is rooted in our upbringing and in what we are taught, all of which in turn influences our perceptions*. So it is that we are taught to interpret things in ways approved by our culture and are rewarded when we conform. Some brave people may decide to be non-conformists, but most will go along with the trend of things. Thus it is that in our culture, the generally prevailing view, taught even from departments of religion and some theological colleges and seminaries, is

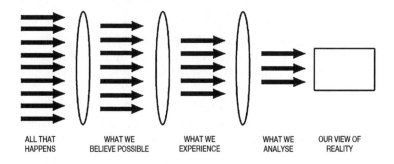

| ALL THAT HAPPENS | WHAT WE BELIEVE POSSIBLE | WHAT WE EXPERIENCE | WHAT WE ANALYSE | OUR VIEW OF REALITY |

that the Bible is not the fully inspired and authoritative Word of God but rather that our enthroned reason which is based on naturalistic presuppositions must sift out what to accept or reject from what we have learned.

Therefore, for example, when the apostle warns in Ephesians 6:12 that "We wrestle not against flesh and blood, but against principalities, powers and thrones", and that there are real demonic forces of evil supernaturalism and a personal force of evil called Satan, then we just screen it all out and conform ourselves theologically to a liberalised understanding of Scripture at that point. The only problem is that our world view in the process is shifting away from that of the Bible.

Fourthly, our world view is shaped by *how we are taught to see and interpret selectively*. Thus in most western societies, things which are material, economic, and political tend to be very much in focus and very real, whereas the existence and influence of the spiritual realm is either minimised or eliminated via our hermeneutical or interpretational grid of preconditioning.

Fifthly, our world view is formed by *the way we analyse what we believe possible and what we experience*. Thus if we have naturalistic presuppositions, and someone seems to be miraculously healed, we would rather say that this has come about by autosuggestion or something like that, rather than acknowledge a supernatural happening.

To sum up, as noted by St Paul, we see reality only dimly and partially through all too human lenses and filters, but one day, we will see and understand everything perfectly (1 Corinthians 13:12). In the meantime the way we are forming our world view is something like this.

Looking at the little diagram above we note that many influences, facts, teachings, perceptions, cultural dictates and so on shape our world view. But we should also note that the number of influences, as indicated by the number of arrows on the left, does decrease as we go from one side of the chart to the other. Thus it is that there are many more things that actually happen in reality than there are things we are taught to believe as possible. This means our view of reality is a much smaller picture than that of everything that does indeed happen.

Above all, we dare not define reality simply by the limits of our own experience, like the two fish in the fishbowl diagram below.

Or take the child learning their arithmetic tables. The father asked what 10 x 10 was, then 11 x 11, and then 12 x 12 and the child got all the right answers. Then the father asked, "What's 13 x 13?" To which the child replied, "Don't be silly Daddy, there's no such thing." Mathematical reality for them ended at 12 x 12. There could be nothing more! Sadly, for lamentable mathematicians like me, there is!

Anyway, for the Christian, it will be different because if our view of reality is drawn from Scripture, and we have a high view of Scripture, then we will be taking into account many realities which are unseen to us but which we receive by faith on the basis of what Scripture teaches.

2. The nature of world views

Summarising the nature of a world view the late South African missiologist David Bosch once wrote:

> World views are shaped by both inculcated (or assumed) faith convictions and by context, social status, emotional health and the like. They are shaped by both "theory" and "practice", which condition each other... A world view in its basic tenets is not argued to but from. It is not the terminus of our quest for insight, but our place of departure.[8]

If we go back to James Sire we find him opening his fine book entitled *The Universe Next Door* noting that: "For any of us to be fully conscious intellectually, we should not only be able to detect the world view of others but be aware of our own – why it is ours, and why in the light of so many options, we think it is true."[9]

This being so, clearly our world view is a set of beliefs which may be true, partially true, or untrue, but which we embrace about the basic nature and shape of our world. And out of this understanding we will answer questions about whether God made the world or whether it is accidental and the result of impersonal energy plus time plus chance. We will ask whether as human beings we are free or determined. We will establish for ourselves a set of morals or values. Our world view will tell us whether we are theists, atheists, materialists, or agnostics. And even if we think we are not embracing a world view, even that will constitute at the very least a philosophical position. This is why, as James Sire has said, "So long as we live, we will live either the examined or the unexamined life."[10]

THE EXAMINED LIFE IS OBVIOUSLY BETTER

For all of us, the examined life is obviously much better because it will bring forth coherent answers as to why we think or do certain things. Our life will have coherence because we know what we are on about and why. All of that is to say that where one starts from in life and in the understanding of it is pretty key. Start to try and climb Mount Everest from the wrong base camp and one will court disaster. Start a journey with the wrong map and one is doomed to get lost.

And so it is with our world view. Get it wrong here, and as with the wrong base camp, wrong map, wrong guide book, or wrong spectacles, so our aims to reach life's summits will be frustrated, our ability to take the right roads in life's journey will be torpedoed, our knowledge of how to make life's inner mechanisms work will be impaired, perhaps tragically, and our vision of what is really there will be perilously distorted. The fact is that our world view tells us where we come from, who we are, why we are here, where, if anywhere, we are going, how we should live, what realities we should keep cognisant of in life and behaviour.

That's why grasping our Lord's world view is so critical, because if He is right in the way He sees things, we imperil ourselves by not putting on the divine spectacles He wore, thereby missing out totally on seeing and comprehending the true nature of the world, reality, and life around us. Most tragic of all, we might miss out on the reality called heaven to which we should be connecting on a regular and daily basis – because there is Someone There, really there, called "Father". And due to his being omniscient and omnipotent, He can help us.

3. Jesus' world view – "heaven"

Let's repeat and note again our Lord's world view: "When Jesus had spoken these words, he lifted up his eyes *to heaven* and said, 'Father'… " (17:1).

What we must say right at the outset is that in both Old and New Testaments, heaven is endlessly referred to as "real"; it is a reality.

And in some ways totally beyond our comprehension, it is a *place*. We remember our Lord's monumental words in John 14:2: "I go to prepare a place for you." Then He added: "And if I go and prepare a place for you, I will come again and will take you to myself, so that where I am, there you may be also" (14:3).

Heaven is alluded to several different ways in Scripture:

THE WORD FOR "HEAVEN" – "*OURANOS*"

The Greek word *"ouranos"*, used here in John 17:1 and translated as "heaven" in our Bibles, is used in several different ways, all speaking of a realm where God is, though to which He is not confined, as Solomon noted when he prayed: "Even heaven and the highest heaven cannot contain you, much less this house that I have built!" (1 Kings 8:27).

THE ATMOSPHERE AROUND US

One use relates to the atmosphere around us, the air we breathe. So in Genesis we hear that "…the windows of the heavens were opened. The rain fell on the earth forty days and forty nights" (Genesis 7:11–12). The psalmist declares the

Lord covers this heaven "with clouds" (Psalm 147:8). This is, as it were, the "first heaven".

THIRD HEAVEN

Next is the third heaven Paul speaks of to the Corinthians as "paradise", which seems to be an intermediate heaven that will precede God's creation of a new heaven and a new earth (Isaiah 65:17; Revelation 21:1). This is the place where God and the angelic host dwell. Says the apostle, "I know a person in Christ who… was caught up to the third heaven… this man was caught up into Paradise" (2 Corinthians 12:2–4).

John MacArthur, an American writer, has made this observation:

> *[God's] dwelling-place – heaven – is not subject to the normal limitations of finite dimensions. We don't need to speculate about how this can be; it is sufficient to note that this is how Scripture describes heaven. It is a real place where people with physical bodies [see 1 Corinthians 15:43–44] will dwell in God's presence for all eternity…* [11]

At this point we must also register that a "spiritual body" is not a contradiction in terms, but rather a type of body, such as Jesus had after His resurrection, which is not confined by time, space, or physical limitations. Thus could He appear and disappear (Luke 24:31) and not be confined by walls (John 20:19 and 26). "He was buried, and… he was raised on the third day in accordance with the scriptures" (1 Corinthians 15:4). We will, in other words, have heavenly bodies suited to the heavenly realm. What a destiny!

The apostle Paul can go further and speak for each Christian believer saying: "Our citizenship is in *heaven*" (Philippians 3:20). In a strange way, all who believe are positionally already living in heaven and in the kingdom of God.

HEAVEN IS ALSO THE PLACE BEYOND

Carol and I remember back some years ago meeting the brave and lovely Joni Eareckson Tada. Joni had broken her neck in a swimming/diving accident and became paralysed from the shoulders down. But she bears an amazing and deeply inspirational testimony and in her book on *Heaven* she writes: "I still can hardly believe it. I, with shrivelled, bent fingers, atrophied muscles, gnarled knees, and no feeling from the shoulders down, will one day have a new body, light, bright, and clothed in righteousness, powerful and dazzling…"[12]

Adds Joni:

> It's so easy for me to "be joyful in hope", as it says in Romans 12:12, and that's exactly what I've been doing for the past twenty-odd years. My assurance of Heaven is so alive that I've been making dates with friends to do all sorts of fun things once we get our new bodies… I don't take these appointments lightly. I'm convinced these things will really happen.[13]

I agree. And it is going to be wonderful and in a strange way scary beyond measure!

WONDERFUL TRUTHS OF 1 CORINTHIANS 2:9

I remember one instructive experience during an early mission in the African Enterprise ministry in 1965 in the small northern Natal city of Ladysmith in South Africa. I preached night after night for three weeks in that city hall. One evening, while preaching, the verse 1 Corinthians 2:9 kept coming into my mind, sort of swooping into my consciousness.

I was not preaching on that, or anything remotely connected to it, but again and again and again as I preached this text its truth pressed itself to the front of my mind. "Eye has not seen, nor ear heard, Nor have entered into the heart of man The things which God has prepared for those who love

Him." After protesting to the Lord a bit that this was not part of my theme, I finally gave up and found a moment at which to speak the text out boldly and clearly.

Next day, at the mission office, a woman, probably in her late sixties, barrelled in and insisted on seeing me. She told me she had committed her life to Christ the previous evening in the city hall meeting and had almost immediately and overwhelmingly come into a sense of encounter with Christ and coming to know Him. Then she continued her story: "You know, it happened for me when you spoke out the verse of 1 Corinthians 2:9 that the 'eye has not seen nor ear heard, neither has there entered the heart of man what God has prepared for them that love Him.'"

She then told me she had been a prodigal daughter and had almost broken her praying mother's heart. Her other siblings had come early in their lives to a knowledge of Christ but she had been a rebel. For years and years and years her mother had faithfully prayed for her daughter to come to know the Saviour. Finally, when her mother was *in extremis* on her deathbed she told this lady that she wanted to give her her Bible. Then her mother added: "But before I do so, I want to write in it a special scripture which I feel God has given me for you." At that point she inscribed 1 Corinthians 2:9 into the flap of the Bible, and there it has been ever since. "When you shared that scripture, all my mother's prayers over multiple years came back to me, as well as her longing for me to repent of my sins and come to Christ. As I heard that verse I knew that this was the night for me. And I committed my life there and then at the end of the message."

It was a lovely and beautiful story of God's faithfulness in answering the prayers of His children, and especially of parents for their offspring. For me, however, this stunning story has always stood in my mind as an awesome reminder of the glories that await us in heaven. So too the Apostle can write in Romans 8:18: "I consider that the sufferings of this present time are not worth comparing with the glory that is to be revealed to us."

HEAVEN IS ALSO A PLACE OF MEETING LOVED ONES

Many years ago my late friend Mick Milligan told me the story of a man on his deathbed. He was a great Christian and had been a wonderful and faithful servant of the Lord. This man's special friend on his earthly journey had been Frank Millard, commonly known around South Africa as Hippo, the head in South Africa of the Children's Special Service Mission (CSSM) – what later came to be known as Scripture Union. He had a marvellous gift with children. He was also the father of my very great university friend, David Millard who died back in 1978. "Hippo" Millard had some years previously gone to be with the Lord and now his great friend was close to the end of his life.

Suddenly, to everyone's astonishment, said Mick, the man on his deathbed sat bolt upright, his eyes radiant and his face alive with joy, and shouted: "Hippo!" Seemingly the Lord had told Hippo in heaven that his good friend was coming home that day and would he not like to go and meet him and usher him into his heavenly home? The picture, the happening and the spiritual reality commended itself to my mind as a real statement of some of the glories of heaven. Among these will be meeting loved ones who have gone ahead of us.

HEAVEN WILL ALSO BE A PLACE OF TOTAL HEALING

St Paul affirms in his classic chapter on the resurrection and the resurrection of the dead (1 Corinthians 15:42) that: "It is sown a physical body, it is raised a spiritual body" (1 Corinthians 15:42–43). "… Just as we have borne the image of the man of dust [Adam], we will also bear the image of the man of heaven [Jesus]" (1 Corinthians 15:49). In other words, the kind of spiritual resurrection body which Jesus had, not confined by limitations of time and space, yet a body for all that (and remember how our Lord could eat and drink), is the kind of healed and perfected body the Lord's children will inherit in heaven.

So it was to this heaven in the atmosphere, air, and sky around him, and as a real place beyond this earth, that Jesus was looking when he lifted up his eyes and said: "Father..." (John 17:1).

The implications of this in terms of both His world view, and how it must affect ours, are awesome. And they are also most marvellously comforting. Let's take a look at John's words in Revelation:

> Then I saw a new heaven and a new earth; for the first heaven and the first earth had passed away, and the sea was no more. And I saw the holy city, the new Jerusalem, coming down out of heaven from God, prepared as a bride adorned for her husband. And I heard a loud voice from the throne saying, "See, the home of God is among mortals. He will dwell with them; they will be his peoples, and God himself will be with them; he will wipe every tear from their eyes. Death will be no more; mourning and crying and pain will be no more, for the first things have passed away."
>
> And the one who was seated on the throne said, "See, I am making all things new." Also he said, "Write this, for these words are trustworthy and true."
>
> **Revelation 21:1–5**

Yes, trustworthy and true. In other words this is actually how it is. And exactly as it will be. True not false. Fact not fiction. Reality.

In Jesus' world view there is one true God who is our Father and he is in heaven.

BUT IS HEAVEN OUR FINAL DESTINY AND RESTING PLACE?

So is heaven really as we are imagining it to be, or – as it is popularly conceived, even in the church – is it the end of the story? Is heaven in fact our final home? Once the so-called "day of the Lord" (see, for example Joel 1:15; Amos 5:18; 1 Thessalonians 5:2; 2 Peter 3:10) has arrived, and once the second coming of our Lord, "the day of Christ", has taken place (Matthew 24:27, 30, 44; Philippians 1:10; Acts 1:11, etc.), as personal, visible and glorious, and once the resurrection of the dead (Revelation 20:11–13) has happened, and once God's final judgment (John 5:22; 2 Corinthians 5:10; Matthew 25:31–46; Revelation 20:11–15) has been rendered, will the redeemed all settle back into this place called heaven to relax and praise God for millennia?

Is that the scenario? Is that where the biblical world view wraps up? Or is that perhaps not a truncated scenario? An incomplete picture?

If we think not, what then of the reference a few moments ago to Revelation 21:1 where John's vision catapults us into new and almost unthinkable vistas of new possibilities and unimaginable realities.

A new heaven and a new earth

Let's revisit John's words: "Then I saw a *new* heaven and a *new* earth; for the first heaven and the first earth had passed away" (Revelation 21:1).

What about 2 Peter 3:11–13: "Since all these things are to be dissolved in this way, what sort of persons ought you to be in leading lives of holiness and godliness, waiting for and hastening the coming of the day of God, because of which the heavens will be set ablaze and dissolved, and the elements will melt with fire? But, in accordance with his promise, we wait for a new heaven and a new earth, where righteousness is at home."

This idea was not new, for had not Isaiah brought this divine revelation even in his day? "Behold, I create *new* heavens and a *new* earth" (Isaiah 65:17).

Most of my life I have just rushed over those verses without stopping to reflect on or ask what they really mean. But if we're seriously thinking about the Bible and Jesus' world view we can't really do that.

What is clear, of course, is that heaven and earth, as normally used, seem to speak of the totality of God's original creation. But now the concept of all that passing away makes us catch our breath, as this picture of a *new* heaven and a *new* earth seems to speak of an even fuller scope of His redeeming and re-creating plan. In fact, as the human world in John's vision of "the new heaven and new earth" will have "no tears, death, mourning nor crying nor pain anymore" (Revelation 21:4), so even the animal world with its violence and threats will also be tamed, redeemed, and brought to peace. Remember Isaiah's lovely and celebrated picture: "The wolf and the lamb shall feed together, the lion will eat straw like the ox; but the serpent – its food shall be dust. They shall not hurt or destroy on all my holy mountain, says the Lord" (Isaiah 65:25).

All this suggests that in the creation of a new heaven and a new earth to which we are ultimately headed after the first heaven and the first earth have passed away" (Revelation 21:1), there will be a renewed and redeemed humanity, alongside even a renewed and redeemed animal kingdom. I always loved C. S. Lewis's notion, shared also by Joni Eareckson Tada, that we will again enjoy our special animal pets in heaven! Why not? In all of this of course, our minds reel in even superficial contemplation. Might I again see Dingo and Shandy, my dogs, and Punch, my horse, and Bhubesi our cat? And again frolic and have fun with them? I wouldn't be surprised.

The British theologian Chris Wright puts it this way:

*The scope of God's redeeming work is as vast as the whole universe He created. It is also a way of telling us clearly that although we are heading for a new reality, it is not a fundamentally different reality. We are not leaving the created order for some other "spiritual" order. Rather, we will be leaving the old sinful order of things and will find ourselves in a renewed, restored, redeemed creation. But it is still "heaven **and** earth", not "heaven instead of earth". Rather, it promises us a whole new creation that includes the earth.*[14]

The old heaven will be home, says Wright "only until the new heaven and the new earth – God's new creation – becomes our eternal home."[15]

He adds:

> Christians who keep on talking about "going to heaven" – as if that were their last great hope – seem to have missed the whole point of the way the Bible ends. Look again at the wonderful picture in Revelation 21–22. It says nothing about us going off to heaven or to anywhere else at all. Rather, it shows us God coming down to earth, transforming the whole creation into the new heaven and new earth that He had promised in Isaiah 65:17, and then living here with us – on earth.
>
> In other words, the Bible's last great vision is not of us going "up" there (to heaven), but of God coming "down" here (to earth)… Immanuel means "God with us" – and that's how the Bible ends. God coming to be with us (repeated three times in Revelation 21:3), not us going off to be with God.[16]

Perhaps for you, as for me until recently (while working on this chapter), such a notion seems very strange. We've always mixed in some literal, physical thoughts of maybe heavenly spiritual bodies with the vague, ethereal non-specific but happy place we've non-reflectively called heaven. That was it. That's where we left it. But it eluded our grasp. Would heaven be some sort of permanent Sunday church service of praise songs and liturgy going on indefinitely forever and ever – in many ways a most alarming prospect? Or would we, sort of ghost-like, as some conceive it, float around midst the sound of Mantovani strings meeting other ghosts, albeit recognisable but incorporeal? And we'd chat spirit to spirit about spiritual things and the Bible for all eternity, occasionally checking in with Jesus for another praise session, or seeking some light on another tricky theological question!

But we'd never really thought or worked our way into

the Bible's full teaching on heaven, least of all into God having an even more startling, incarnational, and semi-physical final purpose of erecting not just a new heaven, the first having been intermediate, but a new earth, the first having been provisional. A new cosmos, one might say. And then bringing them all together.

JESUS IS PREPARING A PLACE

Of course, like the disciples hearing Jesus' teaching in the Final Discourse, we've learned also from Jesus, as mentioned, that He was "going to prepare a place" for us (John 14:2) which would have "many rooms" – a better translation of the original than "many mansions" (NKJV), although I much prefer the poetry and picture of many mansions! To be sure "a place" – with "rooms" (RSV), or mansions all seems physical enough. And if Jesus is indeed preparing a place, surely that place will be the most awesome and special of any places ever prepared by anyone for anyone!

Then we remember reading that Abraham was not looking forward to floating happily towards some sort of ethereal space called heaven, but that he "was looking forward to the *city* with foundations, whose architect and builder is God" (Hebrews 11:10, NIV). We are back to the physical. His descendants "were longing for a better *country* – a *heavenly* one" (Hebrews 11:16, NIV), and not for an invisible realm housing billions of spirits in everlasting doxology. So, a heavenly country. As for Christ's followers, we are told that right now "we do not have an enduring city, but we are looking for the *city* that is to come" (Hebrews 13:14, NIV).

In reality, believers here should not be looking forward to or longing for an unearthly realm, but rather an incarnational and physical *new heaven* and *new earth*.

American theologian Randy Alcorn, who has written an encyclopedic book simply called *Heaven* (termed the most comprehensive and definitive book on heaven to date), writes:

Heaven is God's home. Earth is our home. Jesus Christ, as the God-man, forever links God and mankind, and thereby forever links Heaven and Earth. As Ephesians 1:10 demonstrates, this idea of Earth and Heaven becoming one is explicitly biblical. Christ will make Earth into Heaven and Heaven into Earth. Just as the wall that separates God and mankind is torn down in Jesus, so too the wall that separates Heaven and Earth will be forever demolished. There will be one universe, with all things in Heaven and on Earth together under one head, Jesus Christ...

This is the unstoppable plan of God. This is where history is headed. When God walked with Adam and Eve in the Garden, Earth was Heaven's backyard. The New Earth will be even more than that – it will be Heaven itself. And those who know Jesus will have the privilege of living there. [17]

Writes Dallas Willard: "The life we now have as the persons we now are will continue in the universe in which we now exist." [18]

C. S. Lewis, whose Narnia and other stories, grapple in metaphorical and picture form with some of these understandings believes that "the hills and valleys of heaven will be to those you now experience not as a copy is to an original, not as a substitute is to the genuine article, but as the flower is to the root, or the diamond to the coal". [19]

What Lewis and others are here feeling after is the sense of an incarnational heaven, linked and rooted to life we have known on earth, but all transformed. The nostalgias we feel on earth about wanting our causes or ventures to survive and come to fruition and fulfilment will indeed be one day fulfilled and brought forth. Might my unfulfilled dreams of one day playing the Chopin ballades actually come to fruition?

A. A. Hodges, a theologian of yesteryear had a similar feeling when he movingly wrote:

> *Heaven, as the eternal home of the divine Man and*
> *of all the redeemed members of the human race,*
> *must necessarily be thoroughly human in its structure,*
> *conditions and activities. Its joys and activities must all*
> *be rational, moral, emotional, voluntary and active. There*
> *must be the exercise of all the faculties, the gratification*
> *of all tastes, the development of all talent capacities,*
> *the realization of all ideals… Heaven will prove the*
> *consummate flower and fruit of the whole creation and*
> *of all the history of the universe.*[20]

For the believer, such an incarnational vision of heaven, or of the new heaven and the new earth, if such be rightly understood, must thrill our hearts with anticipation, with wonder, awe, and leave us in some ways, maybe both literally and metaphorically "breathless" with excitement when our moment of death bears in on us and when we "have shuffled off this mortal coil".[21] For this will be our birthday into the new reality, into the real thing, when we will know a richness of experience never previously experienced.

Peter Pan, in J. M. Barrie's classic of the same name, was right when he exulted: "To die will be an awfully big adventure."[22]

When Dietrich Bonhoeffer was being taken to the Nazi gallows, he said to a friend as he went out: "This is the end, but for me it is the beginning of life."

As a teenager once put it to me, "Uncle Mike, heaven's going to be a blast."

I agree!

Of course, all that we have been talking about takes us off the dial of human comprehension, but even making allowances for our difficulties in interpreting apocalyptic language, prophecy, and imagery, and the ease of getting it wrong, nevertheless it reminds us of realities in the biblical world view that are unimaginably awesome, mysterious and glorious. The journey of the believer is the ultimate adventure.

Perhaps then from now on when we quote 1 Corinthians 2:9: "Eye has not seen, nor ear heard, neither has there entered the heart of man, the things God has prepared for those who love Him" (NKJV), we must then be both brave and excited enough to read the next verse (10), "but God has revealed them to us by the Spirit."

And He has. Especially if we read the scripture in its totality.

There is something else. We can most assuredly know one thing, as the apostle puts it: "We shall be changed" (1 Corinthians 15:52). We shall be transformed into the full richness and perfection that God originally intended for us. And that will be glorious! "We shall be like him, for we shall see him as he is" (1 John 3:2).

Now for the next major dimension in our Lord's world view.

4. "Jesus... lifted up his eyes to heaven and said: 'Father'..." (John 17:1)

For Jesus, God is *Father*. This is how the New Testament reveals Him. In other religions, God is viewed as an impersonal Spirit. Or judge. Or "the Force" referenced in the *Star Wars* films. Or simply creator. Or the detached deist, watch-maker God *(deus ex machina)*, in other words, the God who has made the machine of creation but stands outside it. He it is who made the watch of the universe, wound it, but who now stands back disinterestedly while it runs (down) on its own.

No! For Jesus, the spiritual environment is inhabited by one called "Father". It is not empty. Not void. Not bereft of habitation. Not soul-less. Someone is there. Someone real inhabits it. Someone Jesus calls Father. He wasn't talking to Himself. Or to the disciples, or to empty, godless space. He was addressing someone He called "Father".

This address and salutation is a line in the sand. If the "one true God" is not really there, then real notions of truth, morality, meaning, purpose, accountability, and responsibility cannot truly be there either. At least not in any ultimate sense. But if the one true God is really there, all these categories listed above become true and real, once again. Which side of the line we stand on suddenly becomes all-determinative.

POLITICAL CORRECTNESS AND GENDER SENSITIVITY

For those who, in modern times, are gripped with the notions of political correctness and gender sensitivity, or those whose earthly experience of a father has been abusive or oppressive, hackles can rise at this point – at the very first word of Jesus' prayer.

However, our insisting that there be no reinterpretation of the text here is only to stay true to Jesus' revelation here and not to aid and abet the cause of male chauvinism or insensitive conservatism, nor to fuel provocatively the opposing cause of radical feminism, but just to be true to how Jesus reveals the God who is there.

It is important on the other hand, not to load the biblical symbol of God's Fatherhood with notions of an oppressive patriarchal society, whether in the ancient world or now.

BALANCING MALE AND FEMALE

So we do also note that the Scriptures balance the supposedly male characteristics of God with wonderful female images as well. So the psalmist can say: "I have calmed and quieted my soul, like a weaned child with its mother; my soul is like the weaned child that is with me" (Psalm 131:2). Isaiah likewise can report the divine question: "Can a woman forget her nursing child, or show no compassion for the child of her womb? Even these may forget, yet I will not forget you" (Isaiah 49:15). Or as when Jesus rebukes Jerusalem and laments: "How often have I desired to gather your children together as a hen gathers her brood under her wings, and you were not willing!" (Matthew 23:37).

In the light of this, we do well to acknowledge that Jesus addressing God as Father must surely transcend all our inadequate images of earthly fathers, or of a divine being who is predominantly male! He is beyond all maleness and femaleness, all human fatherhood or motherhood.

THE PLACE OF FATHERHOOD AND "ABBA" IN GOD'S SCHEME

In this regard, the fact that our Lord opens His prayer to one He calls Father, and then teaches us to open our own praying to one we are to call "Our Father", alerts us to the place of Fatherhood and Father in God's scheme of things.

This is particularly relevant for modern humans – and even modern Christians, because we live in an age where there has been a massive failure in fathering. The NFI (National Fatherhood Initiative) states that, in the US, "the most consequential social problem of our time [is the] widespread father absence in the lives of our nation's children…"[23]

I remember being deeply moved when I first read the story of the famous James Boswell (1740–94) who became celebrated as a close friend of Samuel Johnson, the writer, philosopher, and wit. Boswell tells in his autobiography of a day when, as a child, his father took him fishing. He records it as the most wonderful and memorable day of his childhood. Later his father's journals were found and they recorded the father's commentary on that day in these terms: "Today went fishing with my son. A day totally wasted." For the father, a day of totally wasted effort, and for the son the highlight of his childhood.

Yes, the hazards of poor fathering.

GOD IS ABBA, FATHER, DADDY

Multitudes in our time experience similar things. Thankfully, significant healing can come for those who suffered poor fathering, not only by forgiving deeply the earthly father who failed, but in finding afresh the heavenly Father who never fails. And this indeed is how our God wants us to know him. He is "Abba", "Father", "Daddy". Indeed the whole redemptive enterprise is to enable us to find Him truly and deeply as Father and be able to address Him as such. Thus Romans 8:14–16 can record that "all who are led by the Spirit of God are sons of God. For you did not receive the spirit of slavery to fall back into fear, but you received the spirit of sonship. When we cry 'Abba! Father!' it is the Spirit himself bearing witness with our spirit that we are children of God."

This is a majorly glorious truth. The whole enterprise of redemption is what makes adoption by God possible so that as noted, we may call Him Abba, Father. And being able to say Abba/Daddy/Father is evidence that we have received both the redemption and the adoption (see Galatians 4:4–7), which is possible through Christ's work on the Cross and that His Spirit is now at work in us with the purpose of enabling us to call Him Father. We thus become by adoption what we are not by nature. By nature we are God's creatures, not His children. By adoption we become His children, and we can then, and only then call Him Abba, Father.

And we are entering and embracing Jesus' worldview.

*** ***

So as Jesus prayed to His Father, so can we. And as we do so we too enter His world view which starts with heaven and one who is really there who is called Father.

Chapter 5

Jesus' World View (II)

His Revolutionary Self-Understanding

"He who has seen me has seen the Father."

John 14:9

"The threefold evidence of his actions, his promises and his claims all set Jesus apart from other men. Who do you say that he is? It is the most important judgment you will ever make. He confronts you head on and says, 'Make up your mind. Decide.'"

Michael Green, _Who is this Jesus?_[1]

"A man who can read the New Testament and not see that Christ claims to be more than a man, can look all over the sky at high noon on a cloudless day and not see the sun."

William Biederwolf

"I am trying here to prevent anyone saying the really foolish thing that people often say about Him: 'I'm ready to accept Jesus as a great moral teacher, but I don't accept His claim to be God.' That is the one thing we must not say. A man who was merely a man and said the sort of things Jesus said would not be a great moral teacher. He would either be a lunatic – on a level with the man who says he is a poached egg – or else he would be the Devil of Hell. You must make your choice."

C. S. Lewis, _Mere Christianity_[2]

Now here's the major shock! We have talked about Jesus praying to God the Father. But what now are we to do with His breath-catching self-understanding? You see:

1. He sees Himself as one with the Father

Jesus sees Himself as having shared glory with the Father before the world was made. Look at verse 5 of John 17: "So now, Father, glorify me in your own presence with the glory that I had in your presence before the world existed."

This is a mind-boggling self-perception. It had earlier been presented to the disciples in order to comfort them, and was said in the most startling and shocking of terms with Jesus' astonishing utterance:

> *Do not let your hearts be troubled. Believe in God, believe also in me. In my Father's house there are many dwelling places. If it were not so, would I have told you that I go to prepare a place for you? And if I go and prepare a place for you, I will come again and will take you to myself, so that where I am, there you may be also. And you know the way to the place where I am going.*
>
> **John 14:1–4**

SHOCKED AND BEWILDERED

It is inevitable and a small wonder that the disciples too in their time were shocked and as bewildered as if they had received an upper cut when they heard these words, for Jesus was allowing them to see – as we said earlier – His own world view: how He saw reality, and how He saw both God and Himself and the nature of their relationship. Said Thomas, still the Doubter, "Lord, we do not know where you are going. How can we know the way?" (John 14:5). Now come Jesus' momentous and famous words: "I am the way, and the truth, and the life. No one comes to the Father except through me" (John 14:6).

He then adds, almost parenthetically, "If you know me, you will know my Father also. From now on you do know him and have seen him" (John 14:7).

Known and seen the Father? God the Father? Jehovah God? The Lord Most High? The creator of the universe? Come now, Lord, no time for fables. Not a moment to pull our legs or tantalise us. Known and seen the Father? What talk is this? We're here in Jerusalem. Middle East. Planet Earth. History. Geography.

Philip has to speak up and says in effect: "Lord, you keep talking about the Father – Father this, Father that – just 'show us the Father, and we will be satisfied'" (John 14:8).

Now listen to this, O Earth, now listen to this third Millennium humankind, now listen to this pluralist pilgrims, now listen to this New Age spiritual searchers, now church, now one and all, listen to this: "Jesus said to him [Philip]: 'Have I been with you so long, and yet you have not known me, Philip? *He who has seen me has seen the Father'*" (John 14:9).

This must have been numbing. Overwhelming. Yes, shocking. Our finite minds are poleaxed. This one revealed to us as Father has in Jesus' self-understanding and in His world view incarnated Himself and stepped onto our planet in the person of the Nazarene carpenter. This Word, or self-expression of God, which "was with God" and "was God" (John 1:1) has "become flesh and dwelt among us" (1:14a). And some who were there and were eyewitnesses to it all "have seen his glory, the glory as of a father's only son, full of grace and truth" (John 1:14b).

2. His death has unique significance in the history of the universe

We see first of all that Jesus assumes His death to be a unique moment in the history of the universe. As this moment arrives Jesus says in the first five words of the High Priestly Prayer,

"Father, the hour has come" (John 17:1).

Jesus is here saying that there is a moment, a time, an "hour" that is consequential above all others. Nor is this just *"an"* hour – one among many – but this is *"the* hour". This is the central moment and hour in the history of the universe.

If we backtrack from John 17, we notice at once that it was towards this hour that Jesus had been moving all His earthly life. Back at the beginning of His ministry, as early as the wedding at Cana of Galilee, He could affirm that His "hour" had "not yet come" (John 2:4).

When some of the Jews tried to seize Him after He had taught in the temple, they could not, because, Jesus' "hour had not yet come" (John 7:30; 8:20).

The notion of "not here yet" pervades most of Jesus' ministry as He speaks of His "hour". But when the die which would take Him to Jerusalem, the Passover Feast and to His death gets cast, His language takes on a different tone. "The hour *has* come for the Son of Man to be glorified" (John 12:23).

And immediately He speaks of death. Says the next verse: "Very truly, I tell you, unless a grain of wheat falls into the earth and dies, it remains just a single grain; but if it dies, it bears much fruit" (verse 24).

At which point, at this talk of death, Jesus finds His "heart troubled" (verse 27a), and shrinking – "shall I say... 'Father, save me from *this hour*?'" (verse 27c). At which point He inserts a conversational and a telegram-like prayer: "Father, glorify your name" (John 12:28).

Somehow this death, now connected unambiguously to this "hour", is also intimately related to the notion of "glorifying" the Father's name. The hour, the death, the glory, the name, the Father. All are interrelated.

SOMETHING ASTONISHING – AND VOID OF PRECEDENT

The "hour" of which Jesus speaks as He enters Jerusalem on His way to His final earthly destiny is so monumental that something cataclysmic and cosmic had to greet it – this arrival in history of the "hour". Something neither you nor I ever heard. The heavens open, the skies split, the atmosphere is rent – and – "Then a voice came from Heaven, 'I have glorified it [His name], and I will glorify it again'" (John 12:28).

This is extraordinary. A voice. Not a voice from a radio. Not a voice from the Jerusalem Broadcasting Corporation or from a loudmouth in the crowd. But instead from this arena of unseen reality we have been talking about. Its boom must have been awesome... because the crowd that was there and heard it said it *thundered* (John 12:29a). Others, not sure of the origin, source or cause of the voice nevertheless felt it was supernatural in origin. Says the text: "Others said, 'An angel had spoken to Him'" (verse 29b). But all knew it was a voice, a voice like thunder.

Now remember what we said just now about world view? All of this speaks ruination to world views which ignore or omit the biblical picture of things. Earth. Heaven. Voices from Heaven. A Father in Heaven. A Son on Earth. Talk between them.

And all linked to an *hour*! An hour interconnecting heaven and earth, Father and Son, sinners and Saviour, physics and metaphysics, natural and supernatural, narrative and meta-narrative, local and universal.

THIS HOUR OF HOURS IS RELATED TO THE DEATH OF DEATHS

Beyond all that, this hour of hours was an hour relating to the death of deaths. The death of a Nazarene carpenter and Galilean country preacher, which in some way beyond finite comprehension would shake all the powers of heaven and hell, affect salvation and judgment, and even address the forces(s) of evil supernaturalism originating from one Jesus calls "the prince of this world" (John 12:31, NIV).

We are caught holding our breaths and are not sure what to make of it all. Least of all this thunderous voice.

Jesus explains: "This voice has come for your sake, not for mine. Now is the judgment of this world; now the ruler of this world will be driven out. And I, when I am lifted up from the earth, will draw all people to myself" (John 12:30–32). Adds John: "He said this to indicate the kind of death he was to die" (John 12:33).

This hour, this death, was just not any hour or any death. This would affect both earth and the realm beyond earth. Something of cosmic, eternal, universal significance was happening. Even the devil himself (the prince of this world) would be affected. Demonic power in its ultimate terms was being broken. The devil was being driven out.

Yes, this was the hour for which Jesus had come into the world – the hour when He would go to the Cross, die, be buried and then rise again to bring redemption and salvation to the human race.

Comments Marcus Rainsford: "Many an hour had passed on the dial of time since time began, but no hour like this."[3]

So the major shock here in terms of Jesus' petitionary utterances is that He sees the Hour of His death as unique in the history of the universe.

Now something else.

3. He had all authority

He assumed and declared He had authority over all flesh, even to the giving and defining of eternal life as knowing both the Father and Himself.

Now if this doesn't shock us, I don't know what will!

And if we had any doubt that Jesus was claiming, assuming, or presupposing His own shared deity with the Father, then all such doubts become for ever banished at this point.

Listen again to His exact words in the Prayer:

*Father, the hour has come; glorify your Son so that the
Son may glorify you, since you have given him authority
over all people, to give eternal life to all whom you have
given him. And this is eternal life, that they may know
you, the only true God, and Jesus Christ whom you
have sent. I glorified you on earth by finishing the work
that you gave me to do. So now, Father, glorify me in
your own presence with the glory that I had in your
presence before the world existed.*

John 17:1–5

So now here again we see Jesus between heaven and earth,
between God and Man, between nature and supernature,
between the physical and metaphysical. Here is Jesus as Man
on earth speaking to God in heaven about giving to humans on
earth an eternal life that will start on earth through knowing
Him and go on into eternity itself in heaven.

All of this stretches our finite minds out to their furthest
limits. Here again we stare into the fathomless mysteries of
what poet G. K. Chesterton called "that incredible interruption
that broke the very backbone of history". But in so doing,
says Chesterton, it "did not shake the world, it steadied the
world".[4]

Yes, as we stare, we are in truth steadied, not shaken or
broken. We don't run away. We don't flee. We don't hide. We
don't deny. We don't rationalise, explain, demythologise, look
for a way out. No, we take off our shoes. We bow. We adore.
We worship. We submit. We receive. We believe. And we
know we are on holy ground.

AND WHY?

And why do we do all that? Well, because our Jesus has had
all authority in heaven and on earth given to Him. That is the
first gift from the Father to the Son. All authority. All power.
As He said elsewhere: "All authority in heaven and on earth
has been given to me" (Matthew 28:18). If the first gift is all

authority, the second gift given by the Father to the Son is that of a people. A people who will receive eternal life as they come to know "the only true God, and Jesus Christ whom you have sent" (John 17:3).

It is to be noted that the words "you have given him" appear twice in verse 2 – the first time referring to "authority over *all flesh*" (NKJV), and the second to the "all" *of a believing people* given by the Father to the Son.

This is overwhelming.

AUTHORITY OVER ALL FLESH

Perhaps the most striking word here, then, is "all". All flesh. That means all humans, and all parts of all humans – body, mind and soul.

Jesus has an authority which in scope knows no limits, not in heaven where even all judgment has been committed by the Father to the Son (John 5:22), and certainly not on earth, over which He could claim to have "all power/authority" (Matthew 28:18).

James Montgomery Boice wrote: "All [flesh] means everyone, everyone who has ever lived or who will ever live. It means the other person. It means me. No one is excepted from the scope of this universal authority of the Lord Jesus Christ."[5]

The same kind of all encompassing authority is vividly conveyed in Paul's famous utterance in Philippians 2:6–7. Here he talks about Jesus who, though in the form of God, could empty Himself, and humble Himself to "taking the form of a slave, being born in human likeness. And being found in human form, he humbled himself and became obedient to the point of death – even death on a cross" (verses 7–8). And then come the celebrated words speaking of this authority over heaven and earth.

Therefore God also highly exalted him and gave him the name that is above every name, so that at the name of

*Jesus every knee should bend, in heaven and on earth
and under the earth, and every tongue should confess
that Jesus Christ is Lord, to the glory of God the Father.*
Philippians 2:9–11

All authority in heaven and on earth. Every knee in heaven
and on earth one day finally bowing to Him. Every tongue
one day finally confessing Him as Lord. All this puts paid to
any temptations we might have to the enticements of religious
pluralism, syncretism, or multi-faith. For these are the claims
and assumptions of both Saviour and Scriptures where
absolutes and not relatives are the coinage of the moment.

4. Eternal life for humans could only be received as *a gift* from Him

Now the authority Jesus has is in this instance sharply focused.
It is authority to be the dispenser and giver of eternal life.

Yes! Eternal life. Nothing more. Nothing less. Eternal life.
And He is the one who gives it.

This to be sure carries the shockwaves further. In many
ways the whole prayer, and the whole redemptive initiative
of God is about eternal life and how humans can find it,
enter it, experience it, enjoy it now, and celebrate it forever.
Jesus could thus sum up His entire incarnational and earthly
ministry saying: "I came that they may have life [Greek *Zoe* –
i.e. eternal life], and have it abundantly" (John 10:10). Jesus'
reason for coming was so that we could find *eternal life*.

John 3:16, the best known and most dearly loved text in
the whole Bible, couldn't be clearer: "For God so loved the
world that he gave his only Son, that whoever believes in him
should not perish but have *eternal life*." Eternal life is what it's
all about. Not perishing but finding eternal life. To miss that
is to miss all. To fail to find that is to fail, period. It's what we
were made for and born for. Eternal life is the one thing we
need – for life, for death, in time, in eternity.

And the giver and dispenser of this ultimate gift, this pearl of most precious price, is Jesus. None other. Indeed. "There is salvation in no one else, for there is no other name under heaven given among men by which we must be saved" (Acts 4:12).

Again we are faced with a claim so daring, so audacious, so brazen and breathtaking that we are tempted to hurry on and leave our reflective capacities at the roadside of neglect or postponement.

But if we pause, reflect, absorb, and register, we are driven once again yet further from the enticements of modern religious pluralism.

JESUS' ASTONISHING DEFINITION OF ETERNAL LIFE

And of course here we find ourselves with the only concise definition of eternal life in the New Testament. It is as plain as the sun on a cloudless day at noon. Says Jesus in His prayer: "And this is eternal life, that they may *know you*, the only true God, and *Jesus Christ whom you have sent*" (John 17:3). Bang! There it is! Eternal life means knowing the Father and Jesus Christ the Son. Not just knowing God, but also Jesus Christ His Son. Other bits of Scripture tell us it happens through the Holy Spirit.

And what is in purview here, let us be clear, is personal, first-hand knowledge and experience of the living God in Christ. This is eternal life. And only this is eternal life.

This is why the question "Do you know Christ?" as put to me by my fellow student Robert Footner in Cambridge on 23 October 1955 is at once the most brazen and yet the most pertinent question of all life. It was certainly the key question for me! It is also the key question for you. For all of us. For every minister even. This is the question – "Does he or she know the Lord?"

That, as they say, is the thousand-dollar question.

And certainly for myself as Robbie Footner led me into commitment to Christ back in October 1955, the discovery of knowing Christ, and coming into a personal knowledge of Him was as different as chalk from cheese to knowing about Him. I knew about the Queen of England, but I did not know her. I knew about Nelson Mandela, but I did not know him personally. That is the key. That is eternal life according to the New Testament and according to Jesus.

Knowing Him. That's what it's all about!

5. This is how Jesus saw and read reality

Jesus brought a certain set of spectacles and lenses to His life here on earth and through His own experience He saw and read reality in a certain way. A reality embracing a real heaven, a real earth, and a "true God" who is also our Father. And a Son who would have a *unique hour* in the history of the universe by which a *unique gift* of eternal life through knowing Him could come to all who would repent and believe.

That was how He saw things. That was His world view.

And in our time the church, I believe, has to own fully His world view and be ready to defend it and do its apologetics "world-viewishly" if we are to help the world find its way from what we believe to be erroneous world views to the Christian and Jesus view of reality.

*** ***

And so we come back again in closing to note by contrast the world view, a wrong one of course, of Carl Sagan, the famous astrophysicist and TV populariser of science. For him "The cosmos is all that is or ever was or ever will be."[6]

That's Carl Sagan's world view. And it is wrong.

Then Richard Dawkins, as previously registered, speaks of our universe as having "at bottom no design, no purpose, no evil and no good, nothing but blind, pitiless indifference".

That's Richard Dawkins's world view. And it is wrong.

Then again, Shakespeare's Macbeth can affirm: "Life

is a tale told by an idiot, full of sound and fury, signifying nothing."[7]

That's Macbeth's world view. And it is wrong.

Of course, most today live and act as if that is in fact their world view and that is how things are.

But Jesus' High Priestly Prayer says: "No! No! You must think again!"

More than that. We also from earth must all lift our eyes with Jesus to heaven... and say... "Father".

Chapter 6

Truth – The First of the Ten Marks of *the Church Jesus Prayed For*

"I think we must attack wherever we meet it, the nonsensical idea that mutually exclusive propositions about God can both be true."

C. S. Lewis, *God in the Dock*[1]

"The truth is a quality of that judgement or proposition which when followed out into the total witness of facts in our experience, does not disappoint our expectations… Truth in its simplest dimensions is a judgement which corresponds to things as they actually are."

Edward John Carnell, *An Introduction to Christian Apologetics*[2]

"These words are trustworthy and true."

Revelation 22:6

"Sanctify them in the truth; your word is truth."

Jesus, in John 17:17

At last now as we move on into the prayer we begin to look at the specific marks that Jesus prayed for to characterise His church. This drives us to ask what Jesus wanted the church to look like and to be. What are the marks that He wants present in the church at this critical time in its history? We find our answer here in this amazing prayer where He prays above all for the *church*, not for the society. "I am praying for them; I am *not* praying for the world" (verse 9).

And I believe that He prays for His church to be characterised, as previously noted, by ten marks, as follows:

- Truth
- Holiness / godliness
- Joy
- Protection
- Mission
- Prayerfulness
- Unity
- Love
- Power
- Glory.

The bulk of the balance of this volume will focus on these marks, starting now with *truth*.

In ordinary, everyday life truth interests us and is of vital importance. Thus we say to our kids: "Now tell us the truth. Did you or didn't you?"

A perplexed teenager asks his science teacher: "Is it true that H_2O is water? Because my dad told me that it's H_3O?"

The little child suddenly blurts out one day: "Daddy, are fairies and Santa Claus really true?"

A little boy in Sunday school asks his teacher: "Miss Jones, is it really true that Jesus rose from the dead?"

*** ***

In everyday life, knowing what is true or untrue is vital if we are to function at all. It is part of daily reflection and decision-making. We accept this. But in our postmodern times we find that the idea of truth invading the religious arena is very problematic, and, for many, is unacceptable.

Thus for example C. S. Lewis, who was deeply devoted to the pursuit of truth, would have been horrified with the contemporary postmodernist notion that ideas of truth, validity, or right reason should no longer be held crucial and that we cannot achieve an accurate *real-world match* between objects, realities, or states of affairs and our concepts of understanding, thought, or verbal description of them. Likewise, that we cannot really make truth statements, but only express opinions.

So maybe Lewis was anticipating our contemporary situation where truth statements are declared either impossible or irrelevant. Thus in *The Screwtape Letters*, Screwtape is the senior devil who advises Wormwood as the junior devil to keep arguments and questions of "true" or "false" away from his patient's mind, the patient being someone Wormwood was trying to prevent from coming to Christian faith.

In fact Screwtape celebrates that while in the past humans were pretty concerned with whether things were true and proven or not, but now in the new present Wormwood needs to focus on keeping his patient content with having "a dozen incompatible philosophies dancing together in his head" without letting him ask, let alone discover, which were true and which were false. Rather, he must keep the patient lazily languishing in notions of "meaningfulness" or "practical helpfulness" or "being contemporary". He must keep him tolerant of everything and whatever happens, keep him strictly away from notions of truth or falsehood.[3]

So Screwtape would counsel Wormwood to ensure that his patient does not ask if the crucifixion really and truly took place as an atonement for the sins of humans, or if the resurrection is actually and historically true. His patient must at all costs be kept away from that sort of thinking or even something as dastardly awful as conversion could take place!

Beyond that, the human patients on whom Wormwood is working must never be allowed to ask whether God is really and truly there. But indeed we do have to ask if He is really there. Or is He there just like Santa Claus? Or like the fairies at the bottom of the garden?

What we *can* say is that Jesus saw truth, whatever He meant by that, as critically important and prayed for it to be a key mark of His church.

We must explore further. So let's note first of all:

1. Jesus' prayer for truth ("Sanctify them in the *truth*" – 17:17)

Jesus' initial affirmation here (verses 6–8) is that the true character of God has been manifested and declared to the disciples. This might be likened to a man manifesting and declaring the truth of his love for a girl. Says our Lord to the Father:

> I have made your name known to those whom you gave
> me from the world. They were yours, and you gave them
> to me, and they have kept your word. Now they know
> that everything you have given me is from you; for the
> words that you gave to me I have given to them, and
> they have received them and know **in truth** that I came
> from you; and they have believed that you sent me.
>
> **John 17:6–8**

We also see here that the truth has not only been manifested and declared by our Lord, but that *the truth has been grasped* by the disciples. The disciples have not only received the words of Jesus but they know that they are true and that it is indeed factually true that Jesus came from the Father. They know it as true "that you sent me" (verse 8).

Now that Jesus can affirm that the truth He has declared to the disciples has been received, grasped, and acted on as factually true, He goes on with a petition to the Father that they should be *kept in that truth.* This relates first of all to the truth of the character of God, "name" here referring, as we said before, to the character of God. Thus in Exodus 33:19 when the Lord says to His people: "I... will proclaim before you my name",what follows in the next verses and in the next chapter (Exodus 34:5–7), is the manifestation of the character and nature of the true God.

Jesus also prays in verse 17 "Sanctify them in the truth; your word is truth." Likewise "that they also may be sanctified in truth" (verse 19).

So then:

2. The nature of truth: what is truth?

So we ask, what is truth? Christians believe that truth is that which accords with reality and with the facts as they are on a one-to-one ratio. It is the properly construed meaning of any reality. Thus I can hold up a watch and affirm "This is a watch." Truth then asks: "Is it? Or isn't it? Could it possibly be a penknife? Or a fountain pen?" Truth answers: "No, those other identities are not true. The truth is that it is a watch." Why? Well because that statement accords with reality and the facts as they are on a one-to-one ratio.

When we put questions like this we are assuming the law of anthesis that A is not non-A and that two contradictory statements cannot both be true at the same time. So I cannot say, "This is a watch and at the same time a knife." The two statements are contradictory and cannot both be true. They are mutually exclusive.

Likewise if a Christian claims that Jesus rose from the dead and the Muslim claims that Jesus did not rise from the dead, then we are forced to conclude that one or other of the statements is true and one is false. Why? Well, because they are contradictory.

My old professor at Fuller Seminary, the late, much loved and greatly revered Edward John Carnell, put it this way:

> *The truth is a quality of that judgement or proposition*
> *which, when followed out into the total witness of facts*
> *in our experience, does not disappoint our expectations.*
> *Thus, if I am told that under a large white basswood*

*tree in the city square, there is now buried a lost
treasure; and if, after dodging the watchful eyes of the
town fathers, I uproot the tree in question, but locate
no treasure, I may conclude that my benefactor has
lied. His judgement, "There is treasure under the white
basswood tree in the city square," is false because it
fails to sustain me in the aggregate of my experience.*

*Again, when little Johnny says that there are fifty
steps leading up to the spring in the park, and actual
scientific count reveals that there are just that number,
then we say that he speaks, or has, the truth. He has
made a good judgement. If, however, the number
exceeds or falls short of the designated fifty, then we
properly say that he speaks falsely. He has made a bad
judgement; he has not the truth.[4]*

WILLARD ON C. S. LEWIS'S VIEW OF TRUTH

Or we can come to C. S. Lewis's take on this as I heard it at a
conference in Oxford and Cambridge called "Oxbridge '98",
which celebrated the 100th anniversary of the birth of Lewis.
Thus we had the first week in Oxford and the second in
Cambridge. Wow! Talk about a treat! Dallas Willard, Professor
of Philosophy at the University of Southern California,
addressed us on C. S. Lewis's understanding of truth known
as "the correspondence theory of reality".

Said Willard: "Lewis held that truth is a matter of a belief
or an idea corresponding to reality. In the course of rejecting
the view that moral laws are social conventions, he insists that
they are, on the contrary (and this is the language he uses)
'real truths'."[5]

Lewis declares:

*If your moral ideas can be truer, and those of the Nazi
less true, there must be something – some real morality
– for them to be true about. The reason that your idea
of New York can be truer or less true than mine is that*

New York is a real place existing quite apart from what either of us thinks. If when each of us said "New York", each meant merely "The town I am imagining in my own head", how could one of us have truer ideas than the other? There would be no question of truth or falsehood at all.[6]

That is a very characteristic statement of what truth as correspondence means. And you have to understand that it is truth as correspondence that provides what sometimes among philosophers today is called "the reality hook" – the connection to reality. But this notion is under attack today.

PEGASUS: TRUE OR UNTRUE?

Willard then took us to the illustration of Pegasus – the winged horse of Greek mythology. Was Pegasus true or untrue? Of course all of us reading this know that Pegasus is untrue and we know that it does not exist. But asks Willard,

What does it mean? It means simply that the relevant properties that we associate with Pegasus do not together belong to anything. Wingedness and horsiness do not together belong to anything. If they did, that thing would be Pegasus and Pegasus would actually exist. Clearly then, being a fact has nothing to do in general with being thought of or being mentioned or being described. Pegasus can be thought of, even thought of as real or as a fact, but that view is mistaken. It is not real, it is untrue.[7]

Willard took another illustration thinking of an empty petrol tank in your car on a lonely road. Challenges Willard:

If you assume or believe your car is well supplied with gasoline when it is not, you may find yourself in great danger or discomfort. And this is true even for a Postmodernist or a relativist. Why is this so, we ask? Well,

> *because the truth of the matter is that the car has*
> *indeed run out of petrol. We do not say, "Oh well, since*
> *you believed there was gas in the tank it shall be so."*
> *The truth is that facts are totally unforgiving.*[8]

Likewise the truth of something is not altered because we may deny it, or because there is no one there to describe it, as when God created the universe (Genesis 1). Or when Jesus was sharing glory with God the Father before the foundation of the world, as per the affirmation of John 17:5.

Likewise, adds Willard, "a universe just like ours, except *devoid* of conscious beings and their language, would still be a universe of true facts and existence."[9]

THE CORRESPONDENCE VIEW OF TRUTH

So we register that denying the existence of our universe (or else not being there at all to describe it in words) will not remove its truth and factualness, any more than denying the resurrection of Jesus will change it from being true and corresponding to historical reality on a one-to-one ratio, as per Christian conviction. It is not our brains or description which make the universe or the resurrection true or factual. Their truth and factualness precede our perception of them as such.

So then, when Christians say "Jesus is lord of the universe", the statement for us is either true or false. Either it honours and accords with reality or it does not. Thus Christians believe it holds true regardless of anyone's opinion on the subject, truth not being determined by subjective views, majority votes, or cultural fashions. For example, it is true and a fact that the world was spherical even when the majority vote of the early Middle Ages said it was flat!

This is the correspondence view of truth, and the one also held by the apostle Paul who could affirm: "and if Christ has not been raised, then our proclamation has been in vain and your faith has been in vain. We are even found to be misrepresenting God, because we testified of God that he raised Christ – whom he did not raise *if it is true* that the dead are not raised" (1 Corinthians 15:14–15). Without the correspondence view of truth, such affirmations carry no meaning.

So then when Jesus speaks in John 17:5 about the glory He had with the Father "before the world was made", the Christian will take that as factually, literally, and truly true.

ALL THIS INCOMPATIBLE WITH POSTMODERN RELATIVISM

All of this stands in obvious opposition to the current relativist and interfaith view that something in the external world can be true for you but not true for me. This latter view, if valid, would mean that the Christian could say "Jesus is Lord and God", and other religions say no: "He is not Lord and God", and all could be asked to receive both statements as true because certain sets of believers sincerely hold them to be so. Under this view the church can then comfortably abdicate its missionary and evangelistic responsibility. How so? Well, because there is no valid constraint to send Christians out to the end of the world proclaiming a message which may or may not be true and which at best could be an invention and at worst plain false.

So we come back to Lewis who insists that

> If I say, "Jesus is Lord and the final divine revelation to our world", and you say, "Allah is God and Muhammad is his ultimate prophet and final revelation", both statements cannot be objectively true because they describe supposed facts or realities which are mutually exclusive. Christians say God has incarnated Himself in Jesus. Muslims say Allah would never incarnate himself. One of these views is true and one is false... I think we must attack wherever we meet it the nonsensical idea that mutually exclusive propositions about God can both be true.[10]

In other words, we are refusing to violate the law of non-contradiction, which says that if an affirmation is true, its negation must be false.

TRUTH CANNOT BE MADE DEPENDENT UPON A GROUP

The above remarks also make it clear that we cannot make truth dependent upon the group, person, or culture holding the belief. If we did that, anything could become true. This is manifestly absurd.

For example, we do not allow *flat-earthists to teach our children* that the earth is flat because we know this to have been falsified by the facts. But if I were a consistent relativist I would have to allow the person to teach this to my children because the flat-earthist, for his part, is sincere about it and holds it as true, and because I for my part, am not allowed by this relativist requirement to produce an objective basis to make them alter their beliefs by presenting contrary argument, facts, or evidence. Such an attitude applied to mathematics, aerodynamics, medicine, or science we would consider nonsensical. Nay, dangerous!

After all, who would want to be flown by a tolerant or broad-minded pilot, unconcerned with the truths of aerodynamics? Or be operated on by a tolerant, broad-minded surgeon unconcerned with the truths of surgery and physiology? Or be taught by a tolerant, broad-minded scientist who was relaxed about whether two times two was either four or five and equally relaxed as to whether H_2O or H_3O could be water. Take your pick. Just be sincere. Use whichever formula is meaningful and which you can feel good about!

Likewise – who wants to rest time and eternity on a "take it or leave it" set of relativist options?

No! While we lovingly tolerate people, we do not tolerate what we believe to be error. We believe there are such things as true facts and such things as erroneous facts and the real facts are "unforgiving". "That is the worst of facts," C. S. Lewis once told his father, "they do cramp a fellow's style!"[11] So we must come to terms with them. For example, with regard to the claim that both the incarnation and the resurrection are facts of history, are they or are they not?

"All I am doing," Lewis once said, "is asking people to face the facts and to understand the questions which Christianity claims to answer."[12]

Francis Schaeffer, speaking at the Berlin Congress on Evangelism in 1966, put it this way:

> Christianity rests upon Truth, not truth as an abstract concept, nor even what the twentieth century man regards as "religious truth", but objective truth. Part of this truth is the emphasis that certain things happened in history… Historic Christianity rests upon the truth of what today is called the "brute facts"… Behind the truth of such history is the great truth that the personal, infinite God is objectively "there". He actually exists (in contrast to His not "being there"): and Christ's redemptive and finished work actually took place at a point of time in real space–time history (in contrast to this not being the case). Historic Christianity rests upon the truth of these things in absolute antithesis to their not being true.[13]

I remember Schaeffer making those remarks at the Berlin Congress not long after he and I and a few others had done a tour round the Berlin Wall during which time Schaeffer, as was his way, continued expounding on issues of truth. Schaeffer was elaborating on something he had said towards the end of his paper:

> Let us never forget that we who stand in the historic stream of Christianity really believe that false doctrine, at those crucial points where false doctrine is heresy, is not a small thing, but is an enemy. If we do not make clear by word and by practice our position for truth and against false doctrine, we are building a wall between the next generation and the Gospel…[14]

In a nutshell, truth really matters.

TAKE THE NEW TESTAMENT ITSELF

So listen to the New Testament and hear plain speaking and words that ring with conviction: "We know… We know… We know." In the Johannine epistles, for example, we are told that we *"know* the truth" (1 John 2:21; 2 John 1; cf. John 8:32).

So if truth is uncertain, elusive, out of reach, lost on us as we live in our own private worlds or post worlds of (post) modern "reality", what on earth are the Apostles talking about? What is it we are supposed to *know* and what is it we are supposed *to obey*? Our own reconstructions of reality? Our own "take" on what life means?

BUT IN THE BIBLICAL VIEW…

We know the *truth* and not just arbitrary rules and approximations. This knowledge of what is "there" includes the truth *about Christ* (1 John 5:20), *about God* (2:13–14), *his character* (3:16), *his redemptive purposes* (3:5), *our own nature* (1:6, 8–11), and the (postmodern) world we inhabit.

On all these matters we have God's truth, and for the church to be shy about saying "We know… We know… We know…" is an act of self-betrayal.

US theologian David Wells observes that

> *Scripture, by contrast, sees itself, and is seen, as the self-disclosure of God that is therefore unlike anything else on earth. It is the truth. What it says corresponds to what happened in the world of which it speaks. It really does reflect what is in the human heart. It is the measure of reality. It is the standard by which we are to judge life's religions and philosophies, its programs and values, its hopes and its fears.*[15]

So the Christian believes that scripture's statements do indeed correspond *truly* to what is out there.

SO BACK TO WHAT JESUS IS PRAYING

First Jesus makes the point: "I came from you" (John 17:8). And He affirms that. The disciples know this "in truth" (verse 8). His prayer also is "that the world may believe that *you have sent me*". In other words, that the world will see this as *true truth* and corresponding with the facts as they are and reality as it is.

So the question for the outside world is – "Is it true? Did the Father really send Him? Is He really one with the Father? Is He really the truth (John 14:6)? Is He really the only Saviour (Acts 4:12)?"

What then we decide about the TRUTH of these statements and claims affects our eternal destiny. TRUTH and error matter for our salvation, and indeed for the salvation of the world to whom we are sent out.

So now from the nature of truth to its source.

3. The living Word as the first source of truth – "for the words that you gave to me I have given to them" (17:8)

In Christian belief truth comes to the human race in two main ways – through Jesus, as the living Word – ("I have given") and through *Scripture,* as the written word ("the words"; 17:8).

Thus as the living Word Jesus could say: "I am... the truth" (John 14:6). We remember too that in John 18:38 Pilate asked "What is truth?" Had he stayed around long enough, he might have heard Jesus reaffirm His claim of John 14:6 "I am... the truth."

In thinking about truth we want to say several things.

I. TRUTH IS PERSONAL

Truth in the first instance is not a system, proposition, set of ethics, golden rule, sermon, not even the Sermon on the

Mount, not a religion, but a Person.

I remember back in 1969 when AE was doing its citywide mission to Nairobi, we had the enormous privilege of the great missionary statesman and writer E. Stanley Jones coming to be with us for some weeks as part of the mission. He told us that during his many years in mission work in India he had got to know Mahatma Gandhi quite well. And he was a great admirer of Gandhi. However, he told us how the mahatma had once told him how much he admired the principles in the Sermon on the Mount. To this E. Stanley Jones replied: "But oh, Mahatma, Mahatma, you have missed the Person." And this is tragic because what finally matters is not the Sermon on the Mount but the Person who preached it. Not the golden rule, but the Person who gave it. Not the morals and ethics but the Person who taught them.

So then in Christian understanding, truth is personal in Jesus before it is propositional about Him or about anything else.

But there is something else of critical importance here.

When we say that Jesus is the truth, we are reminding ourselves that a purely propositional approval of truth, or the declaration of it in evangelism is impoverished indeed unless we are grasping that the truth of Jesus as personal will not be fully understood until we grasp Jesus Himself in personal and transforming commitment.

St Paul did not fully discover the truth of Christ in scripture until he had personally encountered Christ on the Damascus Road. That made all the difference.

Only this way can we prevent our understanding of truth becoming imprisoned in rationalism. In other words, just a thing of the mind. Knowing the truth in Christian terms is not simply to enjoy a conceptual account of reality, but to know it personally through encounter with the one who is behind all reality.

II. TRUTH IS UNIVERSAL

All of God's truth is pervasive throughout all of God's universe, and all of life finds its summary and harmony in Christ. The God of physical law is thus the God of moral and spiritual law. So too the truths of science, mental health, mathematics, music, morality are His truths and originate from Him.

So being the truth, He is the author of all truth. Paul explains: "for in Him [Christ] all things were created... all things were created through him and for him. He himself is before all things, and in him all things hold together" (Colossians 1:16–17).

What this really means as well is that all the material universe is as it were a message in code from God, which mystics and artists and scientists strive to crack – sometimes with a measure of success – but to which Jesus is the ultimate key. So it was that "the Word became flesh" (John 1:14). God became a Person, not a page. So if this universe is His and He made it, it means that His truth is universal in the sense of being throughout the universe.

I remember once reading of a little child given a crossword puzzle with the picture of the face of Jesus on one side of the pieces of the puzzle and the world map on the other. The little child was trying to make sense of the puzzle of the world map and couldn't get it right. Her mother then suggested that she work not so much on the world map as on the face of Jesus. This was much easier to assemble. So after a while she had on the puzzle the face of Christ. Then when she turned the puzzle over there was the world fitting all together and in place and making sense. That's what Jesus does. Einstein once said that "The world is like a well constructed crossword puzzle."

The truth is not only personal and universal, but:

III. TRUTH IS INTELLECTUAL AND HISTORICAL

By affirming that truth is intellectual and historical we are saying that it holds water, it adds up, it makes sense, the mind can accept it, and as far as Christian truth particularly is concerned, it is rooted in history. The historical fact is that the resurrection is history and not a fairy tale. There is no "once upon a time" here. This brings us to stressing strongly the *importance of history for Christianity,* because Christian faith is based on *gospel,* which means "good news" and there is certainly no news, whether good or bad, if something didn't really *happen* in history. Historic Christianity is premised on the fact that at a certain point in history a certain man *died* under Pontius Pilate, the procurator of Judaea, *was buried,* and on the *third day rose again* as a matter of historical fact. If He never lived, died, or rose, then I have no right to my faith. In other words it is untrue.

Ernest Wright of Harvard University once wrote: "In biblical faith everything depends on whether the central events actually occurred. Therefore to assume that it makes no difference whether they are facts or not is simply to destroy the whole basis of the faith."[16]

Archbishop William Temple, one of the great archbishops of Canterbury, put it this way:

> *For Christianity it is impossible to accept the view which makes history of no ultimate importance. For Christianity affirms an act of God within history itself and rests on this affirmation… It is therefore open to attack on the historical plain as no other religion is.*[17]

Professor John Macquarrie, once Lady Margaret Professor of Divinity at Oxford, for his part could put it this way: "Christian theology takes its origin from a revelation given in an historical person, rather than in a dateless myth or a timeless corpus of laws or of philosophical truths."[18]

History is therefore the *locus* of Christian revelation. And Christians believe that the events in the life of Jesus Christ really happened and are true. The great Greek scholar and Bible commentator Brook Foss Wescott of Cambridge once wrote about the Apostles' Creed: "No interpretation of the facts is added. They belong to life. They are in themselves unchangeable. They stand before us forever in their sublime majesty, part of the history of the world."[19]

One writer, Kathryn Lindskoog, produced a very good little summary book on the thought of C. S. Lewis and captured the heart of his thinking saying:

> God became man. This is the central miracle of
> Christianity. All the others fit around it. The Incarnation
> is the Grand Miracle. If the thing really happened, it is
> the central event in the history of the Earth. It is very
> hard to give any historical explanation of the sayings and
> influence of Christ that is not harder than the Christian
> explanation. The credibility of the Incarnation depends
> upon the extent to which it illuminates and integrates the
> whole mass of our knowledge.[20]

And C. S. Lewis himself once said: "I believe in Jesus as I believe in the sun – not merely because I see it, but because by it I see everything else."

JESUS IS ALL-IMPORTANT OR NOT IMPORTANT AT ALL

All of this means in historical terms that Jesus is either all-important or not important at all. The only thing He cannot be is moderately important.

In this regard then the mind can interact creatively and intelligently with Christian truth and be persuaded that it is true. Nothing in Jesus' teachings or the New Testament suggests that we are obliged to commit intellectual suicide while embracing the Christian faith. If it is not true, the sooner we find out about it and stop kidding ourselves, the better. In reality Christians have no fear from intellectual scrutiny of the central facts of their gospel and their message. The one thing Christians do fear is that people will not intellectually investigate it thoroughly enough.

So then Christian truth is intellectual and historical, in

that our intellects can rationally embrace it and our minds can be satisfied that the central events are historical and factual. They really happened in real time, space, and history.

But there is something else critically important to note here, and it is this. The correspondence view of truth, or truth as coherence with things as they are, must also be *linked to the mind of God as the author of all truth* and of all facts and meaning. There is in fact no reality apart from the eternal nature and mind of God whence flows all meaning. And since it is only the mind of God that perfectly knows all reality, we have to add that truth is a property of any judgment that coincides with the mind of God.

What we mean here is that if a person fails to say about any reality what God says about it, then that person is in error, and their statement is not true because it does not correspond with the mind of God. On any level of judgment therefore, we only speak or possess truth when we say about our "supposed" facts what God says about these same facts.

So if a person says humankind's chief end is to eat, drink, and be merry, he or she only tells the truth if God's mind agrees with that. Which it does not! If we say the highest ultimate is matter, it is not true if God says it is spirit. If we say sex is a free-for-all, so you can do whatever you like in this area, it is only true if God's mind is in accord, which it isn't. If we say the universe is the accidental result of impersonal energy plus time plus chance, or that death is the end of everything, our utterances do not partake of truth if God's mind declares it otherwise.

So truth is not just correspondence with facts as they are, but with the mind of God.

And for the Christian that mind is set forth in the Bible as God's written word.

4. The written word – as the second source of truth

Jesus prayed: "Sanctify them in the truth; your word is truth" (verse 17).

Our Lord also affirms in His prayer: "for the words that you gave to me I have given to them" (17:8). He had said that the Spirit would guide the apostles into all truth (John 14:13), and that He would "bring to remembrance all that I have said to you" (John 14:26), presumably as the words were preached and then inscripturated by the Apostles themselves. So it is to the Scriptures that we look for *truth*, and for *authority*. In this we have the precedent of Jesus Himself, and we note:

I. JESUS' VIEW OF THE OLD TESTAMENT

Jesus entered a society already bound by a canon of sacred writings. He never contradicted the prevailing Jewish attitude to the authority of the Law and the Prophets. Indeed He constantly appealed to this corpus of revelation when validating His own messianic claims.

And is it not noteworthy that even radical critics acknowledge Jesus Christ's recognition of Old Testament authority. But they assume His accommodation to prevailing views. However, nowhere else does He fail to correct error. If the Jewish view of Scripture was wrong, the Jesus we know would have corrected it. Instead He uses designations (Scripture, the Scriptures, the Law, the Prophets, the Law and the Prophets, the phrase "It is written" and so on) to refer to the Jewish canonical Scriptures held by all Jews to be sacred and authoritative.

He also sees the details of Scripture as authoritative. In the following verses the whole argument turns on a single word of Old Testament scripture – Matthew 2:15; 4:10; 13:35; 22:44; Mark 12:36; Luke 4:8; 20:42, 43; John 8:17; 10:34; 19:37. He can even bring forth the astonishing utterance that "until heaven and earth pass away, not one letter, not one stroke of a letter, will pass from the law" (Matthew 5:18). Likewise, "Heaven and earth will pass away, but my words will not pass away" (Matthew 24:35).

We also find that He equates "Scripture says" and "God says" with what simply the text says when you look it up. Look at Matthew 18:4ff. Our Lord quotes Genesis 2:24, which in context are the narrator's words, but are here quoted as an utterance of God.

So too does Jesus use Scripture in temptation and answers the devil with the repeated affirmations in Matthew 4:4, 7, 10 of "It is written…"

Scriptural knowledge is vital

More than that our Lord sees scriptural knowledge as vital when He warns the Pharisees that they err "because you do not know the Scriptures" (Mark 12:24, NIV)! He can likewise say in many instances when He is correcting people: "Have you not read…?" as in Matthew 12:3, 5; 19:4; 21:16, 42. The obvious presupposition here in our Lord's statement is that the truth of the matter is found in what is read in Scripture.

Then we find that He gives Moses' writings an authority comparable to His words. Thus He can say: "If you do not believe his [Moses'] writings, how will you believe my words?" (John 5:47).

Particularly interesting is that Jesus endlessly affirmed that He was ministering in fulfilment of the Scriptures, as for example in His *preaching* (Luke 4:18, quoting Isaiah 61:1), in *healing* (Matthew 8:16, quoting Isaiah 53:4), in *going up to Jerusalem* (Luke 18:31), in *dying* with transgressors (Luke 22:37, quoting Isaiah 53:12), and finally in *suffering and dying* (Luke 24:44, 46).

Of course the above material hardly touches the hem of the garment, but it gives us a clear idea of the very high view of the Old Testament Scriptures that our Lord held. French scholar Pierre Marcel puts it this way: "From the manner in which Christ quotes Scripture we find that He recognizes and accepts the Old Testament in its entirety as possessing a normative authority as the true word of God, valid for all time."[21]

We now come to:

II. JESUS' VIEW OF HIS OWN WORDS AND THEIR INSCRIPTURATION

We have already noted how our Lord said in Matthew 24:35 "Heaven and earth will pass away, but my words will not pass away." That said, we have to add that our Lord very clearly anticipated the inscripturation of these same words. And anticipated, I believe, that those who wrote down what He had said would have perfect recall. Thus He could say to the disciples: "But the Advocate, the Holy Spirit, whom the Father will send in my name, will teach you everything, and remind you of all that I have said to you" (John 14:26).

A similar notion comes at John 15:26–27: "When the Advocate comes, whom I will send to you from the Father, the **Spirit of truth** who comes from the Father, he will testify on my behalf. You also are to testify because you have been with me from the beginning."

Likewise a few moments later in the Final Discourse He adds: "When the **Spirit of truth** comes, he will guide you into **all the truth**; for he will not speak on his own, but will speak whatever he hears, and he will declare to you the things that are to come. He will glorify me, because he will take what is mine and declare it to you" (John 16:13–14).

And surely our Lord has to have as a presupposition that His words have been written down when He can affirm to His listeners: "I do not judge anyone who hears my words and does not keep them, for I came not to judge the world, but to save the world. The one who rejects me and does not receive my word has a judge; *on the last day the word that I have spoken will serve as judge…*" (John 12:47–48).

So if we are wanting to know where truth is located and how truth and reality are perceived in the mind of God, so that we may have coherence with that mind, we can rest on sure ground when we turn to the words of our Lord as inscripturated in the Gospels.

But we must go further in terms of the whole New Testament testimony and also look at:

III. THE APOSTLES' VIEW OF THEIR OWN WRITINGS

This is interesting. We find for example that the apostle Paul sees his message as "the word of God" (1 Thessalonians 2:13), as a "command of the Lord" (1 Corinthians 14:37), as "revealed" (Romans 16:25ff; 1 Corinthians 2:10ff; Galatians 1:12; Ephesians 3:3ff) and as "true" (Galatians 4:20).

Luke for his part sees his writings as orderly, true, and accurate as he notes in Luke 1:3, comprehensive (Acts 1:1) and of using the accounts of eyewitness. This is especially evident when we look at the so-called "we" passages where Luke is including himself in the story as a participant and eyewitness. Some of these references are fascinating and to be found for example at Acts 16:10–17; 20:5–15; 21:1–18; 27:1–28.

Then there is the apostle John. He sees his writings as thematic, selective, and evangelistic (John 20:31), as "eyewitness" (John 19:35) and as "true" (John 21:24–25).

As for the apostle Peter he rather succinctly sees his writings as brief and true (1 Peter 5:12).

IV. THE APOSTLES' VIEW OF EACH OTHER'S WRITINGS

It is instructive that Peter viewed Paul's writings as "Scripture" and refers to them as such at 2 Peter 3:16. It is also comforting for those of us who find certain sections of Pauline writings "hard to understand", and it is in a way amusing that Peter says he has exactly the same problem! (see 2 Peter 3:16). Dear old Peter the fisherman struggling with Paul the rabbinic scholar and Hebrew intellectual! But for Peter nevertheless, Paul's writings were Scripture.

So then, what of:

V. THE EARLY CHURCH VIEW OF THE NEW TESTAMENT

"When we turn," says Anglican scholar Geoffrey Bromiley, another of my great professors at Fuller Seminary, "to the Patristic period, we are struck at once by the way in which all writers accepted the inspiration and the authority of the Holy Scriptures as self-evident."[22]

Bromiley adds:

> *The actual writings of the Old and New Testaments are seen to derive from the Holy Spirit and therefore carry the divine message. Nor is this merely a general inspiration; it extends to the detailed phraseology of the Bible in accordance with the saying of Christ in Matthew 5:18. Thus Clement of Alexandria tells us that not one jot nor tittle can pass because all has been spoken by the Lord (Protrepticus, IX, 82, I); and Gregory Nazianzus writes that even the smallest lines in Scripture are due to the minute care of the Holy Spirit, so that we must pay careful attention to every slightest shade of meaning. (Orat., 2, 105) In order to emphasise the perfection and authority of the Bible, Irenaeus can say that they are actually spoken by God Himself through His Word and Spirit. (C.O.H. II, 28,2). What the authors say is really said by God Himself and must be received and studied not merely or primarily as a word of man but as a Word of God.*[23]

He concludes: "There can be little doubt that a sound and Scriptural doctrine of inspiration was for the most part maintained and developed in the Patristic period. The primary fact of inspiration was never in doubt."[24]

VI. THE EXPERIENCE OF SCRIPTURE

Perhaps it is also important here to affirm something we mentioned when speaking earlier about truth as personal – namely that the written word of God does not commend itself to us as true unless the heart is personally confronted by the Living Word in Christ through the Holy Spirit. Paul, as we said, did not see Christ in Scripture until he had met Christ on the Damascus Road. The Bible does not address itself to our hearts as truly the Word of God until Christ is truly met in personal fellowship.

I well remember my own experience as a young undergraduate at Cambridge. I was cycling back to college after some extra tuition from an old retired professor in my abysmally bad Latin. I was praying as I cycled and thinking not about Latin but about Scripture. It was very strange. It was just as if a sudden infusion of the Holy Spirit into my own spirit assured me that the Bible was the Word of God, inspired by the Holy Spirit of God, and therefore to be received as authoritative, reliable, and true. And from that moment I never doubted that this was so.

And my experience has confirmed this conviction.

5. Conclusion

So then, we conclude. The vital thing to affirm is that truth matters. Jesus prays that His church would be sanctified and consecrated "in the truth" (John 17:17, 19). This truth is found in Him and His words. And He is found in conversion and new birth, and His words are found in the Scriptures that are our normative guide and authority in the church for truth, and they give us truth we could not know any other way.

Hence the indispensable necessity of our being a people of truth and being a church bearing the distinguishing mark of truth.

No wonder then the Apostle can warn the young Timothy about those who "swerve from the truth" (2 Timothy 2:18) and urge his young mentee to "guard the good treasure entrusted to you, with the help of the Holy Spirit living in us" (2 Timothy 1:14).

Clearly this posture on truth collides head on with some

of the postmodernist assumptions of our times which say that telling the truth is out of the question because there is no truth to tell.

A FINAL POINT

It also collides with what Alister McGrath describes as *prescriptive pluralism*. He sees this in contrast to *descriptive pluralism*, which simply describes the reality of there being many religious options around us. Christians have always recognised that right from the time of the early church, religious alternatives were on offer.

Notes Alister McGrath:

> *The basic phenomenon of pluralism, then, is nothing new. What is new is the intellectual response to this phenomenon: the suggestion that plurality of beliefs is not merely a matter of observable fact, but is theoretically justified – in intellectual and cultural life in general, and particularly in relation to the religions. Claims by any one group or individual to have any exclusive hold on "truth" are thus treated as the intellectual equivalent of fascism. This form of pluralism is strongly prescriptive, seeking to lay down what may be believed, rather than merely describing what is believed. Significantly… the first casualty of the prescriptive pluralist agenda is truth.*[25]

The biblical Christian will not go with this prescriptive pluralist agenda. The contradictory claims of different religions cannot all be true.

So then for the individual Christian the issue is truth. Likewise for the church Jesus prayed for.

No wonder therefore that He could call on the Father saying: "Sanctify them *in the truth*; your word *is truth*… And for their sakes I sanctify myself, so that they also may be sanctified *in truth*" (John 17:17, 19).

Chapter 7

Holiness – The Second Mark

"...keep them in thy name..."

Jesus, John 17:11

"O God, make all the bad people good, and all the good people nice."

Child's prayer

"As alien and archaic as the idea may seem, the task of the church is not to make men and women happy, it is to make them holy."

Charles W. Colson

"To understand and participate in holiness we go to the source: God is holy... God wants us in on His holiness."

Eugene Peterson[1]

"Make them holy – consecrated – with the truth: Your word is consecrating truth."

Jesus, John 17:17, *The Message*

As Jesus prays for the church to be marked by truth, so He also prays for it to be marked by holiness. As He prays that the church may be kept from error and in truth, so He now prays that it will be kept from evil and in righteousness.

This shakes us up. It is a huge, awesome, and even frightening challenge for each one of us.

Godliness. Hey, wow! This is where we all want to weep. Really. We cannot reach it. We cannot make it.

To be godly. Like God. Manifest godliness and be kept in His name and character. This is the mountain we cannot ascend. The river we cannot cross. The hurdle we cannot leap. The ladder we cannot climb.

And with the Apostle we cry out: "Who will rescue me from this body of death?" (Romans 7:24). We also lament what we know of ourselves saying: "For I know that nothing good dwells within me, that is, in my flesh" (Romans 7:18).

And we want to cry. Really. Give up. Throw in the sponge. Call it a day. You have surely felt this. So have I. Oh, yes!

But our Lord's firm prayer remains – to rally us, haunt us, call us back, arouse us: "protect [or keep] them in your name…" (John 17:11), the name of God, as we have seen earlier in our reflections speaking of the character of God. Our Lord wants us kept in the character of the Father. In other words, in godliness. For this to happen He needs to pray two other things. Firstly, "protect them from the evil one" (verse 15), and secondly, "Sanctify them [make them holy] in the truth" (verse 17). Let's explore this further.

1. God's Godliness in His people

That's what He is after. He wants us like Him. And though we are tempted to despair, we dare not. And we can be encouraged that while we are tempted to despair of reaching the targets He sets us, our Jehovah God encourages us saying: "Surely, this commandment that I am commanding you today is *not too hard for you*… No, the word is very near to you; it is in your mouth and in your heart for you to observe" (Deuteronomy 30:11, 14).

So our holiness is what He prays for. Of course when in the midst of this broken, sin-sodden and cynical world we see real godliness and Christian character we know we are seeing a lovely thing.

MOTHER TERESA

Malcolm Muggeridge, in his book *Something Beautiful for God*, written after he had encountered Mother Teresa in India, tells how he was completely overwhelmed in meeting the little lady.

> *I am very conscious of the inadequacy of my effort to convey in words more than a hazy and inadequate impression of this woman of God and her co-workers... It will be for posterity to decide whether she is a saint. I only say of her that in a dark time she is a burning and a shining light. In a cruel time, a living embodiment of Christ's Gospel of love; in a godless time, the Word dwelling among us, full of grace and truth. For this, all who have the inestimable privilege of knowing her, must be eternally grateful.*[2]

Malcolm Muggeridge knew that in Mother Teresa he was seeing something special and unusual indeed, namely the character of God manifested in a humble human being from whom shined out the spirit of godliness and holiness.

Early in his book Muggeridge describes one occasion when he was seeing Mother Teresa onto a train:

> *When the train began to move, and I walked away, I felt as though I were leaving behind me all the beauty and all the joy in the universe. Something of God's universal love has rubbed off on Mother Teresa, giving her homely features a noticeable luminosity; a shining quality. She has lived so closely with her Lord that the same enchantment clings about her that sent the crowds chasing after Him in Jerusalem and Galilee and made His mere presence seem a harbinger of healing. Outside, the streets were beginning to stir; sleepers awakening, stretching and yawning; some raking over the piles of garbage in search of something edible. It was a scene of desolation, yet it, too, seemed somehow irradiated.*

This love, this Christian love, which shines down on the misery we make and into our dark hearts that make it; irradiating all, uniting all, making of all one stupendous harmony. Momentarily I understood. Then, leaning back in my American limousine, I was carried off to breakfast, to pick over my own particular garbage heap.[3]

In thinking further about the power and impact of godliness, my mind has also turned to two very special men: Billy Graham and John Stott.

BILLY GRAHAM

One chapter in John Pollock's biography *Billy Graham: Evangelist to the World* is entitled "The Man Himself". It's a powerful chapter that in many ways explains and demonstrates how the extraordinary gospel achievements of Billy Graham actually emerge not from his natural or even Spirit-given giftings, but from the godly character of the man himself. This Pollock sees emerging out of Billy Graham's extensive daily reading of the Scriptures, which includes, among other things, "five Psalms and a chapter of Proverbs daily."[4]

Then Pollock refers to Billy's prayer life and quotes him as saying: "I have learned, I believe, to 'pray without ceasing'. I find myself constantly in prayer and fellowship with God, even while I am talking to other people or doing other things."[5] Pollock quotes a letter Billy wrote to John Stott in 1970 saying: "I am most anxious that whatever days I may have left, my life will have more *depth* and less *surface*."

He also quotes Billy Graham's longstanding colleague Walter Smyth, whom I had the privilege of knowing very well. Smyth once noted: "Very rarely is he ever sharp with anyone."[6] Likewise David Kucharsky, once editor of *Christian Herald* and who attended many Billy Graham press conferences and in briefing situations or board meetings said that he had found Billy's "generosity of spirit a wonderful example, because I cannot ever recall him being the least bit cynical even in a private conversation. There are not very many people (Christians or otherwise) about whom that could in truth be said."[7]

In Billy's home, says Pollock, that same spirit pervades how he relates to his family. So Anne Graham Lotz, his daughter, could note that many a man who is gracious in public will often explode in a sympathetic family circle, but

> *I cannot remember one single time that Daddy criticised someone or made a disparaging remark about any particular person. Even those who were outright in their hatred of him, when we asked him about them, he would just say that perhaps they needed our love and prayers more than others.*[8]

So his family could say that he was the same at home as in public. And that's quite something.

My point in sharing all this is to illustrate here in an individual life a little bit of what this godliness looks like. And it's wonderfully attractive.

JOHN STOTT

The same can be said of John Stott. Like Billy Graham, his godliness was rooted in prayer, profound Bible study, and deep Christian devotion. I remember once travelling in ministry for a week with John around South Africa. It meant I had a chance to see him up close. What I particularly remember is that if I rose in the small hours of the morning to answer a call of nature, I found that John had already answered a call of grace. His light was on by 4.00 a.m. and he was having his devotions and an extended time of prayer and Bible study.

Writing of John Stott's devotional life Timothy Dudley-Smith, quotes John in these terms:

> *I think I may say with truthfulness that it has been my practice for many years to pray everyday that God will fill me with His Spirit and cause more of the Spirit's fruit*

*to appear in my life... Almost the first thing I do when I
wake in the morning, when my alarm clock goes off, is
to swing my legs out of bed and sit on the side of my
bed and present my body to God. And I sometimes go
from limb to limb, the hand, the lips, the ears, the eyes,
the feet, and present my body to God afresh for that day
as spiritual worship.*[9]

John Stott's biographer also tells of a story going back to the
1970s when a hard-nosed TV interviewer in Chicago asked a
personal question: "Mr Stott, you have had a brilliant academic
career; Firsts at Cambridge, Rector at twenty-nine, Chaplain
to the Queen; what is your ambition now?" In a five-word
reply, John Stott said it all: "To be more like Jesus."[10]

To Archbishop Donald Coggan the word that summed
up John Stott was "courtesy". And perhaps, adds Dudley-
Smith, "that is simply one aspect of Christian humility...
Humility is a synonym for honesty, not hypocrisy. It implies,
too, submission and dependence, beginning with submission
to scripture: 'an essential element in humility is a willingness
to hear and receive God's word'."[11]

One of John's study assistants, wrote to him later:

*People ask me, "What is John Stott's secret?" I have
taken to telling them that although you have no "secret"
there are several characteristics I have observed in you
that I will seek to emulate for the rest of my life. The
three things I always mention are rigorous self-discipline,
absolute humility and a prayerful spirit. Perhaps the most
important thing I have learnt from you is that, by grace,
faithfulness to God is a combination of these three
qualities.*[12]

The thing in all this is that Stott, like Billy Graham and Mother
Teresa, was a compellingly attractive human being because the
Spirit of godliness radiated from him, and whether it is young
men or maidens, old men or children, white, black, or brown,

Christian or non-Christian, all are powerfully attracted to the person whose key quality is godliness.

So no wonder Jesus prayed for this quality to characterise His people.

Let's see how He put it.

2. Jesus' prayer

First of all our Lord cries out: "protect them in your name" (John 17:11). This means keep them in your character, as we shall see. Then at verse 15 He prays: "protect them from the evil one" (John 17:15).

Thus he prays, but only after He has made certain affirmations about His disciples.

Firstly He establishes His disciples *belong* to Him: "I have made your name known to those whom you gave me from the world" (verse 6a). He adds: " I am asking on their behalf... on behalf of those whom you gave me, because they are yours. All mine are yours, and yours are mine..." (verses 9–10).

Secondly He says that His disciples *obey* Him. Verse 6b states: "they have kept your word" and verse 8a: "they have received them [the words]." Then he affirms that His disciples *know His origin*: "and know in truth that I came from you" (verse 8b).

Next Jesus affirms that His disciples *are in the world*: "they are *in* the world" (verse 11). "I am not asking you to take them *out of the world*..." (verse 15). While His disciples are in the world, nevertheless He adds, but they *are not of the world*. Verse 16 records: "They do not belong to the world, just as I do not belong to the world." He then says that His disciples are *hated by the world*: "the world has hated them because they do not belong to the world" (verse 14).

Finally He declares that His disciples are *sent into the world*: "I have *sent* them into the world" (verse 18).

So it is in those terms that He affirms the state of things among His disciples.

But now He is going to make a very special *petition*. And here it comes: "Protect[or keep] them in your name" (verse 11); in other words in the likeness of the Father's character. That's what it means when it says they are to be kept in His name, as Exodus 33:14–18 makes clear when Moses fears going up towards the Promised Land unless the Lord's presence should go with him. Indeed, pleads Moses: "If your Presence does not go with us, do not bring us up from here" (Exodus 33:15).

Jehovah God replies to His servant: "I will make all my goodness pass before you, and will proclaim before you the name 'The Lord'; and I will be *gracious* to whom I will be gracious, and will show mercy on whom I will show mercy" (Exodus 33:19). The meaning of God's proclamation of His name is then set forth in the following chapter where we are told: "And the Lord descended in the cloud and stood with him there, and proclaimed *the name of the Lord*" (verse 5).

So what then does it mean to proclaim the Name of the Lord? The next verses explain:

The Lord passed before him, and proclaimed, "the Lord, the Lord, a God merciful and gracious, slow to anger and abounding in steadfast love and faithfulness, keeping steadfast love for thousands, forgiving iniquity and transgression and sin, but who will by no means clear the guilty, visiting the iniquity of the fathers upon the children and the children's children to the third and fourth generation."

Exodus 34:6–7

Moses now bows and worships (Exodus 34:8) because he has had a revelation of the character of God and that is what came forth as the Lord proclaimed His name and revealed Himself as a God who was and is *gracious, merciful* and *holy* (33:19). Also *glorious* (33:22), *merciful* (34:6a), *gracious* (34:6b), *slow to anger* (34:6c), *abounding in steadfast love* (34:6d), and *manifesting justice* as well (34:7). But what especially comes through here as we think of the name (or character) of the Lord is the spirit of *love, compassion* and *mercy*.

MORE OF THE CHARACTER OF GOD

But the biblical text has more of the character of God as that which our Lord Jesus wants to see in His people. Thus, not only does Exodus speak of God's *faithfulness* (34:6c), of His *keeping steadfast* love for thousands (34:7), of His forgiving iniquity, transgression, and sin (34:8a), but beyond that it speaks of His justice, because He is "by no means clearing the guilty" (34:7). This latter means He is also committed to *justice and judgment*. There is a moral law of cause and effect built into the moral fabric of the *cosmos* by its creator. By this law, sin and iniquity will have consequences that will go on for generations. Thus do the judgments of history become the judgments of God and vice versa. This of course is why we need to be concerned about both personal and societal sin.

Finally the character of God, the name of God, is seen in His uncompromising holiness as one who does not "make a covenant with the inhabitants of the land… or it will become a snare among you" (verse 12). In other words, there is to be no compromise with the sin of the culture.

This astonishing catalogue and explanation of the nature of God as revealed in the name of God shows us the profound degree of moral and spiritual godliness our Lord Jesus wants from His people.

For this to become a reality, Jesus must pray something else, that something else being, "protect them from the evil one" (verse 15). Our Lord wants His people kept from Satan and evil supernaturalism. The Greek word there for "keep" (*tereo*) means to keep watch over, or guard. It's the same word used in Matthew 26 at verses 36 and 54 when it says that the guards "watched over" Jesus. Just as guards might keep a watchful eye on someone, so our Lord prays that His heavenly Father will guard and watch over his disciples. In Greek, the word *tereo* also speaks of preserving someone or something for a definite purpose, as referred to in 1 Peter 1:4 where the Apostle speaks of the heavenly inheritance that is *guarded*, preserved and kept for us in heaven. And unless God keeps us and we cooperate with Him, evil will contaminate us, and our godliness or holiness will be contaminated.

If that is the negative side, then the positive comes in the prayer at verse 17: *"Sanctify them* in the *truth."* Sanctify, from the Greek verb *hagiazo*, means to make holy, or consecrate, or set aside. It can refer to things being made suitable for ritual purposes, as for example in the Septuagint version of Exodus 29:27. Then in Ephesians 5:26 it is used of the church being sanctified and cleansed (compare also 1 Timothy 4:5).

In other words, Jesus is praying negatively that his disciples will be guarded from the hazards of evil so that positively they may be set aside and dedicated to *His* mission in the world. They are not to withdraw from the world, nor be assimilated by it. They are to be in identification with the world in its need, but not in identity with the world in its sin.

TWO PHRASES, TWO CHALLENGES

These two poles, these two awesome challenges in terms of godliness, are summarised *by the two phrases*:

- "not of" (verse 14)
- "not out of"(verse 15).

Let's revisit the words of our Lord again:

> *I have given them thy word; and the world has hated them because they are not of the world, even as I am not of the world. I do not pray that thou shouldst take them out of the world, but that thou shouldst keep them from the evil one. They are not of the world, just as I am not of the world. Sanctify them in the truth; thy word is truth. As thou didst send me into the world, so I have sent them into the world.*
>
> **John 17:14–17**

It is very significant to note that twice in three verses (verses 14–16, NRSV) our Lord repeats the identical phrase "they do not belong to the world, just as I do not belong to the world". So this is a very important utterance and one we should not miss. Nor should we miss that we have not been taken *"out of the world"*. And not being "out of the world", it is vital that we are protected from the evil one who at all sorts of levels is "the ruler of this world" (note John 12:31; 16:11). The world is thus a morally and spiritually perilous place to inhabit.

So then, we see that our Lord prays for holiness to characterise His people. This means firstly being separated from the world's lifestyle.

3. Separated from the world's lifestyle: "Not of" (verse 14, RSV)

The church is not to be assimilated by the society of the world around it in terms of its *motives, character,* or *methods.* I love J. B. Phillips's translation of Romans 12:2: "Do not let the world squeeze you into its mould."

I. THE CHURCH'S CHARACTER IS NOT OF THE WORLD

This is seen negatively in its lack of corruption

The church is to be morally "set apart" from the world and not a pale reflection of the society around it. If it is, then it is more cultural, ideological, and traditional than biblical and more accommodated than distinct. In fact, it is interesting to reflect back on the Exodus 33 passage referred to earlier in this chapter when Moses is calling on the Lord to grant him His presence as they advance towards the Promised Land (Exodus 33:14).

> If your presence will not go, do not carry us up from here. For how shall it be known that I have found favor in your sight, I and your people, unless you go with us?

In this way, we shall be distinct, I and your people, from
every people on the face of the earth.

Exodus 33:15–16

Moses realised that it was the presence and the power of the
Lord among His people that enabled them to be *different and*
distinct from all other people on the face of the earth. And
thus indeed it should be for the Church of Jesus Christ. People
should know that we are *distinct and different* from the culture
that is around us and we operate what might be called a
Christian counterculture. We have different values, morals,
standards, and ways of living and relating.

Apartheid changed us

Of course, being as I am a white South African, I cannot escape
the fact that the white South African church was massively
tainted by the apartheid ideology and practice and we failed to
change the ideological and moral culture around us. Instead, it
changed us. Thus it is that so many white Christians, whether
Reformed, evangelical, Pentecostal, or charismatic, have to
stand guilty at the bar of history on this point. Apartheid
invaded our ranks, corrupted our political thinking, damaged
and diminished our views of people of colour and their value
and dignity, and we sanctioned, or supported, whether
implicitly or explicitly, the wretched policy of apartheid.
Thankfully there were other Christians who stood firmly and
strongly against apartheid and contributed mightily to its
ultimate downfall.

Society is not to change and invade the church and its
witness. But the church and its witness are to invade and
change society. Society is not to bring its worldliness into the
church, but the church is meant to bring its godliness into
society.

One sees similar types of corruption, for example, in the
churches of the United States where the breakdown of morals,
marriage, and family life in society has now so massively

invaded the church that there is not much difference on this score between the society generally and the church specifically.

So too in many of our African churches where sexual promiscuity has invaded the church, and even some of its leadership, to a degree which makes it often very closely reflective of the sexual mores in the general African culture.

So to all this our Lord declares – No! We are not to be of the world. We have to aim for holiness in our churches. And this is seen negatively in the lack of corruption. One Christian politician said to me after our general elections of 2009: "Our South African churches do not see the importance of social righteousness."

If holiness in the church is seen negatively in the lack of corruption, it is also –

Seen positively in alternative lifestyles

Speaking at the International Congress on World Evangelization in Lausanne in 1974, Dr René Padilla of Buenos Aires, noted that while Jesus' work had both social and political dimensions, He in fact resisted embracing the political alternatives of His world. Dr Padilla went on:

> *An unprejudiced reading of the Gospels shows us a Jesus who, in the midst of many political alternatives (Pharisaism, Sadduceeism, Zealotism, Essenism) personifies and proclaims a new alternative – the Kingdom of God… His kingdom is not of this world, not in the sense that it has nothing to do with the world, but in the sense that it does not adapt itself to human politics. It is a kingdom with its own politics, marked by sacrifice. Jesus is a king who "came not to be served but to serve, and to give his life as a ransom for many" (Mark 10:45).*[13]

Actually in no man-made political groupings will the Christian feel fully comfortable. He or she will always be to some extent a misfit whose absolute allegiance will always be to another king and another lord than Caesar, whoever that Caesar may be.

So as we face the demands of Scripture in this regard we are to become what we are. In other words, as Christians comprising the Church of Christ, we are indeed an alternative messianic community. "Did you not die with Christ?" Paul asks, "Then put to death those parts of you which belong to the earth" (Colossians 2:20; 3:5). After declaring that Christians have been made one (Ephesians 2:3), Paul continues with an appeal to them to act according to that reality. Having been "delivered from this present evil age" (Galatians 1:4), the works of the flesh (such as immorality, strife, enmity, party spirit – see Galatians 5:19) are not to be among us, or we are "behaving like ordinary men" (1 Corinthians 3:3).

So when our Lord prays in verse 14 of His prayer that we are to be "not of the world", which means that we are separated from the world's lifestyle, He is praying a mighty and very difficult thing.

II. A KINGDOM OUTCROP

Because the church is to be kept from evil and the evil one (John 17:15) and sanctified and set apart in truth for God's specific purposes in the world to manifest His kingdom as an outcrop of a new age, it cannot be of the world in either its character or methods. But this does not mean the church is to be withdrawn from the world. In fact Jesus specifically prays that it should not be taken "out of the world" (verse 15), but that the church is to be *in* the world (verse 11) and vitally concerned in Jesus' name for the world's well-being.

John Stott summarised it well in these terms:

*All down history the church has tended to go to
extremes. Sometimes in its proper determination to be
holy, it has withdrawn from the world and lost contact
with it. At other times, in its equally proper determination
not to lose contact, it has conformed to the world and
become virtually indistinguishable from it. But Christ's*

vision for the church's holiness is neither withdrawal nor conformity.

In place of these two extreme positions, Jesus calls us to live "in the world" (verse 11) while remaining like Himself "not of the world" (verse 14), that is neither belonging to it, nor imitating its ways. [14]

The implications of all of this we will explore further in our reflection on mission (in Chapters 10 and 11). But we note that while the church *is to be separated from the world's lifestyle*, it is also to be –

4. Identified with the world's life-need: "Not out of" (verse 15, RSV)

Thus it is that the Christian turns both from the world and to the world. We turn from the world's lifestyle, to the world's life-need. The Christian needs Dietrich Bonhoeffer's celebrated threefold conversion – to Christ, to the church, and to the world. Jesus has left us in the world as salt to arrest decay (Matthew 5:13) and as light to dispel darkness (Matthew 5:14). These demands are included in the demand to be sanctified (or holy or godly) – this requiring not simply separation *from* sin, but separation *for* goodness. This also means faithful service and faithfully declaring the demands of the gospel.

Thus in Romans 1:1, Paul sees himself as "set apart for the gospel of God". The Latin Vulgate's translation of this is interesting: *"segregatus in Evangelium Dei"*. In other words, we are to be *segregated or separated into the gospel of God* and its demands of identification, caring and witness which will involve, as we'll explore more fully later:

- A clear witness to a moral order in the world springing out of the moral fabric of the universe.
- An equally clear witness to God's plan for and protection of the Christian family.

- A commitment to human dignity and societal justice.
- A practical and compassionate caring for the needs of the poor, broken, manipulated and marginalised.
- A clear proclamation of the gospel of our Lord Jesus Christ.

NO SHORTCUTS

It is all very, very challenging. And indeed, none of what our Lord prays to be in us in terms of witness, holiness, and godliness is possible without the supernatural work of the Holy Spirit, plus some old-fashioned steps, and disciplines to keeping us moving along the way. And then of course also in galvanising us to mission: "when the Holy Spirit has come upon you; and you will be my witnesses" (Acts 1:8).

Professor Dallas Willard, one-time Professor of Philosophy in the University of Southern California, and one of the finest, dearest, godliest men it has ever been my privilege to know, noted some of these required disciplines in his landmark volume *The Divine Conspiracy*:

> *Basically, to put off the old person and put on the new, we only follow Jesus into the activities that He engaged in to nurture His own life in relation to the Father. Of course, His calling and mission was out of all proportion to ours, and He never had our weaknesses which result from our long training in sin. But His use of solitude, silence, study of scripture, prayer, and service to others all had a disciplinary aspect in his life. And we can be very sure that what he found useful for the conduct of His life in the Father will also be useful for us. It was an important day in my life when at last I understood that if He needed forty days in the wilderness at one point, I very likely could use three or four.*
>
> *This crucial point carries on down through the ages during which His people have been on earth. The ones who have made great spiritual progress all*

*seriously engaged with a fairly standard list of disciplines
for the spiritual life. There has been abuse and
misunderstanding, no doubt, but the power of solitude,
silence, meditative study, prayer, sacrificial giving, service
and so forth as disciplines are simply beyond question.*[15]

Now a prayer to pray. It comes from Alcuin, the eighth-century British theologian who was assistant to King Charlemagne in educational reform:

*Eternal Light, shine into our hearts;
Eternal Goodness, deliver us from evil;
Eternal Power, be our support;
Eternal Wisdom, scatter the darkness of our ignorance;
Eternal Pity, have mercy upon us;
– That with all our heart and mind and soul and strength
We may seek Thy face and be brought by Thine infinite mercy
To Thy holy presence;
Through Jesus Christ our Lord. Amen.*

Chapter 8

Joy – The Third Mark

"But now I am coming to you, and I speak these things in the world so that they may have my joy made complete in themselves."

John 17:13

"Joy is the gigantic secret of the Christian."

G. K. Chesterton[1]

"Joy is the serious business of Heaven."

C. S. Lewis, *Letters to Malcolm*[2]

"The joy of the Lord is your strength."

Nehemiah 8:10

Midway through His High Priestly prayer, our Lord prays a very mysterious request: "that they may have *my joy* fulfilled in themselves" (verse 13). This I quickly recognised as very startling and challenging. What was our Lord talking about? I knew this prayer request would constitute a special challenge, even though the Bible refers to joy about 540 times!

Not surprisingly then, this chapter has a bit of a story attached to it. You see, when I came to the point of embarking upon it, and thinking more deeply about the meaning of joy, I suddenly registered that I didn't really know where to start. I didn't really know what it meant. So I put it on hold and moved on to the next chapter while I gave this one more thought, did some more reading round it and reflection upon it. All instincts of course took me to C. S. Lewis's *Surprised by Joy*. I then polled numbers of my friends as to their thoughts.

It was an instructive – even joyful – experience!

But in all sorts of ways the mystery remained. The depths were not plumbed. All answers seem incomplete. Partial. Haunting. Calling one further on, deeper in, until finally I saw that all places and experiences in which joy is sought in some way disappoint – *until we are only looking at Jesus.*

"I know now, Lord, why you utter no answer. You are yourself the answer. Before your face questions die away."[3] Thus spake the bitter old queen in C. S. Lewis's strong and pagan novel – *Till We Have Faces.* She had been accusing the gods of being evil and saying they had "no answer". But later she admits the error of her thought, saying now she knows why there is no answer. It's because "you are yourself the answer. Before your face all questions die away."

Speaking of the climax of his search in *Surprised by Joy*, C. S. Lewis says:

> *No slightest hint was vouchsafed me that there ever had been or ever would be any connection between God and Joy. If anything, it was the reverse. I had hoped that the heart of reality might be of such a kind that we can best symbolise it as a place; instead, I found it to be a Person.*[4]

Our seeking Oxford don was spiritually reaching into Bach's conclusion of "Jesu, Joy of Man's Desiring". We are searching for joy. We touch the hem of its garment, but don't quite reach it. We are savouring its scent here and there but not ingesting the blossom. We are pursuing a product, not knowing it is not a product. But a by-product. A by-product of encountering the Producer. The Person.

Lewis wraps up *Surprised by Joy* acknowledging that he had been wrong

> *in supposing that I desired Joy itself. Joy itself, considered simply as an event in my own mind, turned out to be of no value at all. All the value lay in that of which joy was the desiring. And that object, quite clearly, was no state of my own mind or body at all.*[5]

Lewis's confession

This is why Lewis floors us at the end of his odyssey with this confession:

> *But what, in conclusion, of Joy? For that, after all, is what this story has mainly been about. To tell you the truth, the subject has lost nearly all interest for me since I became a Christian… I now know that the experience, considered as a state of my own mind, had never had the kind of importance I once gave it. It was valuable only as a pointer to something other and outer.*
>
> *While that other was in doubt, the pointer naturally loomed large in my thoughts. When we are lost in the woods the sight of a signpost is a great matter. He who first sees it cries, "Look!" The whole party gathers round and stares. But when we have found the road and are passing signposts every few miles, we shall not stop and stare. They will encourage us and we shall be grateful to the authority that set them up. But we shall not stop and stare, or not much; not on this road, though their pillars are of silver and their lettering of gold. "We would be at Jerusalem."*[6]

Lewis was now walking with his Lord. And they were in Jerusalem, and looking together to the New Jerusalem. The "real" had been found. The shadow could now be seen for what it was. And the significance of the sign could now be thanked for with new and deeper doxologies because the destination to which the sign pointed had now been reached. "Jesu, Joy of Man's Desiring" had now been encountered. "Then will I go to the altar of God, to God my exceeding joy" (Psalm 43:4).

As with the steward found faithful in the Lord's parable about the talents, Lewis could surely anticipate the words: "enter into the joy of your master" (Matthew 25:21, 23).

But perhaps, having given the game away, I should go

back to think about all those delicious signposts and precious pointers along the way. But remember, they are only signposts to the one signified, to the Person at whom they point, who is Joy. And in whom all true joy is finally to be found.

1. Old Testament pointers to joy

Perhaps we might call it Jewish joy. It was nothing to do with backslapping bonhomie, raucous laughter, or the boisterous party spirit of wine, women, and song.

The four or five Hebrew words for joy give instructive, almost tantalising clues as to what it was all about. One has a root meaning in "to go round" (Hebrew *chuwg / chagag*) as when colourfully clad worshippers go round in procession during a religious festival and send up their thanksgivings in joyful praise, God himself being the manifest ground of Jewish joy (1 Samuel 30:16).

Psalm 47:5 uses a verb from another root meaning "to give a ringing shout" ("God has gone up with a shout, the Lord with the sound of a trumpet"). The context here is revealing because it presents God as having "gone up" to His throne and evident as having assumed His royal power. When God is revealing Himself in His manifest power He does so with His own mighty shout and joy.

Psalm 96:10 sets forth contextually the ringing cry which greets His accession to the heavenly throne: "The Lord is king!", or "the Lord reigns". When both His presence and His power are thus evident, His people and even His creation enter into God's own joy, "the joy of the Lord" – as it is called in Nehemiah 8:10. And they celebrate it as such, knowing that "the world is established, it shall never be moved" (96:10) – and He will "judge the world with righteousness" (verse 13b). Knowing this releases joy unlike any other.

Says the psalmist:

Let the heavens be glad, and let the earth rejoice; let the sea roar, and all that fills it; let the field exult, and

everything in it. Then shall all the trees of the forest
sing for joy before the Lord; for he is coming, for he is
coming to judge the earth. He will judge the world with
righteousness, and the peoples with his truth.

Psalm 96:11–13

Seeing God as He is, and where He is meant to be and
enthroning Him thus in our hearts, issues forth in us in light,
joy, rejoicing, thanksgiving, and singing. Thus: "Light dawns
for the righteous, and joy for the upright in heart. Rejoice in
the Lord, O you righteous, and give thanks to His holy name!"
(Psalm 97:11–12).

SING A NEW SONG

In consequence of this we have to exhort one another saying:

O sing to the Lord a new song, for he has done
marvelous things! His right hand and his holy arm
have gotten him victory. The Lord has made known his
victory; he has revealed his vindication in the sight of
the nations. He has remembered his steadfast love and
faithfulness to the house of Israel. All the ends of the
earth have seen the victory of our God. Make a joyful
noise to the Lord, all the earth; break forth into joyous
song and sing praises!

Psalm 98:1–4

And this joyful noise and joyous song in the Jewish context
was experienced and celebrated not just with singing but with
clashing cymbals, trumpets, and dancing, with clapping of
hands and shouts of joy. Indeed the full orchestra colourfully
set forth in Psalm 150 with its array of instruments cannot but
critique the contemporary western orchestra in many churches
of a weary organ plus tired old piano, if you're lucky, or on
a good day a poorly strummed guitar! That would not have
passed muster to express Jewish joy, that's for sure. Maybe

African church services with dancing and drums are more to the point!

Note too that this joy was essentially and quintessentially *Jewish* because no Gentile nation could yet rejoice in the Lord Jehovah God because they did not know Him. As yet, no other nation had been dealt with as God had dealt with Israel. This gave their joy not just an individual quality but also a corporate national one. In fact the individual celebrated this joy as a member of a people, a body, a community.

Nor was this just by physical membership of the nation, but by *spiritual* relatedness and obedience to the Lord Himself. So opening his volume of poetry and praise, the psalmist says right at the start: "Happy are those who do not follow the advice of the wicked, or take the path that sinners tread, or sit in the seat of scoffers; but their delight is in the law of the Lord, and on his law they meditate day and night" (Psalm 1:1–2).

This brings the joy of the Lord. And if he or she should rebel against Jehovah, what they will lose, like adulterous David, is the "joy of [their] salvation" (Psalm 51:12).

So for the Jews it was only they who knew this special joy of their Jehovah God.

Other occasions, moments, examples, and causes of Jewish joy are evident everywhere in the Old Testament. Almost all relate to new or deeper encounters in our experiences of the Lord Himself. Thus "the joy of the Lord" himself was imparted to His people as they got close to Him in love, devotion, obedience, repentance, or worship.

Joy was the supreme secret of the Jewish people even pre-Jesus, so not surprisingly it would surely be, as poet G. K. Chesterton once put it, "the gigantic secret of the Christian".[7]

2. New Testament joy

I. THE POINTER OF JESUS' OBEDIENCE

In the New Testament of course we do see Jesus as "a man of sorrows and acquainted with grief". But He was also born a Jew. Yes, He was more than just a human Jew, because within Him was the eternal God, Emmanuel ("God with us"). Nevertheless as a human Jew He still had in Himself everything distinctive about the chosen people. And He had it to perfection, including Jewish joy!

Of course we don't see Him in the biblical text in boisterous, exuberant, cymbal-clashing, trumpet-blowing, foot-stomping and dancing Jewish joy, not publicly anyway. Nevertheless because between Him and His heavenly Father was no obstructive sin, or fellowship-breaking barriers of disobedience, our Lord would have known an unbroken and unfettered joy in His own soul.

In fact even as Jesus' supreme joy and sense of abiding in the Father's love are located as by-products of His obedience to the Father, so the Christian's deepest joy lies in his or her obedience to the Son. John 15:10 is very clear. It all ties up with obedience. "If you keep my commandments, you will abide in my love, *just as I have kept my Father's commandments and abide in His love.*"

Then He adds, again as clearly as it gets, "these things I have spoken to you, that *my joy* may be in you, and that *your joy* may be full" (John 15:11).

Commenting on this remarkable affirmation, US theologian Don Carson, writes:

> This raises Jesus' obedience to his Father to a new and lofty plane. Jesus delights to do his Father's will; His joy depends on pleasing his Father… To please the Father gives the Son the deepest joy and satisfaction. Jesus recognizes this is true of Himself; and He wants this His joy to be shared by His followers. They will drink deeply

of His joy if they imitate His obedience. The ultimate draught is "complete joy," which presupposes complete and unqualified obedience.[8]

Carson then adds something we all know about:

No one is more miserable than the Christian who for a time hedges in his obedience. He does not love sin enough to enjoy its pleasures, and he does not love Christ enough to relish holiness. He perceives that his rebellion is iniquitous, but obedience seems distasteful. He does not feel at home any longer in the world, but the memory of his past associations and the tantalizing lyrics of his old music prevent him from singing with the saints. He is a man most to be pitied.[9]

A by-product of abiding

So when in the High Priestly Prayer our Lord prays that His disciples "may have my joy fulfilled in themselves" (John 17:13), He almost certainly is linking back to the "my joy" of John 15:4 where Jesus' joy, like that of those who are to follow Him and for whom He prays, is to be discovered as a by-product of abiding in the Father's love and in obedience to Him. Jesus really wanted His disciples then, and us now, to know His joy, and celebrate it as one of life's supreme blessings. But it cannot be snatched out of the air, secured by doing some happy thing, but only through full obedience to Him, His Word and His will.

But if we sin or disobey our joy evaporates like the morning mist assaulted by the heat of the sun.

The Cross as the key to joy

Of course one of the most dramatic and poignant linkups of joy to obedience comes in the beginning of Hebrews 12 where the writer is urging: "Let us run with perseverance the race that is set before us, looking to Jesus, the pioneer and perfecter of our faith, who for *the joy that was set before Him* endured the

Cross, despising the shame, and is seated at the right hand of God" (verses 1–3).

The Cross most assuredly in human terms could produce no joy – only blood, sweat, tears, as well as gut-wrenching agony and misery. Yet for Jesus it was a means of joy, because here was the Son of God's supreme act of obedience to the Father, so that the sins of the human race might be forgiven. Thus the ultimate act of obedience produced the ultimate joy – a joy transcending all circumstances.

As we too seek to be fully obedient we can discover this by-product of obedience, the joy of Jesus that runs the gamut from infrared to ultra violet. It is His joy, "fulfilled" in us (John 17:13).

2. THE POINTER OF KNOWING GOD'S WORD

The late James Boice, a wonderful friend and former pastor of the great Tenth Presbyterian Church in Philadelphia, notes that a primary key to joy is of knowing God's Word, because only then can we faithfully obey it.

> *The first remedy for a lack of joy is obvious, for it is on the surface of the text. Jesus says clearly, "These things I speak in the world, that they might have my joy." This means that in one sense the basis for joy is sound doctrine.*
>
> *Moreover, this is found throughout the Bible… many times joy is associated with a mature knowledge of God's Word. David said, "The statues of the Lord are right, **rejoicing** the heart" (Psalm 19:8). Psalm 119 reads, "I have rejoiced in the way of thy testimonies, as much as in all riches" (verse 14).*
>
> *Earlier in these final discourses Jesus declared, "If ye keep my commandments, ye shall abide in my love, even as I have kept my Father's commandments, and abide in his love. These things have I spoken unto you, that my **joy** might remain in you, and that **your joy***

might be full" *(John 15:10, 11). These passages and others teach that joy is to be found in a knowledge of God's character and commandments, and that these are to be learned through His Word.*[10] *(My bold)*

3. THE POINTER OF CONFUSION AND GRIEF TURNED INTO JOY

Our Lord's agonising obedience transmitting into His fathomless and mystery-filled joy alerts us also to another principle of deep relevance for the believer – namely that our own confusions, grief, and pain can turn into joy. Not just be replaced by joy, but be transformed into joy.

So it is that our Lord confuses and bewilders His disciples saying to them:

Is this what you are asking yourselves, what I meant by saying; "a little while, and you will not see me, and again a little while and you will see me?" Truly, I say to you, you will weep and lament, but the world will rejoice: you will be sorrowful, but your sorrow will be turned into joy."

John 16:19–20

Clearly the disciples are very confused. And things can happen to us in life that are very bewildering and confusing to the point where we ask: "Where's God in all of this? None of what's happening to me/us now fits with my/our understanding of the purposes and will of a good and loving God."

So here with the bewildered disciples. Nothing is fitting or making sense. He talks about going and leaving and then about returning and then leaving again. Unthinkable. Abandoning them? Incomprehensible. And of course they have no remote grasp of the three joyful returnings to come, the first after the resurrection, the second in the Person of the Holy Spirit, and the third at the end of the age!

Our problem

Yes, that's our problem. In the context of pain or bewilderment we can't easily get God's perspective on things. But if we do, grief, sorrow, and bewilderment can turn into a transcendent joy, regardless of circumstances.

But for now the disciples in confusion can only mutter and wonder. As we also often have to do.

However there is more to come. Not just confusion but something to make them "weep and lament" (16:20a). No, the believer is not spared even this, even things the world "will rejoice" over (16:20b) because of its alienation from the Christ and His Word.

But when this happens joy is nevertheless just around the corner. Just as a woman's pain, sorrow, and anguish in child-bearing are turned into joy "when she is delivered of her child" (16:21), so for the anguished disciples, who seem to have been left alone in pain "a little while" (verses 16, 17, 18, 19, and so on; seven references, astonishingly, no less!). But when they "see" Jesus again, their "hearts will *rejoice*" (verse 22a). And, adds Jesus, "no one will take your *joy* from you" (verse 22b).

More than that they have the invitation "to ask anything of the Father" (verse 23a), and "he will give it to you in my name" (verse 23b). And it's all part of registering what enormous joy awaits them as they get answers to prayer. Hence His modest rebuke: "Hitherto you have asked nothing in my name; ask and you shall receive, *that your joy may be full*" (16:24).

Goodness me! Does it get any more mysterious or exciting than that?

Joyless times

So when any of us enter those seemingly joyless times when for "a little while", He seems to be absent or missing from the circumstantial landscape of our lives, we need to register that the key for us, as it was for the disciples in this story, was *seeing Jesus again*. He will not leave us in testing times or joyless "sorrow" (16:22) for very long, but only for "a little while". Then everything changes as we "see Him again".

Says the old song: "Turn your eyes upon Jesus". As we do that we see Him who is joy and who enables us again to see ourselves on a joyous journey through the fields of the Lord, even some which hurt our feet by their thorns or stones.

In the disciples' case, unbeknown to them then, there was the imminent Cross. As with a woman in birth pangs where what generated her grief – namely child-bearing – also generated her joy, so what would generate the disciples' deepest grief – namely the Cross – would ultimately produce their deepest joy – a joy which Jesus said "no one will take from you" (16:22).

And so it is with us. If we can see our painful times as Cross, Calvary or Jesus times with His children, and as we "drink the Cup" with Him, and then embrace Him as risen, so too our sorrow is turned into joy, a joy no one can take from us. Even more so when we register that we have a prayer-answering heavenly Father who wants our joy to be full (16:24; compare 14:14 and 15:7ff.). I find when we know the Father through Jesus, and are assured of His love, even in the tough and rough and perplexing patches, then we "have peace" (16:33a), because we know He has "overcome the world" (16:33b), including all that would rob us of joy.

However, from our side if we would consistently know this joy, we must walk with Him in obedience and truth.

IV. THE POINTER OF TRUTH WHEN WE OR OTHERS EMBRACE IT

Now something instructive, especially for pastors, evangelists, or actively witnessing laypeople who seek to bring others to Christ – namely to see what deep joy came to John the apostle when he found his converts were walking obediently in the truth, which would for sure have been bringing joy to them too.

Writes the apostle John to "the beloved Gaius": "It has

given me **great joy** to find some of your children walking in the truth, just as the Father commanded us" (2 John 4, NIV). The elderly Apostle, who remembers from the High Priestly Prayer how Jesus interlinked truth, love, and joy, is eager to see the truth of the gospel progress, and that believers are uncompromisingly committed to it, hence his joy when he hears of the gospel and its truth changing lives.

Likewise he can celebrate with his old friend Gaius saying: "It gave me great joy to have some brothers come and tell about your own faithfulness to the truth and how you continue to walk in the truth. I have *no greater joy* than to hear that my children are *walking in the truth*" (3 John 3–4, NIV).

The converse of course is also true, namely deep distress in the hearts of biblically faithful believers when either their converts, or any in their family, or in their churches, or even among their church leadership are not "walking in the truth". Few things can create greater sadness or threaten our joy more deeply.

I think of the gutting distress of a friend whose children are in a church school where he found the chaplain was telling the kids in all his classes that as Santa Clause is called by different names in different countries, so God is called by different names in different religions and cultures – but all are basically saying the same thing and leading to one ultimate divine goal. My friend's children were terribly upset and confused, while their dad found his joy assaulted.

Muzzy and confused

Clearly the chaplain here was muzzy on the uniqueness of Christ, His exclusive claims, and His historic resurrection. Jesus is made one possible choice in a pantheon of religious options. In fact this chaplain is living post Easter as if all were pre-Easter. This is tragic, because a pre-Easter faith is one of grief and perplexity, not joy and certainty. Moreover to live post Easter as if all were pre-Easter is not only criminally unnecessary and historically absurd, it is also spiritually and theologically shattering and totally destructive of any capacity for real joy.

Looking at the disciples prior to the resurrection of Jesus, they are confused, depressed, fearful, and joyless. The doors which shut them in "for fear of the Jews" (John 20:19) also shut out both joy and peace.

But once they saw and finally got it that He was truly risen, they could "handle" Him and "see" (Luke 24:39), even though "they still disbelieved for *joy,* and wondered" (Luke 24:41). Here is joy overcoming disbelief and enthroning itself in their hearts. Thus could they after our Lord's ascension "return to Jerusalem with *great joy*" (Luke 24:52).

It was all true. The unthinkable, the unimaginable had happened. God had invaded planet Earth. The universe had changed gear. They had been and were in His presence in unimaginably new ways vibrant with joy.

But now, entering into and knowing the presence of the risen Jesus, the New Testament disciples are led through the shadows into the reality, past the latent and into the patent, past the incomplete into the complete, past all the pointers to the one at whom they pointed.

They had come to know what Jesus meant when He prayed that "they may have *my joy* fulfilled in themselves" (John 17:13).

C. S. Lewis, as we noted at the beginning of this chapter, said that all his personal questing after joy only revealed assorted pointers to the one who Himself was joy. Find that one and the pointers are seen to be just that – pointers.

But that does not rob the pointers of their importance, even their joyful importance.

Let's look at a few.

V. POINTERS TO JOY FROM DAILY LIFE

The pointer of music

I remember once at university having my startled room-mate, Alasdair Macaulay, burst in on me when, with tears of joy streaming down my face, I was standing on the couch and conducting Max Bruch's lyrical violin concerto with a bread knife! The extravagant harmonies and melodies were lifting me to the heavens and filling me with joy as I entered into the creator's creativity through the creator–composer. Bruch, Tchaikovsky, Beethoven, Liszt, Sibelius, Rachmaninoff, Chopin, or Brahms could all have the same effect on me. They spawned joy!

Thus could Josef Haydn write: "When I think upon my God, my heart is so *full of joy* that the notes dance and leap from my pen"[11] (my italics).

The pointer of creativity

The creativity may be our own or someone else's. Thus may we find exhilarating joy in carpentry or composing songs, or writing, or photography, or painting. My wife, Carol, as an artist, finds profound joy in painting as an expression of the creator's creativity in her.

Her creative and imaginative gardening in our beautiful garden has the same effect on her. "I feel drawn to God in my garden and joy is the by-product," she says. And this is surely because, as Kipling once remarked: "the Glory of the Garden lies in more than meets the eye".[12] The garden and Carol's creativity, these are pointers from what she sees to the One she doesn't see.

The pointer of nature and creation

Being near God's heart in a garden alerts us in a lovely way to how nature and glorying in natural beauty also produces joy, for one knows one is delighting in the delicious sense of beholding the handiwork of God. We did not create the garden flowers, or the soaring peaks of the Alps or Himalayas, or the expansive stark beauty of the desert, or the icy wonderland of Antarctica, or the multicoloured magic of coral and fish around the Great Barrier Reef of Australia, or the thundering majesty of the Victoria Falls. But we find ourselves in the religious experience of joy when we behold these beauties and know with stabs of delight that they come from on high and point us to the most high God.

Yes, "The heavens declare the glory of God; And the firmament shows His handiwork" (Psalm 19:1, NKJV). Comments the Apostle: "Ever since the creation of the world, his invisible nature, namely his eternal power and deity, has been clearly perceived in the things that have been made" (Romans 1:20). The believer rejoices in this. But the unbeliever who cannot thus rejoice, and who does not see the signature of God in creation only proves that he or she has "exchanged the truth of God for a lie, and worshipped and served the creature rather than the Creator" (Romans 1:25, NIV). Such people have not only lost the plot, they have lost the joy.

The pointer of loving and being loved

When St Paul itemises the fruit of the Spirit, he intimately connects love and joy at the head of the list (Galatians 5:22). Perhaps these two in the Spirit spawn and birth all the rest – "peace, patience, kindness, goodness, faithfulness, gentleness, self-control". Love and joy dance ahead, like Pied Pipers, at the front of this cavalcade of Christian blessings.

So pause with me for a moment and think of some of your "pointers to joy" experiences of loving and of being loved.

Think of a love experience with your mum or dad. I think as a prep-school boy coming home from boarding school for holidays and sitting with my mum by a winter fire as she read some of the classics to me. Oh, the joy, because I knew this was love at work.

I remember likewise during boarding school holidays horseback riding daily with my dad and with my dog Dingo galloping along next to us in doggy delight. Oh, the joy, the bliss! It was not just about riding, but about the love of my dad.

These were activities experienced in the heart-warming context of parental love. Joy was the by-product of the love of God reaching me vicariously through my mum and dad. Want to rob a child lethally or maybe fatally of joy, then rob them of parental love.

And what about when that Magical Maiden is finally met, or when your Prince Charming has finally charmed you sufficiently so that you can each say: "I love you"? When the Lord catapulted my darling Carol into my life, and we said "I love you" to each other, joy inexpressible burst upon our lives and a touch of heaven came down, because "God is love" (1 John 4:16).

Or perhaps you remember when a child first said to you "Daddy, I love you." Or "I love you, Mummy." Joy exploded in your soul, for God Himself and His purposes came close in the innocent beauty and purity of childhood and family love.

Nor must we forget the joy of deep friendships where we love the other with the *agapé* and *philia* love of God and share a world of common interests, shared experiences, and the sustained and dependable meeting and marriage of true minds.

I think of the joy generated through my deep friendships over the years with so many colleagues in African Enterprise. When life's journey is done, the love and loyalty of these partners in the gospel will be recorded as having given me a significant percentage of all life's joys.

No wonder when Paul had been separated a long time from Timothy, he could write: "I long night and day to see you, that I may be filled *with joy*" (2 Timothy 1:4).

The pointer of fun

I want to take a little longer on this, because I think it is quite important, and also generally missed and overlooked. In a sense I want to encourage you to develop a wholesome theology of fun!

Again I recall the Oxbridge '98 conference celebrating the hundredth anniversary of that man of fun, C. S. Lewis. And, yes, it was the "funnest" and perhaps top of the pops conference I ever attended. And, yes, it produced enormous joy, for fun, though definitely not synonymous with joy, must surely at times be at least its second cousin.

In any event, I registered afresh in that fun fortnight that God has given us all things richly to enjoy (1 Timothy 6:17).

So it was that, apart from the fun and laughter punctuating some brilliant presentations of solid stuff, there was built into the programme each morning what they called a "whimsy". Most of us needed educating into the nature of a whimsy, but it turned out to be a fifteen-minute light interlude of skit, musical sketch, dramatic reading, or comedy act.

One memorable whimsy had a highly professional musical group singing through a rollicking script of titles, yes, just *titles* of all C. S. Lewis's major books and essays. Narnia story titles would thus dance along to "Three Blind Mice" or "Hickory Dickory Dock", while *Allegory of Love* would take wings on "I Could Have Danced All Night" and *Surprised by Joy* of course had to come forth on the "Ode to Joy" from Beethoven's Ninth. Lewis's *History of 16ᵗʰ Century English Literature*, part of the *Oxford History of English Literature* (labelled inevitably by Lewis as "OHEL[L]"!), was a mouthful to squeeze into something like the lugubrious "Poor Jud is dead" from *Oklahoma!* Oh, what fun!

Apart from fun seminars on sketching, poetry, and the use of the arts and drama in evangelism, the spirit in the rather heavier content seminars was also buoyant with much laughter.

Of course everyone was urged to have a go at punting. This took me back to my undergraduate days when I had qualified for the Cambridge Damper's Club (which had a tie and an annual dinner) by fulfilling *summa cum laude* the only required membership conditions of genuinely falling off the back of a punt fully clad into the Cam. I was therefore hailed as something of an expert.

But I can also assure you that there are few delights of the soul more exquisite than seeing some world authority on Barth, Brunner, or Buber, hovering between time and eternity as his punt went north while the punt pole, with him hanging on desperately, remained firmly south, solidly embedded in eight centuries of Cambridge mud. As with conversion, holding on or letting go demands a decisive choice, and avoiding either or attempting both is perilous beyond measure. This was discovered by one world authority on something or other succumbing to a baptism, if not of fire, at least of brackish brine, as he sank beneath the surface of the Cam to the immense delight of all non world authorities.

C. S. Lewis as a man of fun

So what then of Lewis as a man of fun? For him, as he allows Screwtape, the senior devil, to lament, "Fun is closely related to Joy – a sort of emotional froth arising from the play instinct. It is very little use to us… in itself it has wholly undesirable tendencies: it promotes charity, courage, contentment, and many other evils."[13]

That is Satan's worry with fun. It connects into and easily resonates with joy and other divinely related gifts of love, courage, and peace. So Satan would discourage fun and obstruct all its expressions because they are pathways to joy. And you know Who joy comes from?

Thankfully Lewis in his fun and playfulness never succumbed to the evil one's blockages of fun.

Listen to his friend George Sayer speaking of Jack's habit (Jack was how Lewis was known to his friends) on coming to a pond or river during a walk of suddenly stripping down, all uninhibited, and plunging boisterously and naked into the water. He loved early morning swims, and would cycle to an Oxford swimming hole called "Parson's Pleasure", with "all the towers and pinnacles gleaming in the sun and bells ringing everywhere." The swim was "without the tiresome convention of bathing things… Even in his own undergraduate years these swims were part of his delight. 'I always swim (on chest) down to a bend, straight towards the sun, see some hills in the distance across the water, then turn and come again to land, going on my back and looking up at the willow trees above me.'"[14]

Those fun swims were surely pure joy!

Think also of the fun and joyful lecturer. Students who had Lewis as a tutor (had I done medieval English instead of medieval French and medieval Latin, he would have been mine – what tragic tricks has fortune played on me!) all recall, also midst his intimidating critiques of their essays, this irrepressible sense of fun. Thus one terrified student who rashly critiqued Matthew Arnold's "Sohrab and Rustum" found his tutor rushing for his brother's old regimental sword to emerge brandishing the weapon and shouting, "The sword must settle this."![15]

My friend, the late Angus Rose, husband of my lovely childhood friend Biddy, had Lewis as a lecturer when he was at Oxford: "Our classes were a riot of fun and laughter," he told me one day.

There then was the teacher who is full of joy!

Inklings and matins

Then of course there were the famous evenings of the so-called "Inklings" when Lewis and some of his friends and colleagues would come together to read one another's new manuscripts. Sometimes they had no new book, chapter, or poem for anyone to read. "On these occasions," says Sayer, "the fun would grow riotous, with Jack at the top of his form and enjoying every minute..." Anyway, Sayer's recollection is that "at the Inklings his talk was an outpouring of wit, nonsense, whimsy, dialectical show-play and pungent judgements."[16] For Lewis, "laughter and the love of friends" was what made the world go round. It all gave him joy.

But even in more obviously serious situations such as a church service, this streak of mischievous fun could be present. At Oxbridge '98, Bishop Simon Barrington-Ward told us how, when he was a young chaplain in Magdalen College, Cambridge, in the mid-fifties, he used to conduct a daily early service of Anglican matins. No one came to these services but C. S. Lewis! But as he left his rooms near the chapel, he would set his whistling kettle to boil water for his tea. As soon as the kettle began to whistle, he would rise and leave both chaplain and matins to their own devices and hasten back to his tea. "Certainly an incentive," said Barrington-Ward, "to get through the proceedings expeditiously!"

I'm sure the Lord of joy forgave him those early exits – and then joined him for the fun of early morning tea!

You see, for Lewis, play and fun were not a frivolous, extraneous, or optional addendum to life, but an important component of our creator God's essence and activity. In Lewis's view of things, seeking enjoyment, fun and play is our appropriate duty as creatures made in the image of a joyful creator.

Narnia and Screwtape

So it is that in the chronicles of Narnia, Aslan the lion (and the God symbol) becomes Lewis's vehicle for showing the mirth and fun side of God as the lion frolics delightedly with Lucy and Susan. After all, in the laws of cause and effect, if we as "effect" know what laughter, fun, and joyful celebration are all about, then God as "cause" must have all those dimensions within Himself, or the "effect" would be greater than the "cause" – which is impossible. This then surely requires of us a theology of joyful fun as we argue back from the phenomenon of fun itself to the ultimate author of it. After all, don't tell me God wasn't having fun the day He created the playful porpoise, the smiling seal, or the ridiculous walrus? And what about the lilac-breasted roller or the gorgeous bush-shrike? Even the owl. Mosquitoes happened on an off day but we'll let that pass. Beyond that, the psalmist can assure us that "in (His) presence is fullness of joy and at (His) right hand are pleasures forevermore" (Psalm 16:11), these being more than fun but surely including it.

This reality infuriates Screwtape, who tells Wormwood that the Enemy (God) is basically

a hedonist at heart. All those fasts and vigils and stakes
and crosses are only a façade, are only like foam on the
seashore. Out at Sea, out in His Sea, there is pleasure,
and more pleasure… He makes no secret of it: at His
right hand are "pleasures for evermore". Ugh![17]

Screwtape Letter number 12, says Sayer, highlights in fact the devil's policy and plan to cut people off from "real pleasures and positive activities, so that when they arrive in Hell, they realise that they spent their lives doing neither what they ought to have done nor what they enjoyed doing."[18]

So we are invited in *Prince Caspian* to celebrate the way, midst a great earthly battle, that the Great Lion (the God symbol, remember?) can be busy organising a grand parade and party.

Everyone was awake, everyone was laughing, flutes
were playing, cymbals clashing…

"What is it, Aslan?" said Lucy, her eyes dancing and
her feet wanting to dance.

"Come children," said he. "Ride on my back again
today."

"Oh lovely!", cried Lucy and both girls climbed onto
the warm golden back. Then the whole party moved
off – Aslan leading, Bacchus and his Maenads leaping,
rushing and turning somersaults, and the beasts frisking
around them.[19]

Well, how's that for an image? Have you thought lately of letting the Lord take you for a ride on His back?

George Sayer sums up the Narnia stories thus – "They are full of laughter and breathe forth joy."[20]

VI. JOY AS ECHOES OF THE HEAVENLY PLACES

Actually, for Lewis, as should be the case with all of us, all things beautiful in nature, art, music, life, literature, love, and spirituality were "echoes of the heavenly places", and foretastes of heaven – where we will know joys forevermore.

Thus did our dear Lord pray that "they may have *my joy* fulfilled in themselves" (John 17:13). Such joy runs the whole gamut from joy as the by-product of Cross-like obedience, or the fruit of transferred pain all the way through to joy in our human loves and creativities.

Then there are our joyful marvellings at nature.

And finally our meeting God and finding the love and peace of Christ, and then waltzing down the pathways of life hand in hand with fun and with all those things our fun and joyful God has given us "richly to enjoy".

Chapter 9

Protection (From Evil Supernaturalism) – The Fourth Mark

"… keep them from the evil one."

Jesus in John 17:15, NKJV

"Do you renounce the Devil and all his works?"

Anglican Book of Common Prayer

"There are two equal and opposite errors into which our race can fall about the devils. One is to disbelieve in their existence. The other is to believe, and to feel an excessive and unhealthy interest in them. They themselves are equally pleased by both errors, and hail a materialist or a magician with the same delight."

C. S. Lewis, *The Screwtape Letters*[1]

"Evil power wars against God's creation, salvation, and blessing. It mangles and destroys, seduces and takes possession."

Eugene Peterson[2]

"And Jesus, full of the Holy Spirit, returned from the Jordan and was led by the Spirit for forty days in the wilderness, tempted by the devil."

Luke 4:1–2

"Be sober, be watchful. Your adversary the devil
prowls around like a roaring lion, seeking some
one to devour. Resist him, firm in your faith."

1 Peter 5:8–9

It is a jump of note to move from the matchless joy of Jesus to the miserable sewers of Satan.

But we cannot and dare not escape this very solemn sentence in our Lord's High Priestly Prayer when He prays: "I am not asking you to take them out of the world, *but I ask you to protect them from the evil one*" (John 17:15).

Protection from evil supernaturalism is the fourth mark for which Jesus prayed to characterise His church.

*** ***

In much of the Christian world at present – even among those who take the Bible really seriously – the devil is a slightly embarrassing figure in both the Old and New Testaments' pictures of reality. We think that the depiction of a personal power of evil by that name can't really be what it seems, so we screen out from our thoughts the devil or Satan, as well as demons, evil spirits, principalities, powers, and strongholds, all of which are very strongly in purview – Ephesians 6 being one of many.

We really just do not want to take on board how Paul sees reality: "Put on the whole armour of God, that you may be able to stand against the wiles of the devil. For we are not contending against flesh and blood, but against the principalities, against the powers, against the world rulers of this present darkness, against the spiritual hosts of wickedness in the heavenly places" (Ephesians 6:11–12).

All of that just seems far too contrary to the modern way of thinking as well as our postmodernist mindset and contemporary secular person's view of the reality around us. So we try to skip over what the Bible is saying at this point and we dismiss the seriousness of what our Lord is praying right here at verse 15 in the High Priestly Prayer: "Keep them [or protect them] from the evil one."

This is not just protection in a general sense from generic evil. Rather, it is protection from a personal force or power of evil. This is not just "evil", but "the evil one". Satan is a real spiritual being – a personal person in the spirit realm; a spiritual person of immense power in the constellation of spiritual beings. In one of the great all-time classics on the Gospel of John, Archbishop William Temple speaks of this reference in John 17:15 as "The Evil One", and not just generic evil.[3]

Likewise William Barclay, in his commentary on John's Gospel, commented on this verse as follows:

> *Jesus prayed that God would keep and protect His disciples from the attacks of the Evil One. The Bible is not a speculative book; it does not discuss the origin of evil; but it is quite certain that in this world there is a power of evil which is in opposition to the power of God, a power which seeks to lure people out of the right way and into the wrong way. It is an uplifting thing to feel that God is the sentinel who stands over our lives to protect us and guard us from the assaults of evil.*[4]

In a sense, what all of this is doing is bringing us back into that which we discussed in Chapter 4 relating to the matter of world view.

Expanding on this, Canon Michael Green, in his penetrating and comprehensive volume *I Believe in Satan's Downfall*, has written:

> *High among the list of traditional Christian doctrines that have fallen into disrepute is belief in Satan. The theologian in his study and the ordinary churchman in his pew are – for once – agreed. It is ridiculous to believe in the Devil in this enlightened age. Such credulity went out with the beginning of the scientific revolution.*
> *At the same time a remarkable thing has been happening. Satan worship, fascination with the occult, black and white magic, astrology and horoscopes,*

*séances and tarot cards have become the rage...
Despite our professed sophistication, there is today in
the West a greater interest in and practice of magic than
for three centuries.*[5]

Scoffing and ridiculing

Michael Green goes on to comment on how people scoff and
ridicule the notion of a "devil with horns and cloven hoof" –
seemingly the belief of those of bygone ages.

*This is a cartoon figure, and has no right to be taken
seriously. The scriptures give no countenance to it, but
they do very seriously warn us of a malign power of
evil standing behind the pressures of a godless world
without and a fallen nature within the Christian.*

*The world, the flesh and the Devil have formed
a crucial part of Christian teaching from the very
beginning. More, they have been embodied in the
baptismal vows of renunciation and repentance. At
the very moment of visible incorporation into Christ
almost all liturgies have a specific act of repudiating
the Devil. Belief in the Devil, is therefore, very much in
the lifeblood of the Christian tradition. We are bound to
ask what justification there may be for believing not in
some cardboard figure of devilish fun, but in a person
(or personification?) so utterly ghastly and wicked, so
totally opposed to our race, that he stands behind all
other types of evil, be they physical, corporate, moral or
spiritual. Is it possible to believe in a unified centre and
focus of evil? I believe it is...*[6]

Let's first recapitulate some of our headlines on Jesus'
worldview.

1. Jesus' and the Apostles' world view

First of all, our Lord assumes the existence of God and He embraced the Old Testament understandings about the nature and activities of God. And this God was, and is, a Father who loves His creation, especially that part of creation that we call human beings. Over such, He wants to have an absolute authority and wants to remove and dispose of the blocks of sin which contaminate human lives. In His own teaching on the Prodigal Son in Luke 15:11–32 Jesus depicts the father who longs and pines for those who have got away from Him; He welcomes them back with joy and delight when they return. God is also one who is actively involved with His creation and loves the world and humankind with an overwhelming love of unconquerable benevolence and invincible good will, as John 3:16 makes clear.

In terms of human sin, there is redemption and forgiveness through the Son, but outside the Son and apart from the Son there is none we know of (John 14:6; Acts 4:12; John 3:16, 18, 36; Luke 13: 3, 5, and so on).

Also in Jesus' world view, judgment and hell (whatever that means) are real and are the unimaginably awful consequences of the rejection of salvation. We are accordingly urged to: "Enter by the narrow gate; for the gate is wide and the way is easy, that leads to destruction, and those who enter by it are many. For the gate is narrow and the way is hard, that leads to life, and those who find it are few" (Matthew 7:13–14).

There is no explanation of the nature or extent of that destruction, but simply a plain declaration of its awful reality (compare 2 Thessalonians 1:5–10; Hebrews 2:3, Matthew 25:46, etc.).

Linked then to all of this in Jesus' world view is the existence of the spirit world. He assumed that angels, demons, and Satan are real (see Matthew 4:11; Mark 5:1–19; 9:14–29).

TWO KINGDOMS

A logical extension of this understanding was Jesus' belief in two kingdoms: the kingdom of God and the kingdom of Satan. This is clear as the Pharisees challenge Him as to where His authority for healing comes from.

> *Every kingdom divided against itself is laid waste, and no city or house divided against itself will stand; and if Satan cast out Satan, he is divided against himself; how then will his kingdom stand? And if I cast out demons by Be-el'zebul by whom do your sons cast them out? Therefore they shall be your judges. But if it is by the Spirit of God that I cast out demons, then the kingdom of God has come upon you.*
>
> **Matthew 12:25–28**

Clearly here Jesus is speaking of two kingdoms, the first being the inferior kingdom of Satan and the second being the superior kingdom of God. But the good news is that in this confrontation between the two kingdoms, the kingdom of God is assured of triumph and victory because of Jesus' death on the cross and His resurrection from the grave (Colossians 2:15; 1 John 3:8).

In this regard it is critically important to register that our Lord Jesus Christ and Satan are not in the same league. Jesus, with His heavenly Father through the power of the Holy Spirit, is the only First League player. Satan, on the other hand, is in the second league with his counterparts for example in Archangel Gabriel or Archangel Michael. Satan himself is a fallen angel and can thus only achieve his ends as permitted by God. So, for example, in the book of Job, Satan tells God he cannot do damage to Job because, "Have you not put a hedge around him and his household and everything he has?" (Job 1:10, NIV). The Lord then speaks a permissive word to Satan, saying, "Very well, then, everything he has is in your hands, but on the man himself do not lay a finger" (Job 1:12, NIV).

In other words, Satan can only do what God allows him

to do. Perhaps that explains how our Lord could also say in His prayer: "*I guarded them*, and not one of them was lost except the one destined to be lost, so that the scripture might be fulfilled" (John 17:12). Judas actively and deliberately used his full and unprogrammed free will to decide to betray Jesus, and as he did so God sovereignly removed "the hedge" and Jesus lifted His "guard" over Judas and allowed "the betrayal" to proceed, as Scripture had prophetically anticipated.

In any event, Jesus curiously in His temptation experience does not dispute Satan's claim that in a sense he is in charge of the world, as when Satan says: "I will give you all this power and all this wealth… It has all been handed over to me, and I can give it to anyone I choose. All this will be yours, then, if you worship me" (Luke 4:6–7, GNB).

This tells us that there seems to be here a mysterious acceptance by Jesus that "the kingdoms of the world" have "been handed over to Satan" and that now "the whole world is under the rule of the evil one" (1 John 5:19, GNB).

Jesus also assumes that this puts the believer at the intersection of a power confrontation between the kingdom of God and the kingdom of Satan and between the power of God and the power of the evil one. The assumption here is that it is a case of power versus power. Thus it was that our Lord constantly exercised His authority in opposition to Satan's activity both in terms of His teaching as we see in Luke 4:32 and His healing as we see in Luke 4:36 and 39.

SENDING OUT THE DISCIPLES

So then when He sends His disciples out as the Father had sent him (John 20:21) He sent them out with "power and authority" to oppose Satan by driving out demons, healing diseases, and preaching about the kingdom of God. Says Luke 9:1–2: "And he called the twelve together and gave them power and authority over all demons and to cure diseases, and he sent them out to preach the kingdom of God and to heal." In Luke 10:9 He says: "heal the sick and say to them 'the kingdom of

God has come near to you.'" Those rejecting the kingdom of God were opting, whether consciously or unconsciously, for the kingdom of the evil one. In consequence, as in Chora'zin and Bethsaida, it would be "more tolerable in the judgement for Tyre and Sidon than for you" (Luke 10:13–14).

Not surprisingly when the seventy returned to Jesus with joy, they express amazement that even the demons (the power of evil supernaturalism and the kingdom of Satan) had been subject to them (Luke 10:17). At which point Jesus gives them the astonishing word that: "I saw Satan fall like lightning from heaven" (verse 18). In other words, during that famous missionary journey of the seventy, the kingdom of Satan was significantly invaded and the evil one experienced a major defeat.

So this wasn't just a case of a sweet little preaching tour. They were engaged in deadly spiritual warfare between the kingdom of God and the kingdom of Satan. It had been a case of the power of Jesus versus the power of Satan. In any event Jesus wanted them to keep perspective and added: "Nevertheless, do not rejoice in this, that the spirits are subject to you; but rather rejoice that your names are written in heaven" (Luke 10:20).

Having heard his Lord speak in this way, it is not surprising that the apostle John later could write: "The reason the Son of God appeared was to destroy the works of the Devil" (1 John 3:8).

PAUL AND PETER

Similarly the apostle Paul can testify before Agrippa how on Damascus Road Jesus said to him:

> I have appeared to you… delivering you from the people and from the Gentiles – to whom I send you to open their eyes, that they may turn from darkness to light, and from the power of Satan to God, that they may receive forgiveness of sins and a place among those who are sanctified by faith in me.

Acts 26:15–18

Delivering people from the power of Satan to God was part of the Apostle's mandate and presumably is part of ours.

Peter, for his part in his talk to the household of Cornelius, tells "how God anointed Jesus of Nazareth with the Holy Spirit and with power; how he went about doing good and healing all who *were oppressed by the devil*, for God was with Him" (Acts 10:38). So as Jesus healed, Peter saw Him dealing not simply with physical problems but with something behind the physical problems and which he calls "being oppressed by the devil".

We note that Peter is also declaring here that what Jesus did in His healing and other ministries was through the Holy Spirit. In His humanity, He was evidently subject to the same conditions and preconditions of power as humans.

THE BIBLICAL WITNESS

In summarising the witness of the Bible which shows that we cannot dispose of, neglect, or ridicule the reality of Satan, Michael Green writes, "This witness is particularly widespread and explicit. From Genesis to Revelation we are confronted by an anti-God force of great power and cunning. He is arrogant and determined, the implacable foe of God and man, who is out to spoil and mar all that is good and lovely."[7]

So the evil supernaturalism where Satan, demons, principalities, and powers are real is central to the biblical world view. And the fact is that if we, as twenty-first-century believers, do not likewise see those powers as real, are not fully aware of them, and are ignorant how to counter them, then we are like the Polish cavalry who galloped on horseback against Hitler's Panzer divisions as they rolled into Poland at the beginning of World War II. In other words, ignorance of Satan and evil supernaturalism is perilous beyond measure. That's why the Apostle can likewise affirm that if we want to "keep Satan from gaining the advantage over us", then we must not be "ignorant of his designs" (2 Corinthians 2:11).

MY THESIS

So my thesis at this point is that real power in the universe is bipolar. There is first and above all our sovereign, Creator God who has all power in heaven and on earth. Then there is the mystery of iniquity personalised in the enormous but not limitless power of Satan and his demonic spirits. These are truly, actively, and really at work in the universe especially among human beings in order to frustrate the plans and purposes of God.

Between these two mighty poles stands the human race capable of entering into and appropriating the power of the living God or else being controlled, often unwittingly, by powers of darkness. Spiritually, morally, personally, relationally, maritally, organisationally, or even nationally, we need to understand the need to appropriate the power of God and the Holy Spirit, thereby overcoming the works of the evil one, and being enabled to live out our lives fully and happily in terms of the purposes and the kingdom of God.

So our Lord was praying something incredibly serious in his High Priestly Prayer when He asked for His disciples – both those of the first century and those of subsequent centuries – that the Father should keep them from the evil one.

TWO EXTREMES

At this point it is worth noting that there are two potential extremes to avoid as we seek to interpret what the Bible says about Satan and evil supernaturalism. The first regards going beyond the Scriptures' real teaching, which may lead to fanaticism. Thus it is that sometimes one meets dear souls where every last negative thing that happens anywhere or to anyone or to themselves is explained in terms of the devil's activity.

The second danger is to fall short of what Scripture teaches. While the first peril leads to fanaticism, the second one leads to scepticism. In other words, people are simply sceptical about whether there really are such realities at work and whether we need to be bothered about such notions.

Thus in the quote at the head of this chapter from C. S. Lewis we find him affirming that:

> There are two equal and opposite errors into which our race can fall about the devils. One is to disbelieve in their existence. The other is to believe, and to feel an excessive and unhealthy interest in them.
>
> They themselves are equally pleased by both errors and hail a materialist or a magician with the same delight.[8]

I agree.

All this says we need to believe in Satan and in His reality. Why? Michael Green answers concisely: "The final, and to my mind, conclusive reason for believing in the reality of Satan is simply this. Jesus believed it. He has more to say about Satan than anyone else in the Bible. He has no doubt whatever of his reality."[9]

2. The powers of evil as experienced in life and ministry

For me personally I am so profoundly thankful our Lord prayed that we would know protection from the evil one, especially when I think of some of the personal and/or ministry experiences we have had over the years in assorted encounters with evil supernaturalism.

MASERU EXPERIENCE

For me the first real awareness of the powers of evil and darkness came when I was in my mid-teens. During our holidays, a group of us in Maseru, Lesotho (then Basutoland) experimented with what some now call a Ouija board game, but what we then we called "Glassy-glassy". Everyone sat round a table with a glass in the middle of the table and a series of letters of the alphabet were displayed around the glass in a circle about half a metre away from the centre point of the glass. We would then call up spirits and ask assorted questions, including name identification, while we all put our index fingers onto the glass.

The glass would then move, sometimes very vigorously to certain letters of the alphabet and spell out an answer, or else race across the table to either a "yes" or a "no" card which were located among the letters of the alphabet. There was no way with our lightness of touch upon the glass that it was being pushed or manipulatively pulled by anyone in the group, particularly as the glass would sometimes delay for a few moments before moving, and then might almost hurtle itself into suddenly spelling out a word or several words completely unanticipated or unplanned by any of us.

I very quickly became convinced we were indeed in touch with evil spirit forces who were playing their wicked games with us while we were playing our wicked games with them. At the end of a week of such games, I remember one night lying in bed before going off to sleep and being terror-struck because of a sense of an evil presence in my room. No one had ever taught me the biblical view on such things, and anyway I was not seriously into the Bible at that stage. But I just knew that what we had been encountering was evil and that the presence in my room that night was evil. I have a strong recollection of resolving that I would never, ever again play with this force we were encountering during our Glassy-glassy games. May none of my readers ever be tempted into this either.

EXPERIENCES OF EVIL SUPERNATURALISM IN OUR WORK

Another example I remember is the time in 1979 when, for some ten days, we were mounting the South African Christian Leadership Assembly (SACLA). We were calling together some 6,000 leaders from right across the denominational and racial spectrums to try and determine what it meant to be witnesses to our Lord Jesus Christ in the context of the anguished and racially shattered South Africa of that time.

As a result of that endeavour I came to believe that when one tackles a national situation and its unique set of problems, one inevitably lands up dealing not simply with a few junior demons, but with the "big boys" in the pantheon of evil. These are "not of flesh and blood", but are "principalities... powers, ... the world rulers of this present darkness... the spiritual hosts of wickedness in the heavenly places" (Ephesians 6:12).

This kind of power is spectacularly evident in Daniel 10 where, after three weeks of intense prayer, Daniel is faced with the Archangel Gabriel who tells him that

> *from the first time that you set your mind to understand and humbled yourself before your God, your words have been heard, and I have come because of your words. The prince of the kingdom of Persia withstood me twenty-one days; but Michael, one of the chief princes, came to help me, so I left him there with the prince of the kingdom of Persia and came to make you understand what is to befall your people in the latter days. For the vision is for days yet to come.*
>
> **Daniel 10:12–14**

Demonic princes over nations

The Archangel Gabriel here is referring to a mighty principality or power, known as the "prince of the kingdom of Persia", who had withstood him in spiritual combat and battle for twenty-one days. Astonishing. This "prince of the kingdom of Persia" is obviously a mighty being in the pantheon of evil powers and he rules or presides over a whole nation. At the end of Daniel's encounter with the archangel, Gabriel tells him "now I will return to fight against the prince of Persia; and when I am through with him, lo, the prince of Greece will come" (Daniel 10:20). These two mighty supernatural generals of evil – the prince of Persia and the prince of Greece

– are beings of evil supernaturalism who have power and assignments over whole nations. Yes, they are the "big boys" and can only be adequately handled by the senior archangels of the heavenly host.

Thus, when we came in a special way to tackle the monumental problems of our nation, as we did at SACLA with apartheid in South Africa in 1979, it was not surprising that we had a sense of coming up against mighty demonic strongholds and spirit powers which came at us with no holds barred. Thus there were endless and sustained attempts to destroy several of us with wicked libel, horrific character assassination via anonymous documents, and so on. Those of us organising SACLA felt that all the furies of hell had been released against us. We were not just coming up against the earthly authorities behind the policy of apartheid, but were coming up against the principalities and powers that stood behind them. The issues thus were not just political but deeply spiritual. Not just natural, but supernatural.

This is why in our own African Enterprise work, for example, when we call for earnest prayer from our prayer partners as we tackle nations or cities, we are not just playing around with religious platitudes. Rather, we are really and genuinely recognising our need for the Lord's people – for His intercessors, for His prayer warriors, for those who understand spiritual warfare – to engage on our behalf with the living God so that we might be protected and saved and kept, as per Jesus' prayer "from the evil one" (John 17:15).

KAMPALA, UGANDA

Another example is that of our Kampala Mission in 1985. The run-up to this mission was extraordinary, bearing in mind that we were tackling a country (Uganda) and a major city that had been gripped by some of the most monumental violence inflicted on any population in several centuries. This was the violence generated by Idi Amin in which some 400,000 people died. This was followed by the violence of the so-called liberator, Milton Obote, under whom even more people died – perhaps as many as 450,000. So we were in a country where the principalities or powers or nation princes were profoundly characterised by the spirit of violence.

Once again I don't think we had ourselves adequately covered by our intercessors and prayer warriors against the spirit of violence. Thus it was that we had to cope with the assassination of John Wilson, the lead set-up director for that mission. This was horrific, John being one of the finest African Christian gentlemen and friends it has ever been my privilege to know. Not long after that, Stephen Mongoma, one of our major leading evangelists, was viciously stabbed, nearly killed, and certainly put out of action for the mission. Then Festo Kivengere, the great Ugandan bishop and co-leader of AE at that time, became critically ill and could not participate in the mission. We knew we were really up against it in terms of demonic powers coming against us.

Interestingly enough, when I preached in one of the lunch-hour mass rallies in the middle of Kampala, a witch doctor came forward to give his life to Christ and brought all his witch doctor paraphernalia with him, laying it all down just below my pulpit. I announced there and then that next day I would have a public burning during the lunch-hour rally of all the witch doctor's paraphernalia and we would demonstrate the superior power of Jesus over witchcraft.

This happened the next day before a huge crowd. I took the inverted lid of a rubbish bin, put all the witch doctor's claptrap into it, then set it alight, holding it up in front of the crowd as it burned. The place went wild with both delight and fear. One soldier in the crowd was overheard saying to another: "That preacher will be a dead man tomorrow." This was reported to me and in the rally the next day. At the same place, same time, I announced that I was still very much alive, thus confirming that Jesus' power was greater than that of the devil. Again, the place exploded with praises to the Lord, and, I like to think, with some relief that preacher Michael was still in the land of the living! The witch doctor, for his part, still remained thoroughly converted to Jesus Christ and was rejoicing mightily in being freed of his demonic doings.

MANZINI, SWAZILAND

Then, when we were conducting a mission to Manzini in Swaziland in 1988, Neil Pagard, an amazing and wonderful brother who was doing the major mission set-up, was involved in a horrific episode just weeks before the mission began. A huge sixteen-wheeler truck on an open freeway ploughed into his wife just when Neil and she were changing drivers on a wide and open stretch of road. Neil's beloved Billy never recovered from the accident and was permanently brain damaged. This of course drastically curtailed Neil's ministry and finally took him out of set-up work altogether. Billy never came right and died some years later.

LUSAKA, ZAMBIA

Another example I remember is when we were gearing up for our mission to Lusaka in 1989. A young man from England, an intern working with us who was playing a major role in mission set-up, was nearly killed by electrocution through an electrical short that had somehow freakishly electrified the shower where he was showering. A few days before that same mission started, I came the closest, maybe ever in my life, to being killed in a car accident. I was at a crossroads when an enormous truck travelling at high speed at night, without headlights, missed our vehicle by just a few centimetres. I was sitting on the side that would have taken the direct impact. It seemed that two of us who were playing key roles in the mission had almost been taken out in the first few days before the proclamation phase had even started.

HOW SATANISTS OPERATE

Once in Pietermaritzburg, South Africa, a former Satanist who had come to Christ told my colleague, David Peters, that in some of their so-called prayer sessions to the prince of darkness, they specifically and regularly prayed for the downfall of Michael Cassidy and African Enterprise, as well as for the destruction of Michael's marriage.

At an African Enterprise conference in 1990 we were told a similar thing by Ed Murphy of California. Ed was a prominent lecturer around the world on evil supernaturalism and how to combat it and he told us how he was once on an aeroplane to San Francisco and found himself sitting next to a man who declined the airline lunch because, he said, he was praying and fasting. Ed was impressed and asked him to elaborate. The man replied: "Well, I am not praying and fasting for the sort of thing you might anticipate, because I am not a Christian. I am a Satanist. And in our San Francisco Satanist group we are praying for the marital destruction of the six leading pastors in the Bay Area." Ed told us how this episode had taken place three or four years previously, but by the time of his lecture to us several years later, five out of six of those targeted ministers had already gone down the marital tube with both their marriages and their ministries destroyed.

MY SISTER'S EXPERIENCE IN THE UK

Another very frightening experience for me came in 1992 when my sister Olave Snelling was involved in producing a television programme on Satanism and satanic ritual abuse for Channel 4, a major British TV channel. Her research took her into the strangest places with the most shocking discoveries. Her interviews with scores of people who had come majorly out of Satanism or been victims of satanic ritual abuse revealed a terrifying network of people involved in this practice and abuse, especially of women and children.

Some of the abusers happened to belong to the highest circles of British and European Union politics. The more my sister explored the realities of this phenomenon in Britain, the more appalled and horrified she was with the demonic darkness she was discovering on so many sides, as well as, in some cases, with its politically explosive potential.

When the programme was finally aired by Channel 4, fifteen helplines were opened up for five hours at the end of the programme, with a further five helplines being opened the next day. The calls were to represent merely the tip of the iceberg in terms of demand. British Telecom recorded 595 attempted calls in the first five minutes after the helpline number appeared on screen. Counselling lifelines were opened and 4,700 calls were received within the first hour, hopelessly jamming up the lines with people seeking help. The counselling lines in fact were open and busy that night for five hours, and the next day for a further five hours again. Apart from significant counselling and spiritual help being given, these calls unearthed massive new evidence of Satanic practice and ritual abuse around the UK.

MOST HORRIFIC OF ALL

But then, for me personally, came the most horrific experience of all. Word from survivors of satanic ritual abuse indicated that what Satanists around Britain would be doing after this sensational public exposure was to focus in their rituals on seeking Olave's destruction. About this time I was due to pass through London en route to the United States and I encountered in my sister, in a terrifying way, a person I scarcely knew. Her reactions, behaviour, and responses were bizarre and frightening, and she was suffering chronic panic attacks. I felt I was seeing someone under massive satanic assault and whose whole being and inner person were under threat and in deep spiritual peril.

Olave sought here and there to get prayer from others but it seemed of little avail. I told her that on returning from the

States ten days later I wanted to take her back to South Africa and out of England to have three or four weeks where we could just surround her with love and care and prayer until the demonic assault lifted and left her. And that is exactly what we did. After a couple of weeks in South Africa, the massive spiritual assault and oppression left her, her spirit and personality were released and freed again, and she sang doxologies of joy and thanksgiving for the Lord's deliverance out of what was unquestionably the most terrifying spiritual experience of her entire life.

Looking back on it Olave writes:

As the Lord was healing me during my time in South Africa with Michael, I heard the Lord say speaking through Matthew 10:26: "Therefore do not fear them. For there is nothing covered that will not be revealed and hidden that will not be known... But the very hairs of your head are all numbered. Do not fear therefore, you are of more value than many sparrows!" That was it! I fell back onto my pillows and heard something akin to a bar of iron breaking. I knew that the victory was the Lord's and He would deal with the situation. He had spoken! I had heard and obeyed. I didn't die. I lived! I got better. The Lord is evermore our Rock and our High Tower, and is our salvation. He said: "In this world you will have trouble, but behold, I have overcome the world."

I remember concluding afterwards that when Olave had embarked upon this research project for Channel 4, she had not managed to secure adequate spiritual covering through intercessors deeply experienced in spiritual warfare. She had gone into the den of the evil one insufficiently protected spiritually. And she had paid a price. Not only had the price been the most horrific attack of demonic darkness upon her, almost like a stranglehold upon her soul, but she had found herself deeply suicidal and perilously close to self-destructing.

Once delivered, nothing like that ever happened to her again.

For me it was one of the most instructive experiences of my life in making me profoundly aware of how much every believer needs for themselves our Lord's prayer: "*Protect [keep] them from the evil one*" (John 17:15).

ETHIOPIA

Let me share another couple of instructive experiences, one of which came out of our ministry in Ethiopia some years ago. Then I am done with these personal stories which I find most distasteful discussing and difficult to record, but which are necessary to relate in order to bring home the reality of these things and the critical importance of our understanding this arena of spiritual life, even as we celebrate with thanksgiving our Lord's prayer at this point for our protection.

We were doing a sort of double-whammy mission to two cities at once in southern Ethiopia, the first Debrezeit and the second, Nazareth. I don't think anywhere I have ministered in my life have I seen such demonic manifestations as we saw during some of our missions in Ethiopia. I remember one day preaching at an open-air rally in Debrezeit. No sooner was I into the message and preaching Jesus than assorted demonic manifestations began in several sectors of the crowd. People would scream, or yell, or writhe, or fall on the ground. One man crawled across the ground on his belly, as if he were a snake. Another with a wild face bounced round the open space in front of the pulpit on his hands and knees, crawling and barking like a dog.

Ethiopian believers are thankfully well experienced in dealing with such situations and in each case of such manifestation several men would come in and bodily remove the demonised person to a room adjacent to the open-air area where the meeting was being held. Then intercessors would begin to pray for the demonised, usually asking the demons first to identify themselves by name, as happened in the New

Testament, and then begin to pray in the name of Jesus for them to be cast out.

Debrezeit demoniac

I recollect after this particular meeting going to the prayer room. There were five or six such people being prayed for, several of whom appeared already to have been delivered. However, the man who had been crawling round the ground barking like a dog was still in a fearful state, still crawling, and still barking, his face a horrified and twisted contortion of evil and darkness, with eyes wild and blazing and a demeanour enough to terrify to death any except the spiritually initiated and experienced – which I happened to be. Likewise these Ethiopian prayer warriors.

I joined with two or three other men in the prayer process. I remember saying to the Lord: "Lord Jesus, we haven't come to Ethiopia to preach your word in your name and then be defeated by a demon such as this one. I want to see you deliver this man." One thing I remember was that the demon had identified himself with the name of an area beside a lake close by where Satanists regularly met for major sessions of witchcraft practice. This demon gave its name as identical to that of the area.

As we prayed and called on the name of the Lord, commanding the demon or demons to come out in the name of Jesus, all of a sudden, when we had been praying for about forty-five minutes, this man suddenly fell unconscious on his back with his hands outstretched in a cruciform pattern. He looked as if he were dead.

New Testament precedent

Needless to say this brought immediately to mind the story in Mark 9 of the demoniac boy brought to Jesus by the lad's anguished father: "Teacher, I have brought my son to you, for he has a dumb spirit and whenever it seizes him, it dashes him down; and he foams and grinds his teeth and becomes rigid" (verses 17–18). You will recollect that the disciples had not succeeded in exorcising the spirit so the boy was brought to Our Lord:

> *And when the spirit saw him, immediately it convulsed the boy, and he fell on the ground and rolled about, foaming at the mouth. And Jesus asked his father "How long has he had this?" And he said, "From childhood. And it has often cast him into the fire and into the water, to destroy him; but if you can do anything, have pity on us and help us." And Jesus said to him: "If you can! All things are possible to him who believes." Immediately the father of the child cried out and said, "I believe; help my unbelief!" And when Jesus saw that a crowd came running together, he rebuked the unclean spirit, saying to it, "You dumb and deaf spirit, I command you, come out of him, and never enter him again." And after crying out and convulsing him terribly, it came out and the boy was like a corpse; so that most of them said "He is dead." But Jesus took him by the hand and lifted him up, and he arose.*

> **Mark 9:20–27**

In fact, in the margin of my Bible, even as I now record this story and note again this passage, I see I have written "Debrezeit demoniac – Fell and rolled about, 8 December '95."

New Testament glory

So here with this biblical precedent in mind, I saw our Debrezeit demoniac on his back, his hands, as I say, outstretched in cruciform pattern, with all the raging storm of demon possession suddenly stilled. I watched mesmerised. Suddenly the man opened his eyes. His face suddenly lit up like a Christmas tree, his eyes radiated joy and relief and his demeanour was almost instantaneously filled with New Testament glory. We lifted him to his feet and he stood up radiant with the certainty of rescue and deliverance. The contrast to what he had been in the previous hours was not the difference between chalk and cheese but the difference between hell and heaven, between darkness and light, and between the spirit of Satan and the superior Spirit of Jesus.

Being an addicted camera clicker, and hardly ever being without a small camera in my pocket, I asked the man if I might take a picture of him so that I would remember him and the glory of this moment. He was more than willing. In fact he had a fine and handsome face, a beautiful face one might almost say, and certainly not the face of the wild animal we had seen in him minutes previously.

As we spoke to him he told us he had known he was demonised and that this had happened to him on and off in a nightmarish and terrifying way for twelve years. He had felt irrevocably trapped and imprisoned. It all began, he said, when he was a student at a local teachers' training college. The students were putting on a play in which there was one character who was a witch doctor. Our friend said nobody was willing to play the part of the witch doctor until he himself piped up and said that as he did not believe in all that nonsense, he would be happy to play the part of the witch doctor. And this he did. To get himself into the role he visited witch doctors, got caught up in their activities, and finally in calling on spirits he suddenly found himself demonically gripped and inescapably demonised. It was a spine-chilling story, but an instructive one. No one tampers with this stuff and gets away unscathed, unless mightily protected by Jesus Christ and the power of the Holy Spirit.

That night in my little room in Debrezeit I read Mark 5, about the demoniac whose name was Legion and whose demons came out and entered the herd of swine that had rushed down the bank and entered the sea. "And people came to see what it was that had happened. And they came to Jesus, and saw the demoniac sitting there, clothed and *in his right mind*" (Mark 5:14–15). And again I wrote in my Bible and I see it again at this moment "Debrezeit demoniac – 8 December '95 – 'in his right mind' – PTL."

RADIANT AND LOVELY

Then there was our experience in Nazareth, not far from Debrezeit. My preaching text, not surprisingly, was "Can anything good come out of Nazareth?" (John 1:46). At the end of the service I prayed for people who had come forward in response to my appeal. As I touched one young woman and began to pray for her, she fell down screaming sounds of demonic and desperate darkness. As I reached down to pray for her again, she coughed up horrific phlegm and spat it in my face and clothes before lunging up like a panther to seize me by the throat. Though a slight and spindly young lady, with very thin arms, yet her strength was prodigious and only the full might of several men could prise her loose from my throat.

Some of the counsellors then carried her out to a counselling room and began to pray for her while I continued praying for other people who had responded to my appeal. After a while I felt constrained to go through to the back room while the service continued and was led by other colleagues. I found this woman standing and looking radiant and lovely, a beautiful young woman actually, with some of the counsellors around her. The demon had come out and she was freed and ecstatic. She told us that she was the wife of a Satanist and had come secretly to the service seeking help. She said she had been demonised for some time but knew that now she was free. She asked us to pray for her as she went back to her home and to cope with her Satanist husband whose reactions to her conversion and deliverance she clearly feared. Locals said they would get a Bible to her and follow her up. How profoundly I hope that happened. I am sure it did. Again, I have a lovely photograph to remember both this happening and this person.

*** ***

Given the kind of stories shared above, it is clear that we would agree with several statements emerging from the

Lausanne Movement for World Evangelization.

Clause 12 of the Lausanne Covenant opens with this credal affirmation: "We believe that we are engaged in constant spiritual warfare with the principalities and powers of evil, who are seeking to overthrow the church and frustrate its task of world evangelisation."

Then at the Second Lausanne Congress, which took place in Manila, the Philippines, in 1989, the following statement appeared in the Manila Manifesto: "We affirm that spiritual warfare demands spiritual weapons, and that we must both preach the Word in the power of the Spirit and pray constantly that we may enter into Christ's victory over the principalities and powers of evil."

At the Lausanne Consultation on Spiritual Warfare held in Nairobi, Kenya, in 1993, for which mission leaders from all across the world and from all denominational backgrounds attended, this statement of agreement came forth: "We agreed that evangelisation is to bring people from darkness to light *and from the power of Satan to God* (Acts 26:18). This involves an inescapable element of spiritual warfare."

LESSONS FROM JOB

Perhaps in all this it is worth registering some of the instructive insights that come to us from the book of Job. The whole story of Job is set against the backdrop of Satan's challenges to God. Satan is basically saying to God that He is not intrinsically lovable and that all of creation, especially the creation of man, is a failure because humans will not love Him unless He constantly behaves towards them as a sort of cosmic Father Christmas or benefactor, blessing them and doing good things for them all the time. And certainly they won't love God if He is nasty to them.

This is the whole gist of the conversation in chapter 1 of the book of Job. Job of course does not realise that he is on stage before a watching universe and that he is a key test case as to whether God is intrinsically lovable and creation intrinsically successful. So, says the book of Job:

*The Lord said to Satan, "Have you considered my
servant Job? There is no one like him on the earth, a
blameless and upright man who fears God and turns
away from evil." Then Satan answered the Lord, "Does
Job fear God for nothing? Have you not put a fence
around him and his house and all that he has, on every
side? You have blessed the work of his hands, and his
possessions have increased in the land. But stretch out
your hand now, and touch all that he has, and he will
curse you to your face." The Lord said to Satan, "Very
well, all that he has is in your power; only do not stretch
out your hand against him!" So Satan went out from the
presence of the Lord.*

Job 1:8–12

Everything imaginable

Everything imaginable, as we all know, then began to happen
to Job. And we see the extent of Satan's power with the
forces or instruments he was able to harness against God's
servant Job. First of all there were the Sabeans who fell on
Job's sons and daughters and slew them (1:15). Then there
was a lightning strike on Job's sheep and servants (1:16). Then
came a raid from the Chaldeans on Job's camels and servants
(1:17). And then finally a *whirlwind* destroying both family
members and the house of the eldest son (1:18–19). Satan thus
exhibits power over both human instruments as well as forces
of nature. This is scary.

Of course we who know the end of the story know how
magnificently Job, even with his physical afflictions, came
through his horrific ordeal and could affirm the intrinsic
lovability of God when he says: "Though He slay me, yet will
I trust Him" (Job 13:15, KJV). Furthermore Job can add: "He
knows the way that I take; and when He has tried me, I shall
come forth as gold" (Job 23:10). "For he will complete what he
appoints for me" (Job 23:14). Beyond that Job can affirm his

massive confidence in the sovereignty of God and even sees into the future to the coming of the Messiah when he says: "For I know that my Redeemer lives, and He shall stand at last on the earth" (Job 19:25, NKJV).

"Upstairs" and "downstairs" plays

In a sense what the book of Job shows is that in the total reality of things, there is an "upstairs play" and a "downstairs play". The conversation in heaven between God and Satan reveals something of the upstairs play. Then downstairs another play is worked out in the life of Job and his family. And of course the people in the downstairs play don't understand everything that is happening around them because they don't know, see, or understand the upstairs play.

In China, I am told, there is an interesting type of theatre whereby the audience looks at an upstairs and downstairs pair of stages, as if the wall had been knocked out of one side of a double-storey house. The audience then sees two plays going on at once and they see how all sorts of things happening in the downstairs play are inexplicable to the people downstairs because they don't understand the upstairs play which the audience, who are watching both plays at the same time, are able to see. Fascinating.

Of course in biblical terms the downstairs play is indeed invaded by both God and Satan, as the Christian believer knows and understands, even when he or she does not comprehend the interactions and actions upstairs between the two major players of God Himself and Satan.

New Testament

Coming back into the New Testament we find that in the Gospels there are twenty-nine references to Satan, twenty-five of them coming from the lips of Jesus Himself. In fact, in reading the Gospels one grasps that Jesus and all the New Testament writers saw His whole ministry as a power encounter with Satan and demons. This is especially evident in our Lord's temptation experiences in the wilderness (Luke 4:1–12), where Satan even quotes, or in fact misquotes, Scripture to Him, and Jesus replies addressing the evil one specifically. Our Lord had no doubt about the existence of the one He was addressing.

Book of Acts

The book of Acts is likewise laced with similar references. Thus in Acts 5:1 Ananias and Sapphira, who had cheated and lied about the money from their sale of property, are asked by Peter: "why has Satan filled your heart to lie?" (verse 3). In 5:16 we are told that the apostles received people "afflicted with unclean spirits and they were all healed." In 8:7 Philip, now in Samaria, deals with demonised people and Luke comments: "For unclean spirits came out of many who were possessed." In 13:10 Elymas, the magician in Cyprus, is called "You son of the devil."

Acts 19:12 records the interesting story of the Jewish exorcists trying to exorcise in the name of Jesus. The evil spirit replies: "Jesus I know, and Paul I know; but who are you?" (verse 15). Adds verse 16: "And the man in whom the evil spirit was leaped on them, mastered all of them, and overpowered them, so that they fled out of the house naked and wounded." This apparently "became known to all the residents of Ephesus, both Jews and Greeks; and fear fell upon them all; and the name of the Lord Jesus was extolled" (Acts 19: 16–17).

Book of Revelation

Perhaps before leaving this difficult and unsavoury subject it is worth registering that in four out of the seven letters to the churches in the book of Revelation, our Lord refers to the works of Satan going on in those churches, with some of these things being related very specifically to false and erroneous teaching. Even teachers in a church can be wittingly or unwittingly demonically directed.

Conclusion

These references, and scores of others which one could adduce, along with dozens of other stories I could share out of fifty years of Christian ministry, underline for us the reality of the power of evil supernaturalism and the reality of Satan himself. How hugely important is it therefore that Christian believers should be alert to the reality and machinations of the evil one, even being aware that at times "Satan disguises himself as an angel of light. So it is not strange if his servants also disguise themselves as servants of righteousness" (2 Corinthians 11:14–15). Satan can thus come in the guise of goodness and light and deceive unwary or undiscerning believers.

Noted the Reformer John Calvin: "The devil doesn't have to be nasty. Just godless." So too we register again the apostle Peter's exhortation: "Be sober. Be watchful. Your adversary the devil prowls around like a roaring lion, seeking someone to devour. Resist him, firm in your faith" (1 Peter 5:8–9). And he's a trickster too, striking not randomly and thoughtlessly, but waiting, as he did with our Lord, "until an opportune time" (Luke 4:13).

We can let the apostle Paul summarise for us: "though we live in the world we are not carrying on a worldly war, for the weapons of our warfare are not worldly but have divine power to destroy strongholds. We destroy arguments and every proud obstacle to the knowledge of God, and take every thought captive to obey Christ" (2 Corinthians 10:3–5).

So of course we register finally and afresh the Apostle's clear injunction: "Finally, be strong in the Lord and in the strength of his might. Put on the whole armour of God, that you may be able to stand against the wiles of the devil" (Ephesians 6:10–11).

To be sure each one of us should lift our hearts, minds, and lips to heaven in the traditional so-called Lord's Prayer and call out to our heavenly Father: "Father, keep us from the evil one." And we sing mysterious praises of gratitude to our all-powerful Saviour that He very specifically prayed for us in His High Priestly Prayer saying, "Father… keep them from the evil one" (John 17:15).

Chapter 10

Mission – The Fifth Mark (I)

Jesus' Attitudes in Mission

"The church exists by mission, as fire exists by burning."

Emil Brunner

"The Spirit of Christ is the spirit of missions, and the nearer we get to Him the more intensely missionary we must become."

Henry Martyn

"The Living God of the Bible is a sending God."

John Stott

"Recognizing that mission has at its heart a sense of sending and being sent only raises another question: sent to do what?"

Christopher J. H. Wright, *The Mission of God's People*[1]

"We are committed to world mission because it is central to our understanding of God, the Bible, the church, human history and the ultimate future."

The Cape Town Commitment, post the Third Lausanne Congress on World Evangelization – October 2010

"As you have sent me into the world, so I have sent them into the world."

Jesus in John 17:18

Jesus prayed not simply for the church to be marked by truth and holiness, joy and protection from evil supernaturalism, but He also prayed that the church would be very clearly characterised by the mark of Mission: "As you have sent me into the world, so I have sent them into the world" (John 17:18).

Indeed, only by bearing the mark of mission can the church avoid the two extremes of withdrawal from the world, like the Essenes of old, or assimilation by it, as per much of what is happening in the modern church which all too easily becomes an echo of the society around us with our hats endlessly doffed to the spirit of the age.

In fact, however, truth, holiness, joy, and spiritual protection without mission lead to a spiritual lopsidedness in the church whereby it focuses on its own orthodoxy and purity, its own maintenance systems, and its own status quo standing in society, but neglects the world which "God so loved", for which Jesus died, and into which we are sent as Christians.

So most famously in His prayer, and we repeat it, He prayed: "*As* you have sent me into the world, *so* I have sent them into the world" (John 17:18). This was later reiterated as a command: "*As* the Father has sent me, *so* I send you" (John 20:21). The pattern of His ministry is to be ours. Jesus is not only the message, He is also the model. We are to look at how *He* did it. A pretty staggering challenge, I would say!

A sent people

In any event we cannot come to Jesus Christ without coming to His mandate to *mission*. This word of course comes from the Latin *mitto* meaning "I send", or *missio*, which means "a sending". We are in other words a *sent people*. In fact, each one of us could consider ourselves either a missionary going out to the mission field or else part of the mission field. In reality, then, we are either one or the other. That's why I often encourage churches to put a sign at the exit door of their church for people to read as they leave Sunday worship, saying: "You are now entering the mission field." The fact is that this task of mission is not that of a small professional ministerial or ecclesiastical élite. It is the task also of each and every layperson. This is why the main responsibility of the minister/pastor and the other giftings in the body of Christ is "to *equip the saints* for the work of the ministry" (Ephesians 4:12). Ministry, we thus discover, is the main task of ordinary believers. And we are to carry it out "Jesus style".

Of course, it is obvious – if we believe in Jesus at all – that we believe He was *sent* into the world by the Father. So if we go as He came, we know at once that we are a sent people. No standing still. No sitting back. No luxuriating in armchairs of apathy or spectating from a pew with a view! We are commissioned. We are assigned. We are sent. We are not the people of "in-drag" but of outreach. Before we ask people to crash the stained-glass barrier of our building, or our medieval songs, or pop band or whatever, we go out and find and meet people where they are. Like Jesus, we are to go out – "to seek out and to save the lost" (Luke 19:10). We fish where the fish are.

Great Commission

If we are in any doubt about this we have the "Great Commission" in various forms at the end of all four Gospels to remove those doubts. This is especially capped by Acts 1:8 where our Lord says to the waiting and apprehensive disciples: "But you shall receive power when the Holy Spirit has come upon you; and you shall be my witnesses in Jerusalem and in all Judea and Samaria and to the end of the earth."

Insofar as these were His *last* words, they need to become our *first* concern. I remember speaking in a missions conference in Raleigh, South Carolina. When I gave an appeal for people to respond to "the possibility of full-time mission service" a young lad came forward saying he had seen among the national flags draped around the auditorium the South African flag which, when suspended vertically, has a Y-shaped configuration. As this young man saw that Y configuration in the flag, he said it became Y for "Yes". And he stepped boldly forward to say "Yes" to Jesus Christ for the possibility of entering full-time mission work. Yes, that's the spirit!

Another young eleven-year-old lad from Tennessee, USA, showed a similar spirit in a letter he wrote me saying: "Dear Mr Cassidy, What is it like in Africa? Thank you for preaching about God. If you need any help, let me know!" Another willing recruit, perhaps, for the work of mission!

So we ask ourselves afresh. Are we witnesses? Are we in mission? Are we missionaries? Formal? Or marketplace? In fact, whether we are the butcher, the baker, or the candlestick maker, we are as believers nevertheless part of the mission enterprise of the church of Jesus Christ.

Archbishop William Temple once remarked "The church is the only organisation on earth which primarily exists for the benefit of non-members."[2]

So, church member, your job is to go after those non-church members and make them members!

So let's think about it. How was Jesus sent? How did He come? How did He go? How did He witness to the love and power of the Father?

We note first of all that:

1. Prayerfully in the power of the Spirit Jesus fleshed out grace, truth, holiness, and compassion

I. HE MOVED PRAYERFULLY

This is so central that we will have cause to devote the whole of a chapter to it. However, for the moment we note that the prayer of John 17 is typical of our Lord's prayer life. Right after talking to the disciples in His final discourse He stops with them, and "When Jesus had spoken these words, he lifted his eyes to heaven and said, 'Father...'" (verse 1). In other words, He is praying.

At verse 9 He says: "I am *praying* for them." In verses 20 and 21 He emphasises "I do not *pray* for these only, but for those who believe in me through their word, that they may all be one."

In Luke 6:12 He goes out into the mountain alone to pray and to pray all night. And of course He began His ministry with forty days and forty nights of prayer in the wilderness. Thereafter, in all His ministry, He moved prayerfully in communion with the Father, and was in consequence led by His Father in all He said and did.

What a huge challenge to us to "go and do likewise!"

II. HE MOVED IN THE POWER OF THE HOLY SPIRIT

We register here that everything Jesus was and did flowed from the power of the Spirit working in Him and through Him. Later we'll give this a whole chapter.

Thus at His baptism by John the Baptist "the Spirit of God descended on Him like a dove" (John 1:32–34). Then Luke tells us that, "Jesus, *full of the Holy Spirit,* returned from the Jordan and was *led by the Spirit* in the wilderness where for forty days he was tempted by the devil" (Luke 4:1f.).

Then back in Nazareth, as He went to the synagogue (Luke 4:18f), we find Him testifying: "The *Spirit of the Lord* is upon me, because he has anointed me to preach good news to the poor. He has sent me to proclaim release to the captives and recovering of sight to the blind, to set at liberty those who are oppressed, and to proclaim the acceptable year of the Lord." All of that spoke of His mission to the world which He knew could not be carried out unless the *Spirit of the Lord* was upon Him.

So too, our own mission out there to the world is as

unthinkable as it is impossible to accomplish without the *Spirit of the Lord* being upon us. That is the indispensable enabling power without which we are as weak as water and as feeble as flax.

And if the disciples had not got the point in His pre-death and resurrection utterances, they certainly got it in His major post-resurrection utterance when He says: "when the *Holy Spirit has come upon you,* you will be witnesses in Jerusalem and in all Judea and Samaria and to the ends of the earth" (Acts 1:8). Here again is the indispensable enabling and the indispensable prerequisite of effective ministry.

This is why in my view we should not get too worked up over the Pentecostal / charismatic or evangelical controversies related to a fresh experience and empowering of the Spirit. Our Lord wants us simply to claim the fullness of the Spirit and move in that fullness so we can get the job done. I don't think getting ourselves in a lather about some of the vocabulary is very enlightening or helpful, because once heat comes in, light tends to go out.

Don't run on empty

But the big point here is that we dare not allow ourselves to run on empty in terms of the Spirit's fullness, empowering, and presence in our lives. That not only produces manifest ineffectiveness but enormous stress. I remember when our middle child Debbie was a student at Cape Town University that I found myself from time to time coming into that lovely city on ministry assignments. Dear Debs would often come to the airport to collect me in her old student jalopy. As a vehicle it was a seriously beat up little piece of former engineering!

But it ran. Anyway, once, when Debs had fetched me, we set off for the city, but I noticed the petrol gauge flickering violently several centimetres below the empty sign. Lights were flashing and the whole thing looked dreadfully ominous. We were definitely running on empty. Debbie casually announced: "Don't worry Dad, when it does that I know there are still 15.8 kilometres of fuel in the car, and getting to town is only 12 kilometres! In between having a personal fit, I ordered Debbie into the nearest garage. I mandated the tank be filled. Debbie would then give me that pathetic look student daughters, who have not only run out of petrol but out of money, reserve for agitated fathers! At which point I would hand my credit card to the petrol attendant, pay for the full tank, settle back and relax knowing we were now running on the fullness of petrol.

As all of us know, running on empty in a car is very stressful and traumatic, so too in Christian ministry and service. We can't run on empty. We have to be filled and constantly refilled with the Holy Spirit.

III. HE FLESHED OUT GRACE, TRUTH, AND HOLINESS IN ACTION

Everything about our Lord's earthly ministry was about incarnation and fleshing out the Word of God. Indeed, He was the Word made flesh. John is clear in his prologue (1:14): "the Word became *flesh* and dwelt among *us*". And the hard fact is that in terms of mission and effective ministry, every word coming from us to the world has to become flesh. People need to see and hear things fleshed out.

I remember reading the story of a little girl whose father became wearied with her reiterated requests for him to tell her a story. Finally, in desperation over the time-consuming nature of these repeated assignments, he decided to put a mass of children's stories on to a CD. If she wanted a story from Daddy she should just push the "On" button on her little CD player. This dispensation was tried for a couple of weeks. Then his little daughter came to him in disgust and protest. "Daddy, I want *you* to tell me a story. You see, Daddy, the CD player hasn't got a lap." She needed the story and the words fleshed out to her in the physical arms and lap of her daddy. The word just had to become flesh in order to be truly receivable.

Our Lord did this. And none of us concerned for the work of mission can avoid or evade it. Wherever we are, the challenge before the Lord's people is to flesh out their witness.

The nurse

I remember when my dear dad was dying there was one nurse, a wonderful young Christian woman, who was particularly caring for all the patients who were *in extremis*. This included my dad. No little acts of kindness or care were too small or insignificant for her. I will never forget her one comment to me when she said: "They all really love it when I help them clean their teeth." I never forgot that remark. That is incarnational ministry.

The doctors in Libya

Another vivid memory comes to mind out of my first tour around Africa with a friend in the summer of 1961 as we were getting African Enterprise established. We began our tour in Tripoli in Libya before heading 50,000 km round the continent into dozens of countries.

I will never forget our first stop in Tripoli when we met a missionary couple, Pat and Patsy McCarthy, who were doctors labouring in the back streets of the city among the poorest of the poor and the most needy of the needy. The laws of the strongly Islamic republic made it almost impossible to verbalise their witness. But their medical ministry to physical needs of every sort could not but have been a significant incarnational ministry and testimony to those needy people, especially when they discovered Pat and Patsy were Christians and were doing what they were doing out of a love for Jesus Christ.

Did they win lots of souls? I don't know. But I do know that their radiant faces bore the marks of New Testament glory and hundreds of people received their incarnational ministry knowing that this came at the bidding of and in obedience to Jesus.

Then John 1:14 and many other Scriptures show how He fleshed it out in a particular way with *grace, truth, holiness and compassion*. As He did this there was a manifestation of glory. Says the apostle John: "and we have seen his glory, the glory as of a father's only son, full of grace and truth."

People must see

A little later on, when the disciples were being called, Philip said to Nathaniel: "We have found him of whom Moses in the law and the prophets wrote, Jesus of Nazareth" (John 1:45). Nathaniel's astonished response was: "Can anything good come out of Nazareth?" To this, Philip replied with the most convincing and irrefutable answer of all: "*Come and see*" (John 1:46).

The fact is that in the postmodern world in which we live most people sadly tend to be down on truth and argument. Only opinions are allowed. So throwing our truth at people, or our fancy apologetics and arguments for the resurrection and so on will not be in and of themselves enough, important though argument and apologetics are. Our postmodern world is more likely to be convinced by the *demonstration* and *incarnation* of truth and argument.

The early Billy Graham film, *Souls in Conflict*, tells of Dr Graham's Harringay Crusade in 1954 in London. There was an airline pilot who had been converted to the faith and was facing the scepticism and intellectual counterblasts of the airline personnel around him. Finally he said to them: "Have you any argument against a changed life?" They agreed that they had none because in him they had seen an astonishing change.

Thus it is that our mission to the world will abort if people do not see grace and demonstration along with truth.

IV. THEY SAW ALL JESUS' MINISTRY FLOWING OUT OF INCREDIBLE COMPASSION.

Matthew tells us: "When he saw the crowds he had *compassion* on them, because they were harassed and helpless, like sheep without a shepherd" (9:36). The English word "compassion" comes from two Latin words: *cum* meaning "with" and then *passus*, being the past participle of the Latin verb *patior* meaning "to suffer". *Patiens*, is the derived noun, meaning "suffering". So compassion means "to suffer with", or "to enter into the suffering or pains or needs of others". That was how Jesus ministered. He entered in a heartfelt way into what people were feeling and going through. And certainly it is a rough and painful thing to see people who are "harassed, helpless, and like sheep without a shepherd". This aroused Jesus' compassion.

Every one of us therefore needs to pray: "Lord, baptise me with new compassion."

Tears for Chris

Tears of compassion can at times make a poignant difference. I remember many years ago, when I was involved in ministry in Toronto, Canada, I was invited to breakfast with a very dear former Cambridge friend of mine called Chris. He was in fact the very first person from whom I heard the gospel clearly as I arrived at university. But now here was Chris inviting me to breakfast with him and then sharing with me the startling and traumatic news that he had "lost his faith".

"Chris, have you just lost faith at the edges, or at the centre?"

"At the centre," he answered with grief and pain in his eyes. After being one of the most ardent members of the Christian Union at Cambridge, he later went on to a particular American theological college (which shall remain nameless), that basically destroyed his faith. Such happenings in certain theological colleges around the world make my blood boil as almost nothing else. I find myself wanting to see the proverbial millstone round their necks as they are cast into the depths of the sea.

I told Chris that almost everything I was and am had started with his first decisive act of witness to me. My whole life had been shaped by that testimony. He looked back at me with monumental sadness in his eyes. At which point I found tears rolling down my cheeks. The waitress came to check our table and then scurried away without a word, embarrassed and confused.

When I left Chris I said to him I believed the Hound of Heaven would pursue him and in due course bring him back to his Saviour. Later that morning I went walking and praying in the streets of Toronto and asked the Lord why he had allowed me to weep in a rather embarrassing way in that restaurant. Then I felt I heard a very distinct word from the Lord into my heart. "You see, my son, I knew it was the only language he would understand." While I know that seven or eight times out of ten I might not feel compassion for someone or for different situations, nevertheless compassion for my brother and friend Chris is what I felt that morning.

Delight

Anyway, imagine my ecstatic delight a good many years later when I heard from Chris that he had come back to a rediscovery of our Lord Jesus Christ. He was over the moon, as was I. And a couple of years after that came yet another letter, saying Chris had been ordained and was fulfilling the call placed upon him early in his life and he was now back in the ministry.

What part my tears of compassion played I have no idea, but I believe they were hidden somewhere in the equation of Chris's final return to his Saviour and Lord.

So as we receive His compassion, so we are called to extend it to others whenever we can and in any situation. In the case of Jesus we see that very same compassion in how He addressed the crowds; how He changed water into wine in the wedding at Cana of Galilee when the host was in a state of embarrassment; how He took time out with Nicodemus in secret to help the questioning theologian through his perplexities; how he stopped in the noonday sun with the morally broken Samaritan woman; and how He raised Lazareth from the dead. The list, of course, is endless.

V. ALL JESUS DID WAS DONE IN THE SPIRIT OF FORGIVENESS

Thus did Jesus forgive the woman taken in adultery. Thus did He forgive the disciples their blunders and blindness. Thus did He forgive even those who nailed Him to the cross.

Likewise as we minister it has to spring from the forgiveness we have received from our Lord, and out of the forgiveness we extend to those who have offended us – even to naughty people who have done bad stuff and to whom we are seeking to witness. When we thus minister we open up the pathways of penetration into their souls.

The prisoners preach

I remember an episode in the 1980s when our team was caught up in the dramas of Idi Amin's cruel regime and its aftermath. My dear and great and late friend, Bishop Festo Kivengere, co-leader with me in our African Enterprise work, was down in his home area of Kabale when it was announced on a certain day that three men were to be publicly executed by firing squad in a local stadium for protesting at the injustices of the Amin government. Here were these three men, awaiting execution.

Festo went to President Amin and protested, to no avail. Festo then asked the authorities if he could speak to the men before they were executed. Permission was granted. As the three men were led into the stadium, hobbling, with rope at both their wrists and feet, and followed by nine soldiers with AK47s, they called out to the crowd the message of Jesus and the gospel of forgiveness. The people were flabbergasted. The doomed trio were led into the centre of the field. Then Festo was told he could go and address them. He came up to them, and as he later reported to me, "Michael, I saw on their faces New Testament glory." Then before Festo could minister to them, they asked if he would interpret for them from their dialect into Swahili so that all would understand. Festo of course agreed.

Then to the amazement of all, each of these men in turn began to give their testimonies as to how they had found Jesus Christ in prison and how the spirit of love and forgiveness had in consequence been birthed in their hearts. They told the crowd they forgave Idi Amin, and they forgave the soldiers who were about to shoot them. And they were excited because within minutes they would be meeting Jesus in glory. The crowd was stunned. One could have heard a pin drop. Festo then shared a few words of his own with them before he was asked to step aside.

After Festo had stepped aside, nine shots rang out. The three men fell dead to the ground. But their miraculous spirit of forgiveness had left the crowd spiritually overwhelmed and reminded of our Lord's own words on the cross, "Father, forgive them; for they know not what they do" (Luke 23:34).

Festo then told me that for weeks after this episode there were multitudes who came spontaneously to Christ, so powerful was the forgiveness testimony of the prisoners as they were about to die.

So then we declare rightly that our Lord prayerfully in the power of the Spirit fleshed out grace, truth, holiness and compassion. And in our labours of mission we are called on to do likewise.

Then we register that:

2. In love He broke barriers, went where people were, and started a new community

In breaking down these barriers and starting a new community, Jesus led His disciples into unthinkable relationships and fellowship. All of this was classically seen in the extraordinary bunch of disciples that Jesus called. They were an impossible crew.

Thus there were the shy and retiring Philip, the doubting

Thomas, the betrayer Judas, the sons of thunder, James and John, Matthew the tax collector and government man, and Simon, the zealot, the violent revolutionary bent on overthrowing the status quo and the government system.

The bunch of disciples represented our Lord's alternative community.

And then they produced groups of people who were bonded across impossible barriers so that we can read that people did not know what to call them. After all, they were neither Jews nor Gentiles, but in effect a "third race" who needed a new name. So "it was in Antioch that the disciples were first called 'Christians'" (Acts 11:26). This is not surprising when one sees some of the members of the church in Antioch as recorded in Acts 13:1–2.

Thus there were "prophets and teachers", in other words different sorts of charismatic giftings, then Barnabas the Jew, then Simeon called Niger – in other words a black person – Lucius of Cyrene, who would have been an Arab Libyan (present here of course with Jewish people), then Manaen, a member of the Court of Herod the Tetrarch, this gentleman being a member of government and a high official. Then around him were people whom he governed!

Saul and Barnabas were also there as ministers to this group among whom were also people strong in worshipping the Lord (Acts 13:2) and in the discipline of fasting (verse 2). So together, so spiritually sensitive, so ready to obey were they, that the voice of the Holy Spirit could be audible saying: "Set apart for me Barnabas and Saul for the work to which I have called them" (verse 2b). Clearly the church was also a missionary group who were ready at the instruction of the Spirit to move out in mission (verse 3).

AN ALTERNATIVE COMMUNITY

So this is the kind of extraordinary cross-cultural, non-racial group, differentiated in economic and educational level, no doubt, that our Lord had called together to be a kind of exemplary missionary sending body and a glorious gospel precedent for all time. An alternative community.

These sorts of challenges remain for the church today. I remember once preaching in Cairo in shared ministry with Festo Kivengere. The two of us, as noted, were co-leaders of African Enterprise. Festo was a black person, I was white. Festo was a bishop, I was a layman. Festo was an older man, I was a younger one. Festo was from independent Africa, I was from the polecat tyranny of apartheid South Africa. Yet we were able to minister together both in Egypt and across Africa and around the world.

After one of our meetings in Egypt, when Festo and I had shared the message – I taking the prodigal son to the far country, and Festo bringing him home – one of the Egyptian believers came up to us and commented as he looked at my pale skin and Festo's dark one: "Michael, you are the milk of the gospel, and Festo is the chocolate!" A milk chocolate gospel!

When people asked Festo how he could travel the world with a white South African, thereby prejudicing his witness and credibility, he used to reply: "Michael is my miracle brother. He has come to Jesus, and I have come to Jesus, and so we have come to each other. That's why we must be together." In many ways Festo and I were an impossible combination – as were our African Enterprise teams with their massive mix of different backgrounds. But we were able to minister effectively across this continent and well beyond its shores.

We were part of an alternative community for Africa. The Christian church should be that visible alternative community. If we look back to the early church, evangelism and mission were the spontaneous, effervescent overflow of the fellowship among believers. So it is that Luke can tell us that, "They devoted themselves to the apostles' teaching, and fellowship, to the breaking of bread and prayers" and all "who believed were together" (Acts 2:42, 44).

The consequence of all this can be found in verse 47: "And

day by day the Lord added to their number those who were being saved."

It is exactly this sort of thing that we still need today, with the church not only being a spiritual movement, but a cultural alternative too.

KIGALI PRISON

I remember another occasion in our mission to Kigali in Rwanda a year after the 1994 genocide. We preached in many devastated and dramatic contexts during that mission and saw the Lord do many astonishing things. But I recollect one particularly poignant experience preaching in a prison jammed with some 7,000 or 8,000 men in a space that should have basically never had more than 500 people. The congestion was cruel and terrifying, and for some fatal. Literally.

I found myself standing on a rickety table in a jammed courtyard with people crammed into every nook and cranny craning their cramped heads out of porthole sized windows in the cells. Of course I preached about the blood of Jesus shed on the cross for all, including those who had committed murder, some of these men having committed upwards of several hundred murders. And I told them of the forgiveness that was available in Jesus Christ at the Cross. Of course half of my inmates were Hutu and the other half Tutsi and it had been their internecine tribal strife that had led to the tragic genocide in which 850,000 died.

After my message I gave an appeal to those who wanted to respond to Jesus Christ. Almost everyone put up their hands. This made me suspect they weren't fully understanding the full import of my message. Not only did they have to come to Jesus Christ, I said, but they had to come to one another in reconciliation and forgiveness. I accordingly called up several of my colleagues to stand on a strong bench alongside the table from which I was precariously preaching. I called up a black colleague, a white colleague, a coloured colleague, an Indian colleague and an Asian colleague from Singapore.

As I stood with these brothers next to me, everyone from a different racial background, I told these spiritually panting prisoners that if they came to Jesus Christ as their Lord and Saviour, then this, as I pointed to my racially diverse group of colleagues, was what they were also coming to. They had to come to a multiracial, multi-tribal, multi-ethnic fellowship. Tutsi would have to forgive Hutu, and vice versa. I left them for a few moments in a sobering silence as they reflected on what I was demonstrating to them.

I then repeated my appeal. Again, the vast majority responded, but perhaps with more comprehension. I then led them in a prayer of commitment to our Lord and to the multifaceted Christian fellowship into which they were being called. And to the model.

This was how our Lord ministered. And as He had been thus called by the Father, so likewise He calls us. Again He was not only the message, He was the method.

SAMARITAN WOMAN

These kinds of principles are dramatically set forth in our Lord's encounter with the Samaritan woman in John 4. Here our Lord broke down national barriers. He, a Jew, ministered to this woman, a Samaritan, knowing full well that: "Jews have no dealings with the Samaritans" (John 4:9).

Our Lord was also of course crossing a gender barrier. And He ministered across this barrier, as must we.

More than that, He went to where she was. He didn't wait for her to come to Him, He went into her world, not just the physical and geographical world of the well at Sychar but into her world of seeking out water. Now he connects directly to her world by saying: "Give me a drink" (verse 7). And from there He moved on to connect her and her world to His, as He spoke to her about the possibility of receiving "living water" (verse 10). This water, He explained, could be received so that people would "never thirst". And it would become a "spring of water welling up to eternal life" (verse 14). Unsurprisingly she was inevitably moved to say: "Sir, give me this water" (verse 15).

Thus did our Lord minister to people where they were and in the context of their needs. The monumental and strategic challenge remains for us to do the same.

OUR SAMARITANS

All this puts on us an inescapable pressure to ask ourselves who constitute our own Samaritans. Whether racial, ethnic, tribal, gender, economic, educational, or whatever. As the Father sent Him, so He sends us.

Then as the Lord blesses our ministry, we will seek, win, and draw all kinds and conditions of people into this new messianic community of love, of acceptance, of mutual care, of fellowship, of understanding, and of belonging. In our contemporary postmodern world people are longing for community, connectedness, care, love, acceptance, and fellowship. This is available uniquely and in a totally special way in the church of Jesus Christ.

All of this reveals the basic attitudes and spiritual postures our Lord bought to the work of mission. He is saying: "This is how I saw and viewed my mission. These were my attitudes and commitments. Now they must become yours. Especially must you take them into your actions and acts of mission itself.

So to this we now turn.

Chapter 11

Mission – The Fifth Mark (II)

Jesus' Actions in Mission

"For the Son of Man came to seek out and to save the lost."

Jesus, Luke 19:10

"The highest service that men may attain on Earth is to preach the Word of God."

John Wycliffe

"If God calls you to preach, do not stoop to be a king."

Anonymous

"Mission will not happen unless the Church goes beyond its own life out into active care in the local neighbourhood."

David Sheppard

"As the Father has sent me, so send I you."

Jesus, John 20:21

In looking at Jesus as not just our message of mission, but also our model (John 17:18), we turn from His attitudes in mission to His *actions* in mission.

1. In the name of the Father He called a few to be with Him, to watch and copy Him in seeking out the lost, in preaching, teaching, healing, and delivering

HE CALLED A FEW TO BE WITH HIM

Mark 3:14 tells us that Jesus "appointed twelve, to be with him".

The key aspect of this training was that they were primarily "with Him". That was the main thing. They were with Him, close to Him, alongside Him, and in daily companionship with Him. As a result, they could observe what He said, what He did, how He did it, and how He related both to His heavenly Father and to those around Him. Beyond that intimate inner circle He seems also to have invested time and training into a further *seventy* (see Luke 10:1). Then by the time we are heading towards the day of Pentecost and the outpouring of the Spirit, the group ready for that experience "was in all about a hundred and twenty" (Acts 1:15).

In a nutshell, our Lord was concerned to equip a relatively small number of disciples who would go out and become an overwhelming minority! And thanks to that faithful little few, we – as a body of Christ – are here today, some 2.5 billion of us with 125,000 new believers added daily. We are the descendants of the few, the faithful few. The few he trained.

HE TRAINED THE FEW

And this principle of training "the few" has to be our basic and most key model still today. The apostle Paul makes this crystal clear when he says: "And his gifts were that some should be apostles, some prophets, some evangelists, some pastors and teachers, to *equip the saints for the work of the ministry for building up the body of Christ*" (Ephesians 4:11–12). The omnicompetent, omnipresent, overworked, overstretched, and frantic "do it all yourself" ministers are not the New Testament model, which explains why the Christian church is not growing and multiplying in all parts of the world as it should. The New Testament model is that the fivefold giftings in the body of Christ of apostles, prophets, evangelists, pastors, and teachers are there not to do the whole job themselves, but rather to equip the laity in the churches to carry out the work of the Christian ministry.

I remember sharing in a seminar/workshop on evangelism with Michael Green at Wycliffe College, Oxford, back in 1999. I remember that day being told of a random survey conducted in the UK of some 1,000 laypeople who were asked, among other things, the question as to whether they felt they had been trained in their churches for ministry in the marketplace or the places where they daily worked and served. Only 3 per cent replied that they felt thus trained. The other 97 per cent declared themselves at sea in terms of know-how as to carrying out the work of witness and discipling in the marketplace.

The secrets of the Indian church

In June 2009 I had the great privilege to go with two African Enterprise colleagues to India to research how it was that the Indian church had grown from some 15 million to 75 million in twelve to fifteen years, with much of it being reasonably well-discipled. My two AE colleagues and I had the educational and inspiring privilege of meeting many key leaders in Hyderabad, Chennai, Mumbai, and Delhi.

It was extraordinary how the same message was repeated again and again and again. When we asked how they had done it, the reply was "Training, training, training". Thus, for example, had the New Life Centre in Mumbai grown from a single congregation to 700 congregations with a total membership of 76,000.

The dynamic and inspirational leader, Pastor Susai Joseph told us:

*First of all, there is character training. People have to
know clearly what it means to make Jesus Christ Lord
of their lives and to reflect His character and godliness
to the wider world. They also need strong assurance of
salvation.*

*Secondly, we seek to establish the callings and
giftings of each believer and release these into where the
Lord wants to place each person. But they must know
their giftings and then use them. For this they receive
training.*

*Thirdly, they are taught very strongly the principles of
church planting and how to bring forth a church from a
prayer cell. The key notions are:*

- *win*
- *consolidate*
- *disciple/train*
- *plant.*[1]

Pastor Joseph said it took about nine months to a year to train
someone to plant a church and lead it, "But then there is much
ongoing, on the job training."

Making disciples

Likewise in Hyderabad we heard from Doctors Chiree and
Kamalal Chiranjeevi that their Mission India programme
has as its mission statement "Making disciples to transform
India for Christ". In other words, everything is focused into
training and making disciples. They have also produced what
they call The Institute of Community Transformation (ICT).
These are onsite church planting and training schools. Their
aim is that in two years each training programme (ICT) must
plant two churches.

Mission India now has over 160 ICT schools with
ten people in each school being trained along the lines
described.

Or again, I think of Pastor William Carey and his radiant

wife Hebsiba. The pastor was, of course, named after the famous nineteenth-century missionary to India, William Carey. Pastor Carey and Hebsiba together head up a ministry called Aenon, also located in Hyderabad. They too have developed an extraordinary and mushrooming ministry. Describing the key to it they said the most important things for them were:

- preaching the Word of God clearly
- discipling and training the people thoroughly
- training people to plant other churches diligently and systematically.

The Company of the Committed

Then there is Pastor Stanley Mehta of Bombay Baptist Church. Again the ministry of this particular congregation is burgeoning and exploding. Pastor Stanley told us how they run training courses for their own congregations, which they draw up themselves, and which focus strongly on discipleship and the Person and work of the Holy Spirit. This is what takes people from general run of the mill members in the congregation into what he calls the "Company of the Committed" where each person is expected to take responsibility for a ministry according to their gifting and find a place in which to serve within the twenty-five different departments of the church.

So, same story. Training! Training! Training![2]

OUR LORD'S MODEL

I rehearse all of the above so as to give some modern and contemporary examples, which are known to me personally, where our Lord's model of training a few has been deeply put to work with astonishing consequences.

Yes, Jesus prayed, "As you sent me into the world, *so send I have sent them into the world*"(John 17:8). This means that as He came with a methodology of powerfully training a limited few, so we need to do the same. God's arithmetic is not addition, but multiplication. This is the model. And if this model is not operated because the minister is either too unaware of this biblical principle, or too insecure, or too selfishly preoccupied with doing it all themselves, then you get what one Indian leader calls "Live chicks under a Dead Hen"! The live chicks want to get out and live and contribute and fly, but the mother hen won't sanction it. This finally leads to the decline and death of the mother hen as a result of exhaustion or burnout. But in the process the live chicks finally get killed off as well. It is a sad and unbiblical scenario. And it is certainly not our Lord's model and method.

HE PREACHED

Then obviously we register that He *preached*. Thus at the beginning of His ministry He could say, "The Spirit of the Lord is upon me, because He has anointed me to *preach good news to the poor*" (Luke 4:18). Speaking of the very beginning of his ministry, Mark can testify that, "Jesus came into Galilee *preaching* the gospel of God" (Mark 1:14). Mark also reports that when Jesus was at Capernaum, "he was preaching the word to them" (2:2).

And if Jesus came preaching it is hardly surprising that in turn, He sent His followers out to preach. Says Mark 6:12, "So they *went out and preached* that men should repent." And His final exhortation before His ascension after His earthly ministry was: "Go into all the world and *preach* the gospel to the whole creation" (Mark 16:15). They obeyed and "went forth and preached everywhere" (Mark 16:20).

PREACHING'S REVOLUTIONARY POTENTIAL

I must say that in our contemporary church, it saddens me that many disparage preaching or diminish it. For myself, I never could, and never will. The reason is that something very unique indeed happens via the Holy Spirit when people sit under the preached and faithfully proclaimed Word of God. In fact, I know of no single activity of which humans are capable, other than preaching the gospel, which can in such a short time produce a right about-turn of such revolutionary consequence that lives are changed forever.

Thus could John Wycliffe say: "The highest service that men may attain to on earth is to preach the Word of God."[3] Likewise the great Alexander Whyte of Edinburgh could admonish a discouraged Methodist minister with these words: "Never think of giving up preaching. The angels around the throne envy you your great work."[4]

Interestingly enough in the Second Vatican Council, Roman Catholic clergy were summoned to preach the gospel saying: "Since no one can be saved who has not first believed, priests, as co-workers with their bishops, have as their primary duty the proclamation of the Gospel of God to all."[5]

THE CONTENT OF WHAT WE PREACH

A wise someone once said that before you tell the story, make sure you get it right.

Likewise Mark 3:14: "And he appointed twelve, to be with him, and to be sent out to *preach*…"

At this point it is critically important to register that it is not just the act of preaching that is important if people are to be saved and brought into a personal knowledge of Christ, but it is the *content* of what is preached.

This is made clear in the vitally important scripture of 1 Corinthians 1:21. But we must get the translation right. The King James version says: "it pleased God by the foolishness of preaching to save them that believe." The Greek word used there, which the King James version translates as "preaching", is *kerygma*. But in reality the word *kerygma* does not mean the act of preaching but the *content* of what is preached. So the RSV, for example, has it right when it says: "it pleased God by the folly of what we preach to save those who believe". Thus people do not get saved if a watered down, erroneous, or liberalised reconstruction of the gospel is preached. Or any other religion or philosophy.

Very clearly *kerygma* is all about content. It is a word derived from another Greek word *keryx*, which speaks of the *herald* in the ancient world. The herald was the town crier who got his news from the king or nobleman or town authorities. The herald was not the author of that news. All he had to do was go around the town with a billboard, crying out the headlines of news someone else had given him. He couldn't produce an invention of his own ideas!

In the case of the New Testament, it is therefore extremely important that we know the content of the *kerygma* produced by the *keryx*, because it is only by that content, and no other, that people may be saved.

Kerygma summarised

One can explain the New Testament *kerygma* in different ways. Thus one could say that it involves:

- telling the story
- explaining the meaning of the story
- securing a response to the story.

Or else we could say that the *kerygma* involves:

- a historical proclamation (such as Jesus lived, died, and rose again)
- a theological explanation (such as when He died, it was in order to bear our sins in His own body on the tree)
- an ethical summons (such as: what are you going to do about this historical proclamation and what that means?)

I like to summarise the *kerygma* in a simple 1–2–3–4 outline.

- One Gospel fact (the life, death, resurrection, and return of Jesus Christ)
- Two Gospel promises:
  - » Forgiveness (Acts 2:38a)
  - » The gift of the Holy Spirit (note Acts 2:38b and Peter's sermon on the day of Pentecost. Here in this scripture

he declares: "Repent, and be baptized every one of you in the name of Jesus Christ *for the forgiveness of your sins; and you shall receive the gift of the Holy Spirit.*" The two gospel promises are very clearly set forth there).

- Three Gospel demands:
  - » Repent (Mark 1:15)
  - » Believe (Mark 1:15)
  - » Follow (John 1:43; Luke 5:27; Matthew 4:19; Luke 9:23).
- Four Gospel relationships:
  - » A new relationship with God (Matthew 19:37)
  - » A new relationship with oneself (Matthew 22:39b)
  - » A new relationship with one's neighbour, both in the church and in the world (Matthew 22:39b)
  - » A new relationship with the world (we are to leave its lifestyle but minister into its life need – 1 John 2:15; Mark 16:15; John 17:18).

So while we insist on the importance and central place of preaching, the New Testament also insists that its content should be right for the simple reason that it is by the folly of what we preach that God saves those who believe (1 Corinthians 1:21).

PEOPLE MUST HEAR THE PREACHED WORD

Thus in our churches we need to make every possible effort to bring people under the sound of the preached Word of God. Beyond that we have to go out to where people actually are in the marketplace and preach the gospel there as well. Thus in our African Enterprise citywide missions we have a methodology we call "stratified evangelism". By this strategy we establish the many different contexts, strata, and locations of society where we can go and preach the gospel. This might be on a street corner, in a marketplace, in a hospital, a high school, a clinic, a prison, a mayor's parlour, a parliament, a factory or business house, or whatever. The point is to fish where the fish are.

When I was a student at Fuller Seminary, I would often see Dr Charles Fuller, founder of the seminary, in the corridors. When he passed me, he would always say: "Hello Mike! Preach the Word, Mike. Preach the Word!"

It was sound counsel. And it lined up with what Jesus did and laid on others: "Go into all the world and preach the gospel..." (Mark 16:15).

JESUS TAUGHT

Jesus not only came preaching, but He also came *teaching*. He was supremely a teacher and was known to His disciples and others as "Teacher". When Luke is opening up the book of Acts as the second of his two volumes of New Testament history, he says in verse 1, referring to the Gospel that he had written: "I have dealt with all that Jesus began to do and *teach*" (Acts 1:1).

Mark writes: "On the sabbath He began to *teach* in the synagogue" (6:2). Matthew tells us: "he went about *all* Galilee *teaching*" (Matthew 4:23). Luke tells us that He "was *teaching* them on the Sabbath..." (Luke 4:31). When it comes to the matter of how best His followers ought to pray, His disciples say to Him: "Lord, *teach* us to pray..." (Luke 11:1). Historian Luke tells us that people "were astonished at his *teaching*..." (Luke 4:32).

And He taught them about everything: about the character of the Father; the divine identity of the Son; the Person and work of the Holy Spirit; heaven and hell; about history and the Last Things. He taught about the kingdom of God, about conversion, repentance and faith, and new birth. He taught about ethics, morality, and Christian behaviour. He taught about family life and marriage – as permanent, monogamous, and heterosexual. He taught about justice in society, about church and state, about a moral order in the fabric of the universe over which He had all authority. He taught about prayer, about mission, about evangelising.

Indeed in His Great Commission he affirmed: "All authority in heaven and on earth has been given to me. Go therefore and make disciples of all nations, baptizing them in the name of the Father, and of the Son and of the Holy Spirit, *and teaching them* to obey everything that I have commanded you. And remember, I am with you always, to the end of the age" (Matthew 28:18–20).

THE EARLY CHURCH TAUGHT

Then as the early church gets underway we find that "they devoted themselves to the apostles' *teaching,* and fellowship, to the breaking of bread and the prayers" (Acts 2:42). Likewise Paul can exhort in 1 Timothy 4:13: "attend to the public reading of scripture, to preaching, to *teaching*". The New Testament leaders were supremely preachers/teachers, or teachers/preachers. And they were to "labour in preaching and *teaching*" (1 Timothy 5:17).

While the gospel or "evangel" (in Greek, *euangellion*) and its saving content (Greek, *kerygma),* a body of content for the unbelieving world, is primarily *preached,* the *didache* (Greek, "teaching"), on the other hand, the content primarily conveyed to Christian disciples, is something primarily *taught.*

LITTLE COMMITMENT IN CONTEMPORARY CHURCH

One of the great tragedies of many sections of the modern church is that there is so little commitment to extensive and intensive *teaching* and explication of the Word of God. On the other hand, where you find churches and their ministers deeply committed to teaching, expounding, and faithfully exegeting the Word of God via *teaching,* there you will find churches full of eager and hungry people who know they are being fed and built up in the faith. Preaching the gospel to unconverted people brings commitment to Christ. *Teaching* the Bible brings spiritual depth and deeply committed discipleship. Preaching produces converts. Teaching produces disciples. And sermonettes produce Christianettes!

If a congregation has both good evangelistic preaching and solid discipleship teaching vigorously active, plus a strong life of prayer and the administration of the sacraments, then all four New Testament commitments of the thriving New Testament church – as per Acts 2:42 – will be in place.

Of course in our modern technical times, teaching can also be done by any number of new, novel and imaginative ways.

Over the past twenty-five years we have witnessed many advances in technology. New, portable "take everywhere" forms of technology allow people to access the internet and download or upload any form of media, at any time, almost anywhere in the world!

This, of course, has huge implications for the propagation and proclamation of the gospel. As Christians, these technologies should not be shunned but rather embraced and understood, so that our timeless message will continue to spread no matter what changes in technology come about in the world around us.

Back now to how our Lord in fact did it, even without a computer, iPad, BlackBerry, or weekly TV programme plus robed choir! Our Lord not only preached and taught, but –

HE HEALED

Matthew 4:23 tells us that Jesus went through all Galilee "teaching", "preaching", and "*healing*". So here then is this critically important triad of ministry activities all brought together in one very succinct verse describing our Lord's ministry.

Now if the average contemporary church tends to be weak on both preaching and teaching, it is almost certainly completely delinquent when it comes to the obligation of healing. But in our Lord's ministry it is centrally there right from start to finish.

In Mark's Gospel one of the first acts of his public ministry is the healing of Peter's mother-in-law (Mark 1:30–31). In the very next verses Mark tells us that, "That evening, at sundown, they brought to him all who were sick or possessed with demons. And the whole city was gathered together about the door. And He *healed* many who were sick with various diseases, and cast out many demons" (Mark 1:32–34). Just a few verses later we find the leper coming to him with that moving affirmation of faith and saying: "If you will, you can make me clean" (Mark 1:40). Then we find that Jesus "moved with pity, stretched out his hand and touched him… And immediately the leprosy left him, and he was made clean" (Mark 1:40–42). Then after the paralytic took up his pallet and went out before them all, "they were all amazed and glorified God, saying, 'We have never seen anything like this!'" (Mark 2:11–12).

I should think not! Never had they seen a preacher and teacher who could also *heal*. In reality, if you were to press through the gospels, and remove all references to healing, hardly a single chapter would emerge unscathed!

HEALING CONTROVERSIAL

Now I know this whole thing of healing is a bit controversial and many believers are nervous of it, because often it has been open to abuse or extravagant claims, or even falsified or exaggerated claims. We should acknowledge this, but that apart, nevertheless nowhere in Scripture are we informed that the ministry of healing was to stop with the New Testament. Thus, when the apostle Paul is listing the special giftings in the church he includes healers. He writes: "And God has appointed in the church first apostles, second prophets, third teachers, then workers of miracles, then *healers*, helpers, administrators, speakers in various kinds of tongues" (1 Corinthians 12:28).

So healing is there all the way through the Gospels, all over the book of Acts, key in the early church, and clearly present in the epistles as one of the charismatic gifts.

PERSONAL TESTIMONY

For myself, I do not feel I have any particular so-called gift of healing. But I have certainly learned in fifty years of ministry in Africa, particularly in many places where there aren't doctors, nurses, or clinics and suchlike that we need to be willing to exercise a ministry of healing. And this we have done over the years in our African Enterprise ministry and have indeed seen many such healings, especially in evangelistic contexts. Really.

In this regard it is important to remember that whenever healing happens, the ultimate healer is Jesus Himself. And this healing can often be most effectively mediated when not just one person prays for the healing but several join together in laying hands on the person in need, perhaps in addition anointing them with oil and then praying the prayer of faith. This can happen immediately, or overnight, after the prayer has taken place, or else perhaps even over a period of time.

So as we ask why we *don't* see more healing in the modern church, perhaps we need to remember our Lord saying: "According to your faith let it be done to you" (Matthew 9:29). This being the case, it is unsurprising if the modern church, which does not believe much in healing, does not see much healing! But if our faith and expectation levels could be raised, lifted, built up, and if we more seriously embraced both New Testament precedents and exhortations about healing, then there is no reason why healing should not become much more commonplace.

The hard fact is, coming back to Matthew 4:23, that "Jesus went throughout all Galilee teaching, preaching and *healing*". And if He meant it, as obviously He did, that "As the Father has sent me, so send I you" (John 20:21), then even as He came **healing** so should we go **healing**.

*** ***

Now as we move forward, there is something even more challenging to face. Not only did Jesus preach, teach, and heal, but –

HE DELIVERED

Yes, He constantly delivered people from demonic oppression and demonisation. And He did it again, and again, and again.

Coming back again to one of those summary statements about His ministry we find Mark writing, "he appointed twelve, to be with him, and to be sent out to preach and *have authority to cast out demons*" (Mark 3:14–15).

Once again in modern times, as with healing, we find not only fear and nervousness, but misunderstanding about this arena of exorcism or casting out demons. The problem is that there has been much confusion, abuse, excess, erroneous understandings of Scripture, or sometimes just plain agnosticism as to whether this is still part of the mandate of our Lord to His church.

However the Bible speaks constantly, and of course most notably, in the New Testament of the reality of evil supernaturalism and of Satan and demons. Having been involved in over five decades of ministry, mainly in Africa, but also in many other parts of the world, I am assured from personal experience and the evidence of my eyes as to the existence of demons and their activity in the world today.

This may be more obvious and evident in Africa, but the world of the demonic and of evil supernaturalism is just as operative in Western and other sophisticated societies, although less obviously so (see Chapter 4). That probably makes the world of evil supernaturalism that much more dangerous because it is that much less obvious. Sometimes the devil is most devilish when respectable and demons could even be most demonic when working through someone with a PhD!

MY CONVICTION

However, I reiterate here my conviction that if in the contemporary church we do not pay deeper attention to the spiritual realities that are part of the world around us, then we betray the gospel. And because He has sent us as the Father sent Him, and He tackled these realities, so we need to do likewise.

*** ***

There is something else exceedingly important to note, namely, that:

2. In the humility of sonship He ministered prayerfully in constant fellowship and communion with the Father and under the authority of Scripture

I. JESUS CHRIST OPERATED ONLY IN THE WILL OF THE FATHER

Thus He could say: "I have come down from heaven, not to do my own will but the will of him who sent me" (John 6:38). Here in our John 17 prayer He reaffirms this principle: "I glorified you on earth by finishing the work that you gave me to do" (verse 4).

When I think of our Lord I am so struck – in contrast to our frenzied style – by the measured, surefooted, and seemingly relaxed pace at which He moved and in which He ministered. Thus the New Testament records no story of a bystander spotting a donkey galloping through the streets of Jerusalem, stones and dust flying from beneath its feet, people leaping for protection or cover, or ricocheting off the side of the little four-legged creature, with the rider beating the beast forward faster and faster and shouting to everyone to get out of the way. No record of that, or of a bystander then asking someone in the know: "Who and what was that?"

"Oh," says the well-informed local, "that is Jesus rushing late as usual to His next counselling appointment. He is very busy, these days. Just seems He can't cope with it all."

Well, there just ain't no report like that anywhere in the New Testament!

In his landmark volume *The Overload Syndrome*, Richard Swenson addresses the problem of overload and what he calls "margin", which he describes as

> the space that once existed between our load and our limits. Margin is the space between vitality and exhaustion. It is our breathing room, our reserves, our leeway. Margin is the opposite of overload, and therefore the antidote for that vexatious condition.[6]

Swenson adds:

> If Jesus had chosen to live in modern America instead of ancient Israel, how would He act?... Would He have worn a watch? Would He have carried a beeper? Can you imagine being paged out of the Last Supper?
>
> When I look deeper at the life of Christ, I also notice there is no indication that He worked twenty-hour ministry days. He went to sleep each night without having healed every disease in Israel and He apparently slept well. Neither did He minister to everybody who needed it. Neither did He visit or teach everybody who needed it. There were many needs that He simply chose not to meet. Even when Lazarus became sick, Jesus was shockingly slow to mobilize. I would have had a helicopter there in twenty minutes. But Jesus delayed for two days.[7]

The fact is that Jesus lived within limits because He moved at a measured pace, was constantly in tune with His heavenly Father, and only did *what the Father led Him to do or say* (see John 12:50). That was His secret, and it needs to be our secret in ministry as well.

Getting it wrong

Years ago, after a very convoluted, fruitless, and unhappy mission in a church near Johannesburg, I sought the Lord's face, searched His Word, and heard from Him via a very powerful little passage in Jeremiah 23. The context reveals the Lord's lament for shepherds of the flock who were failing both Him and their people. Says verse 1 of that chapter: "'Woe to the shepherds who destroy and scatter the sheep of my pasture!', says the Lord." The Lord's lament continues at verse 9: "Concerning the prophets, My heart is broken within me." Then comes a chilling warning: "Thus says the Lord of hosts: 'Do not listen to the words of the prophets who prophesy to you, filling you with vain hopes; they speak visions of their own minds, not from the mouth of the Lord'" (verse 16).

Divine indictment

Now here comes the major component of the divine indictment on the prophets – in other words the religious leaders of the time: "I did not send the prophets, yet they ran; I did not speak to them, yet they prophesied. But *if* they had stood in my council, *then* they would have proclaimed my words to my people, and they would have turned them from their evil way, and from the evil of their doings" (Jeremiah 23:21–22).

In other words, the prophets were running and speaking in ineffectual, wasted, non-mandated, and not divinely directed religious activity. This is hectic, frenzied, ever-so-busy religious activity. Here are these prophets giving not divinely mandated or God-guided content to the people. Wasted words, in fact. Big religious energy expended, but without God behind it. Therefore fruitless.

In fact, just like the mission I was leading near Johannesburg. I had not been sent, yet I ran. I had not been spoken to by the Lord, yet I was prophesying and preaching to others. All vain, empty, wasted religious activity, energy, and money.

The great condition

Coming back to the Lord's word to Jeremiah's contemporaries, He can declare the great condition and consequence of what happens when He guides the things we do and say in Christian ministry. The text states: "But if they had stood in my council", meaning, if in other words they had sought God's will ahead of time in prayer, and asked for His guidance, *"then* they would have proclaimed my words to my people"; they would have said what the Lord wanted them to say. Beyond that there would have been a completely different outcome; namely effective and fruitful ministry because "they would have turned them from their evil way, and from the evil of their doings" (verse 22). In other words, the messages would have gone home and produced real spiritual results for both time and eternity.

Book of Acts

After that same desperate mission near Johannesburg, I found myself looking into how things operated in the book of Acts and in particular how the apostles only went where the Lord wanted them to go. Acts 16:6–7 gives us a classic illustration of this principle: "And they went through the region of Phrygia and Galatia, *having been forbidden by the Holy Spirit* to speak the word in Asia. And when they had come opposite Mysia they attempted to go into Bithynia, *but the Spirit of Jesus did not allow them.*"

So as they were just about to go off in the wrong direction, the Lord intervenes through the Holy Spirit. His servants are listening to His Spirit and seeking His will, but Jesus stops that particular course of action for there was somewhere else they were meant to be: "...so, passing by Mysia, they went down to Troas. During the night Paul had a vision: there stood a man of Macedonia pleading with him and saying, "Come over to Macedonia and help us." When he had seen the vision, we immediately tried to cross over to Macedonia, being convinced that God had called us to proclaim the good news to them" (Acts 16:8–10).

The apostolic servants of the Lord were determined, in the model of Jesus Himself, to be in the right place at the right time and saying and doing the right things as guided by the Spirit.

Our congregations and organisations

Such actions, by the way, would diminish the burnout and sadness factor in the lives of many Christian workers, rectors, and pastors. Thus can Richard Swenson express his deep concern that only one in three pastors "finishes well". Burnout is so common that Focus on the Family's H. B. London Jr has called the pastor "an endangered species". It is reported that

> *ninety percent of pastors say they are inadequately trained to cope with ministry demands, eighty percent say their ministries have had a negative effect on their families, and seventy percent have a lower self-image now than when they started in the ministry. Ministry hours are long, while expectations are often conflicting – and sometimes impossible. These pressures inevitably wear on pastors, who frequently feel no permission to reveal their distress. At least twenty-two organisations exist for the sole purpose of pre- or post-burnout counselling for pastors.*[8]

Mounting on wings like eagles

Perhaps the point comes home to us vividly when we register the Old Testament principle in Isaiah 40:31 where the prophet's word says: "They who wait for the Lord shall renew their strength, they shall mount up with wings like eagles, they shall run and not be weary, they shall walk and not faint." The eagle analogy here is most instructive, because eagles mount up into the heights of the sky not by mad flapping of wings, like pelicans for example where huge energy is expended for very little lift-off, but by setting their wings and waiting for the upward thermals of wind which can carry them effortlessly to enormous heights. They mount to such heights on an energy and a power that is not their own – namely the energy and power of the upward wind draft of the thermal.

Finding the thermals

In Christian life and ministry, then, the key is to find the upward thermals of the Spirit of God and to mount on those rather than the furiously energetic administrative flappings of the average church's wings where the massive input and expenditure of energy produces almost minimal lift-off. We are to move where the Spirit is moving. We are to go where our Lord is going. Thus could Jesus tell His disciples that if they would die to their own plans and purposes, and instead embrace His, and fall into the ground like a grain of wheat and die, then they would "bear much fruit" (John 12:24).

Then our Lord adds something critically important: "If anyone serves me, he must follow me; and where I am, there shall my servant be also" (John 12:26). The pointed principle here is not that we move along with our own plans and agendas and have the Lord tagging along behind us, but because we have died to our own plans and purposes and are seeking only His, it is we who move along behind Him so that where He is, there are His servants also! This is what it means only to speak and act in the will of the Father. That's how He did it. That's how we are to do it. "As – and – so!" This is the key notion.

II. JESUS ONLY OPERATED UNDER THE AUTHORITY OF SCRIPTURE

At the beginning of His ministry, Luke tells us that He was led into the wilderness by the Spirit to be "tempted by the devil" (Luke 4:1–2). During that horrific ordeal Jesus responded to each one of the devil's temptations by quoting Scripture at him. Three times He responded with the reiterated, "It is written."

The point is, as I have noted elsewhere, that Jesus entered a society already bound by a canon of sacred writings. He never contradicted the prevailing Jewish attitude to the authority of the Law and the Prophets. Indeed, He constantly appealed to this corpus of revelation when validating His own messianic claims. He uses designations such as "Scripture", "the Law", "the Prophets", or "It is written", to refer to the Jewish canonical Scriptures that were held authoritative by all Jews.

Furthermore, Jesus equates "God says" with what the text says, as in Matthew 19:4ff. where He quotes the narrator's words in Genesis 2:24 as an utterance of God Himself. Jesus also gives Moses' writings an authority comparable to His own words when, in John 5:47 He says, "But if you do not believe his writings, how will you believe my words?"

French theologian Pierre Marcel, as noted in Chapter 6 ("Truth"), bears repeating,

> *From the manner in which Jesus Christ quotes Scripture, we find that He recognises and accepts the Old Testament in its entirety as possessing a normative authority, as the true Word of God, valid for all time. Said Jesus, "Scripture cannot be broken" (John 10:35). Thus Jesus rebuked the Sadducees, saying, "You are wrong, because you know neither the Scriptures nor the power of God" (Matthew 22:29). These two deficiencies often go together.*[9]

Fulfilment of Scripture

It is also arresting to both our hearts and our minds that even on the Cross Jesus had the fulfilment of Scripture in the forefront of His mind: "that the Scripture might be fulfilled, He said, 'I thirst!'" (John 19:28, NKJV).

Then most dramatically we have this principle pre-eminent when our Lord meets with those two startled and perplexed disciples on the road to Emmaus; they are all the more so, when the stranger before them, "beginning with Moses and all the prophets, interpreted to them in all the scriptures the things concerning himself" (Luke 24:27).

And then, just before the awesome moment of giving His disciples the Great Commission, He said to them, "'These are my words which I spoke to you, while I was still with you – that everything written about me in the law of Moses, the prophets, and the psalms must be fulfilled.' Then he opened their minds to understand the scriptures, and said to them, 'Thus it is written, that the Christ should suffer and on the third day rise from the dead…'" (Luke 24:44–46).

The implication of all of this is as clear as the sun on a cloudless day at noon. Jesus operated in subjection to and under the authority of the Scriptures.

And He expects us to do the same.

And so we pray: "Lord, may we too, like you, operate in humility, in prayerful communion with you, in the will of God, and in submission to the Bible as the Word of God."

*** ***

And now finally, we note that –

III. IN THE SPIRIT OF SACRIFICE HE MINISTERED AS A SERVANT AND GAVE ALL

For Jesus, all was sacrifice. Thus did He sacrifice the safety and security of heaven. Thus did He sacrifice the riches of heaven for the poverty of earth. Thus did He sacrifice the praise and acclaim of heaven for the calumny, rejection, and abuse of earth. Thus did He sacrifice the recognition that "in him dwells all the fullness of the Godhead bodily" (Colossians 2:9, NKJV) and instead "emptied himself, taking the form of a servant… he humbled himself, and becoming obedient unto death, even death on a cross" (Philippians 2:7–8).

Servanthood and servant leadership

Likewise, and related to His sacrificial posture, everything in our Lord reflected servanthood and servant leadership. Thus could He wash His disciples feet during the Last Supper

(John 13:1–10). In so doing, He gave His disciples a brand new concept of leadership as He noted that, "The kings of the Gentiles exercise lordship over them; and those in authority over them are called benefactors. *But not so with you;* rather let the greatest among you become as the youngest, and the leader as one who serves" (Luke 22:25–26).

The ancient world knew nothing of this and was staggered by it. Thus could Julius Caesar once say: "I would rather be first at Brundisium than second at Rome." For Caesar, as for so many strong personalities in the world – and even sometimes nowadays in the church – the important thing is to be first. The key thing is to be the top dog. Underdogs and coming second have no place in our world. Thus the ego-tripping and self-inflating of some Christian leaders in our time is out of character with their Lord.

Sacrificial self-giving

Beyond all that, the sacrificial self-giving of our Lord who "gave his life as a ransom for many" (Matthew 20:28; Mark 10:45; 1 Timothy 2:6) challenges us to the depths of our beings.

Of course, we offer not just our ability, but also our availability. We are His, and not our own, because we are bought with a price. In other words, we give Him our life agenda to be settled as He should choose. Asked Saul of Tarsus on the road to Damascus: "'What am I to do, Lord?" (Acts 22:10).

We also give Him our possessions, human resources, finances, our time, and our times (compare Psalm 31:15). To Him belongs not just a tenth of our money, but all of it. The tenth or the tithe is the specific amount we give Him for His service but the other nine tenths are His also to use and dispose of as He sees fit. It all comes from Him anyway, so it all goes back to Him. "What do you have that was not given to you?" He asks us (1 Corinthians 4:7, NCV).

A friend of mine once had an opportunity of bringing

a witness for Christ to a great and wealthy Greek shipping magnate who owned a whole fleet of ships. This man was impressed with my friend's witness to him for Christ and asked: "Do you think Jesus would like me to give Him a ship?"

"No," said my friend, after a moment's deliberation. "I think Jesus wants you to give Him yourself. But of course He knows that if He gets you, why, He gets *all* the ships!"

Give it away – get it back

I also remember when I was an undergraduate I was very challenged by the story of an exceedingly fine rugby player and fellow student. In his early weeks at the university he was challenged with the Christian gospel and gave his life to Christ. One day, when encountering the great Dr Basil Atkinson, the legendary father figure of the CICCU (Cambridge Inter-Collegiate Christian Union), he said to the old saint: "Dr Atkinson, now that I've given my life to Christ, do you feel that I need to give up my rugby?"

"Yes," replied Dr Atkinson without a second's hesitation, "but I am sure He will give it back to you and say 'Play it to my glory!'"

Conclusion

So then, we see the monumentally challenging ministry lifestyle of our Lord. All of us are a hundred million light years away from how He did it, the standards He set, and the sustained sacrificial love in which it was all carried out.

But at the very least we need to try and get a grasp on how He did it so that we might begin to try and model out in our own lives something of what we see in His. At the very least we need to be constantly studying how He went about things and seeing how to apply those methodologies in our churches corporately, and in our own personal lives individually.

Chapter 12

Prayer – The Sixth Mark

"More things are wrought by prayer
Than this world dreams of."

Alfred Lord Tennyson, "Morte D'Arthur"

"If Christ himself needed to retire from time to
time to the mountain top to pray, lesser men and
women need not be ashamed to acknowledge that
necessity."

B. H. Streeter

"Lord, teach us to pray…"

The disciples, Luke 11:1

"[He] went up on the mountain to pray."

Luke 9:28

"I do not pray for these only, but also for those who
believe in me through their word…"

Jesus, John 17:20

The High Priestly Prayer of John 17 is a prayer, and therefore about prayer. It is also a demonstration of prayer, a supreme example of prayer, and the ultimate precedent showing the importance and centrality of prayer for all believers who would walk in the ways of their Saviour.

In this prayer of prayers, our Lord does not in fact pray to the Father that His disciples would be prayerful, but rather He demonstrates practically – and in a way which dramatically caps all He has previously taught them – that if they follow

Him they too must be characterised by the same life-posture of prayerful engagement.

So we are absolutely sure that we can know that the practice of prayer as seen in John 17 only completes the endless precepts on prayer that reached the minds and hearts of the disciples from the lips of their Lord. He wanted prayer to be a central characteristic in the life of His people and both His precepts and His practice powerfully conveyed this. Supernatural provision was the prerequisite of pulling off the superhuman task. The disciples had to discover for themselves His secret strength and make it operative in their own lives.

We remember too the opening of John 17: "When Jesus had spoken *these words*, he lifted up his eyes to heaven and said: '*Father…*'" The prayer that followed was placed in the context of "*these words*" (that is, the Final Discourse – John 14–16), which He had just spoken.

Indeed that Final Discourse, which, as we have repeatedly said, gives the clue in terms of meaning to so much of what He prays in the prayer, is laced with prayer exhortations. For example: "Whatever you *ask* [that is, in prayer] in my name, I will do" (John 14:13). That is *precept* about prayer: "If you love me, you will keep my commandments. And *I will* pray the Father, and he will give you another Counselor" (John 14:15–16). This is the *practice* of prayer. Then we have John 15:16: "I chose you and appointed you… so that whatever you *ask* the Father in my name he may give it to you."

So following the *precepts* of the Final Discourse, He now prays Himself and demonstrates the *practice*.

Our Lord's example

For our Lord, prayer was the air He breathed. And it shines through His life like the prevailing colour in a painting, or the dominant melody in the movement of a symphony.

So at the very beginning of His public ministry, Luke tells

us, "When all the people were baptized, and when Jesus also had been baptized *and was praying*, the heaven was opened, and the Holy Spirit descended upon him in bodily form, as a dove" (Luke 3:21–22). Thus Jesus went from His baptism straight into prayer. And during that prayer the Holy Spirit descends upon Him and the Father speaks from heaven: "You are my Son, the Beloved; with you I am well pleased" (Luke 3:22). The whole Trinity is caught up in conversation and action with the Son talking to the Father, and the Father to the Son, and the Spirit making Himself evident in visible form.

And indeed at every significant moment in His ministry from then onwards, prayer (the conversing of the Son with the Father) was in evidence.

One thinks, for example, of the selection of the twelve apostles. Luke tells us that before making the critical decisions relating to the apostolic dozen, he went out to the mountain to pray; and all night he continued in prayer to God (Luke 6:12). Then when it came to our Lord seeking to elicit from His disciples the response of confessing His Messiahship, Luke tells us "it happened that as *he was praying alone* the disciples were with Him; and He asked them, 'Who do the people say that I am?'" (Luke 9:18). He then asked them, "But who do you say that I am?" And Peter answered, "The Christ of God" (verse 20). So that breathtaking question and universe-changing answer came out of the context of Jesus "praying alone".

TRANSFIGURATION AND THUNDER

Or else just move a few verses on to where Luke records the amazing happening of the Transfiguration when Jesus was transfigured in front of Peter, John, and James. Then Moses and Elijah appear (verse 30) and then the Father speaks from heaven saying, "This is my Son, my Chosen; listen to him" (verse 35). Now all of that, once again – and unsurprisingly – took place in the context of prayer. Listen to Luke. "Now about eight days after these sayings he took with him Peter and John and James and *went up on the mountain to pray. And as He was praying, the appearance of his countenance was altered, and his raiment became dazzling white"* (verses 28 and 29).

As our Lord begins to face His imminent and upcoming death and the Calvary experience, He speaks in prayer to the Father. John records this as follows: "Now is my soul troubled. And what shall I say – 'Father save me from this hour'? No, for this purpose I have come to this hour. Father glorify thy name. Then a voice came from heaven, 'I have glorified it and I will glorify it again'" (John 12:27–28). This prayerful, conversational interchange between the Son and the Father had such volume in it that "The crowd standing by heard it and said that it had thundered" (verse 29). Again the supernatural ingredient here was prayer.

PRAYER AS HE MOVED TOWARDS THE CROSS

Next we can think of His institution of the Lord's Supper when He took the bread and blessed it and then took the cup, and only gave it to them "when he had given thanks" (Matthew 26:27). Thus in this institution of the most solemn ceremony known to humankind, our Lord was found in the posture of giving prayerful thanksgiving to the Father.

Then with the anguish of Gethsemane in prospect, what could He do but fall "on his face and pray" (verse 39)? "My Father, if it be possible, let this cup pass from me; nevertheless, not as I will, but as thou wilt"(Matthew 26:39). And imagine at that point finding His disciples not alert with electric attention, but *sleeping* (Matthew 26:40). And imagine how Peter felt as the rebuke reached him: "So, could you not watch with me one hour? *Watch and pray…*" (verses 40–41). Then Matthew: "Again, for the second time, he went away and *prayed*: 'My Father, if this cannot pass unless I drink it, thy will be done.' And again he came and found them sleeping, for their eyes were heavy. So, leaving them again, he went away and *prayed* for the third time, saying the same words" (verses 42–44). Everything happening in this ultimate drama of planet Earth is imbued and impregnated with prayer from the Saviour juxtaposed right next door to a chronic prayer failure from the disciples.

Then as He faced the Stygian and multiple darknesses of Calvary, He could find it within Himself to pray for others. "Simon, Simon, behold, Satan demanded to have you, that he might sift you like wheat, *but I have prayed for you* that your faith may not fail" (Luke 22:31–32). Indeed, if anyone ever needed to pray exclusively for themselves at such a time, then it was Jesus. But no, His prayers are focused on a disciple whose faith would shortly be profoundly tested.

And of course the ultimately mysterious prayer in the ultimate moment of agony came on the Cross itself: "My God, my God, why have you forsaken me?" (Matthew 27:46). Then finally prayer was in the very last pre-resurrection breath that our Lord took: "Then Jesus, crying with a loud voice, said, 'Father, into thy hands I commit my spirit!' And having said this he breathed his last" (Luke 23:46).

Prayer the perpetual motion

Prayer, prayer, prayer, prayer was the perpetual motion and the all-embracing context of His life and living, His preaching and teaching, His healing and exorcising, His death itself, along with His every tender touch upon the lives of broken and damaged people.

My friend Robert Coleman, in his masterly classic *The Mind of the Master*, notes that for Jesus, "Prayer was His way of getting things done."[1]

LESSONS FROM WHAT AND HOW HE PRAYED

While our Lord was not setting out here in the High Priestly Prayer to give lessons on how and what to pray, His example, precedent, and petitionary content are instructive for us. Some of these, from this real Lord's Prayer, find obvious echoes and parallels in the Disciple's Prayer (normally and erroneously known as the Lord's Prayer), which we'll look at shortly. But let's note here:

The addressee: "Father" (verse 1)

This is His heavenly Father whom He addresses as "Father" (verses 1, 4), "Holy Father" (verse 11) or "Righteous Father" (verse 25). We have had cause to comment on this when we looked at our Lord's world view (Chapter 4) and we'll observe more in a moment in the Disciple's Prayer.

Our concern for truth: "The only true God" (verse 3)

This is an integral notion in Jesus' praying, namely that the God and Father to whom He is praying is a true God, indeed "the only True God", and not a false one. The Bible warns everywhere of false gods (see, for example, 2 Chronicles 15:3). In our praying, we rejoice to focus on "the only true God". In all things to do with our faith we are concerned for truth, and the spread of it. So in our praying, we pray for people to come to understand and receive the truth.

The context: "The hour has come" (verse 1)

Our Lord prays out of the desperate needs of His context and the imminent ordeal of His trials, Calvary journey, and then the Cross itself. When we pray we likewise do so out of the real-life context of where we are, what we are facing, and the complex mix of emotions and happenings in our lives. These we bring to the Lord as we pray. The real stuff of life is the real stuff of prayer.

Our motive: "Glorify your Son that the Son may glorify you" (verse 1)

Our Lord's motive in praying and in all He did was to glorify the Father. Ultimately, this has to be our own primary motive in praying. We do not come to God primarily to secure answers for our own shopping list needs for this or that, or sundry goodies. We are endlessly exhorted to "ask" but if we lose sight of praying and living primarily for the glory of God, then we have lost the primary prayer and life motive reflected here as our Lord opens up His prayer.

Rehearsing to God our theological premises – the premise of spiritual power: "you have given him authority over all people" (verse 2)

Our Lord was conscious of the power and authority He had received from the Father. When we pray we are privileged to know we have access to the power of our Lord. We are not praying to an impotent God, but rather to an omnipotent one. Said our Lord: "All authority in heaven and on earth has been given to me... And remember, I am with you always, to the end of the age" (Matthew 28:18, 20).

Penned John Newton:

Thou art coming to a king
Large petitions with thee bring.
For His grace and power are such,
None can ever ask too much.

The premise of dealing with eternity: "And this is eternal life, that they may know you, the only true God, and Jesus Christ whom you have sent" (verse 3)

Our Lord is immediately conscious that what is in purview here are eternal things. Likewise when we pray we need to be praying for people we know, family or friends, or the unevangelised to find eternal life which is discovered only as people come to "know" the Father, "and Jesus Christ whom [He] has sent." Martin Luther had a saying, and I keep it on top of my own diary and day planner: "I have only two days in my diary – Today and That Day." In the midst of time Luther had his eye daily on eternity. Our Lord did the same. So must we.

The premise of having a work to accomplish: "by finishing the work that you gave me to do" (verse 4)

Jesus had a work to do, as assigned to Him by the Father. From beginning to end in His earthly ministry, Jesus was deeply conscious of this. Now the important thing was to complete and accomplish it fully. In our praying, too, we need daily to have the same consciousness. We each have a task to accomplish and our daily prayers must play into this. We must be seeking both His will and His way and His strength for the task in hand. And like Jesus our prayerful concern must be to accomplish the earthly task(s) He's given us and finish well. The late Ted Engstrom, a great friend and mentor, always taught me to pray: "Lord, may I finish better than I started."

The premise of special prayer concerns for certain people one is specially responsible to pray for

This premise comes in verses 9 and 20: "I am asking on their behalf; I am not asking on behalf of the world, but on behalf of those whom you gave me, because they are yours… I ask not only on behalf of these, but also on behalf of those who will believe in me through their word" (verses 9, 20).

We cannot pray for everyone. Nor are we obliged to. Not even our Lord prayed for everyone. He prayed for those for whom He had a special responsibility, and who had special claims on Him – namely His immediate disciples, and then those who would become believers down through the ages through them. Other prayer needs He ignored.

Likewise with us. We pray for those with special claims on us – family, friends, loved ones, people in need in our circle. Thereafter the Lord will put others on our hearts; those who need to come to Him. In the case of my family, a special prayer must firstly be, "Protect them from the evil one" (John 17:15), and then I must also pray for their growth in Christian character and loyalty to biblical truth. "Sanctify them in the truth: your word is truth" (verse 17). These prayer concerns and our Lord's praying must be reflected in our own.

The longing in prayer for unbelievers to come to faith: "that the world may believe that you have sent me... so that the world may know that you have sent me" (verses 21 and 23)

This kind of longing needs to be in us and it will play out in our praying for people we know to come to Christ and in lifting to the Lord missionary needs, missionaries, and unevangelised contexts. And in this we should persist; the evangelist D. L. Moody, for example, prayed for over forty years for two men to come to Christ and eventually both were converted at his funeral. After an evangelistic service in Cambridge when I was an undergraduate, I said to Dr Basil Atkinson, under-librarian of Cambridge University, "You must have been thrilled tonight to see those two men from the University library commit their lives to Christ." "Yes," he beamed with the famous Basilean beam, "I've been praying for those men for thirty-seven years!" Carol and I prayed for over thirty-five years for her dad to come to faith. Then one day I had the privilege, over the phone if you please, of leading him to Christ when he was eighty-eight!

*** ***

OUR LORD'S INSTRUCTION

Not surprisingly, as the disciples observed and were blessed by prayer as the habitual lifestyle of Jesus, they would sooner or later put the penetrating request to Him: "Lord, teach us to pray" (Luke 11:1).

His answer was to give them the Disciples' Prayer (more commonly known as the Lord's Prayer; the Lord's Prayer is in fact the one which is found in John 17 and which starts out "Father" – or "Our Father" compare Luke 11:2–4; Matthew 6:9–13).

And Dallas Willard notes:

There is, of course, much more to prayer than the Lord's Prayer. But it is a prayer that teaches us to pray. It is the foundation of the praying life: its introduction and its continuing basis. It is an enduring framework for all praying. You only move beyond it provided you stay within it.[2]

Yes, indeed. So the Disciples' Prayer is not just a prayer but a teaching and instruction about prayer.

Let's set it out before us first of all in the traditional version:

*Our Father, who art in heaven,
hallowed be thy name;
thy kingdom come;
thy will be done;
on earth as it is in heaven.
Give us this day our daily bread.
And forgive us our trespasses,
as we forgive them that trespass against us.
And lead us not into temptation;
but deliver us from evil.
For thine is the kingdom,
the power and the glory
for ever and ever.
Amen.*

Now let's set before us Dallas Willard's version of it. Willard's version is, incidentally, a prayer that I use daily in my own devotions.

*Dear Father always near us, and filling the heavens
may your name be treasured and loved,
may your rule be completed in us –
may your will be done here on earth
in just the way it is done in heaven.*

Give us today the things we need today,
and forgive us our sins and impositions on you
as we are forgiving all who in any way offend us.
Please don't put us through trials,
but deliver us from everything bad.
Because you are the one in charge,
And you have all the power,
And the glory too is all yours – forever –
which is just the way we want it![3]

Willard adds:

"Just the way we want it" is not a bad paraphrase
for "amen". What is needed at the end of this great
prayer is a ringing affirmation of the goodness of God
and God's world. If your nerves can take it you might
(occasionally?) try "Whoopee!" I imagine God Himself will
not mind.[4]

Willard in his lovely classic *The Divine Conspiracy* testifies about his use of the Lord's Prayer in these terms:

I personally did not find the Lord's Prayer to be the
doorway into a praying life until I was in my mid-
twenties… But at some point, for reasons I cannot
explain, I began to use it in a new way: taking each
phrase of it and slowly and meditatively entering into the
depths of its meaning, elaborating within it important
details of my current life.[5]

I think that's beautiful. And very helpful.

It all starts out with saying:

"Our Father…"

The first, loveliest, and most important thing our Lord here teaches is that we not only can, but must, address God as "our Father". The wonder and glory of this we discussed at some length in Chapter 4 on world view, which for Jesus included a place called heaven and a person there called Father. So we won't repeat all that.

But we can observe with Dallas Willard that:

> the "address" part of prayer is of vital significance. We dare not slight or overlook it. It is one of the things that distinguishes prayer from worrying out loud or silently, which many, unfortunately, have confused with prayer.
>
> When we speak to someone, we use a name to call to that person in distinction from everyone else. We thereby indicate that we wish to speak to that particular person. The name also calls attention to our standing in relation to the one addressed.[6]

Willard goes on:

> When we speak to God, Jesus tells us, we are to address Him as "Our Father, the one in the heavens." This is the configuration of reality from within which we pray. The overwhelming difficulties many people have with prayer, both understanding it and doing it, derive from nothing more than their failure or their inability to place themselves within this configuration and receive it by grace...[7]

Before moving on, it is worth noting here that our Lord speaks of God as Father 170 times in the Gospels, of which twenty-one of these pertain to how He personally addresses God. So if that was our Lord's way in praying, it clearly also needs to be ours. And what a blessing it is to greet Him daily saying, "Abba/ Our Father/Dear Father, always near us and filling the Heavens."

"Who art in heaven", or "Always near us and filling the heavens"

A couple of points here. First of all, calling Him our Abba Father speaks of deep intimacy. But when we add "who art in heaven" – or "the one filling the heavens", we are now adding the dimension of cosmic respect to the name Abba. In other words, while we can be deeply intimate with God, we cannot be casual, flippant, or disrespectful. This wonderful Father we have is also *in heaven, and filling the heavens*. We need to remember that.

We are praying on earth to a Father who is really and truly there in a place or places called heaven. That's the way things are. That's our reality. And it's the configuration from which we pray.

"Hallowed be thy name", or "May your name be treasured and loved"

Again as we have noted earlier (Chapter 7), God's name in both the Old and New Testaments speaks of His character. In other words that character is to be kept in purview and in constant consciousness as we pray. We do not want to see His character defamed, or defiled, or blasphemed against, or distorted. When we pray we hold His character before us as holy, just and loving. And when we pray things "in the name of Jesus", we are obliging ourselves to make requests which are not inconsistent with, or in distortion or violation of, the character of God as revealed in Scripture.

So praying in Jesus' name is to pray as He himself would pray if He were in our situation.

"Thy kingdom come", or "May your rule be completed in us"

Our request for the kingdom to come is tied immediately in with the petitions that follow. To follow Willard's translation again: "May your will be done here on earth in just the way it is done in heaven." The kingdom of God is a complex notion in the New Testament, but at the very heart of it is the understanding that it is present where the kingly rule of Christ is effectively operative. And that might be in an individual, a family, a church, an organisation, or a company or business.

And one thing is for sure. Jesus made the kingdom

the central plank or pillar of His preaching. In fact the first recorded words of His public ministry are these: "the *kingdom* of God is at hand: repent, and believe in the gospel" (Mark 1:15). Then Matthew tells us that "He went about… preaching the gospel of the *kingdom*" (Matthew 4:23).

Indeed He used the phrase the "kingdom of God" or its equivalent about a hundred times. And at the very end of His earthly ministry, Luke tells us that He spent six weeks with His apostles teaching them about the *"kingdom* of God" (Acts 1:3).

Cosmic Christ

Way back in 1969, when our African Enterprise team was having its first Pan African citywide mission outside South Africa (at this point in Nairobi), we had the privilege of having with us on the team the famous missionary statesman, E. Stanley Jones for a few weeks. What I was so profoundly struck by in his teaching was that Jesus was the "Cosmic Christ", being as He was Lord of the cosmos. He had accordingly established a cosmic order in which all laws – whether physical, scientific, moral, psychological, spiritual, or whatever – were His. His creative and cosmic stamp was on everything so that the cosmic reality of law and order around us worked His way and only His way.

So morality was not something imposed, but exposed. Jesus simply showed us how things were and are in the cosmic order around us and how they worked. To be moral, good, and holy was simply a matter of cooperating with the moral environment around us. While Stanley Jones profoundly understood that the kingdom of God operated where the kingly rule of Christ was being worked out, nevertheless he also saw this cosmic order behind everything as itself being an expression of the kingdom. This cosmic orderly context is God's and it is His statement and expression of the way things are and the way He has arranged things in obedience and submission to His will.

The order and the Person

So in his classic book *The Unshakable Kingdom and the Unchanging Person*, E. Stanley Jones testifies as to how he himself

> *had discovered two absolutes; the Unshakable Kingdom, the Absolute Order; and the Unchanging Person, the absolute Person. There were two absolutes then, now they have coalesced and have become one. [Thus Jesus could use] interchangeably "for the kingdom of heaven's sake", and "for my name's sake" (e.g. Matthew 19:12, 29)... We had to see the Kingdom in operation in a person. Jesus is the kingdom of God taking sandals and walking.*[8]

The kingdom built into our make-up

What all of this means then is that the kingdom of heaven is around us in the cosmic order and is accordingly built into our own very make-up, into the laws of our being and into the nature of the world, reality, and universe in which we live. This means then that when we rebel or sin against God we rebel and sin against ourselves and against the universe. That's why apartheid could never work, as I once wrote to one of P. W. Botha's Cabinet. Because it went against the grain and the moral fabric of the universe and the kingdom rule of Christ, it was doomed to failure. And the cause and effect judgments of history became also the judgments of God.

God wants His kingdom order that is *out there* to be internalised by His Kingdom *in here* – and within us – as we submit to the kingly rule of Christ both in our personal lives and in society.

So when we pray "Thy kingdom come" we are asking that there be a coinciding within us of the moral fabric of the universe and of our own moral make-up with the moral choices controlling our behaviour and the way we live both individually and in society.

"Give us this day our daily bread " or "Give us today the things we need today"

This is what Richard Foster most imaginatively calls "praying the ordinary". This makes clear that this prayer (the Disciples' Prayer) is indeed one which each of us needs to pray regularly on a *daily basis*.

So, yes, every day, we can and must pray about ordinary things. We can pray about our food, our finances, our physical and emotional strength, our sleep, our diligence (that there be no laziness in us), our health, our physical protection, our efficiency, and yes, a parking place, or something we have lost! Incidentally, in terms of the latter, I have found the Lord to have an almost 100 per cent track record in helping me find things I have lost or misplaced. I always say to him: "Lord, you with your all-seeing eyes know exactly and precisely where that particular lost item is. So please lead me to it, or have someone get it back to me." And yes, bingo, almost always, there it is, or it comes back somehow or other! That's praying the ordinary.

Cricket!

My wife and I have a standing joke – almost a theological difference, one might say – on whether one can pray about sporting events or happenings. With our son-in-law, Gary Kirsten, having played cricket for South Africa for so many years and then thereafter becoming the coach of the Indian cricket team, and after that the South African one, there have been many opportunities to pray about sporting events, or his part in them! Carol thinks I am a bit heretical, and maybe she is right, she usually is, that God is not involved in sport. But I say that may be generally true, but one can get Him involved! After all, He says we can pray about anything.

Daily needs

Beyond that I can testify, and I know many others can too, of a God who really does hear our prayers for ordinary things such as our finances, our health, our protection, or the health needs of ourselves, our children or our friends. Richard Foster sees this as praying about the "untheatrical realities" of the "uneventful" and comments:

> The discovery of God lies in the daily and the ordinary, not in the spectacular and the heroic. If we cannot find God in the routines of home and shop, then we will not find Him at all. Ours is to be a symphonic piety in which all the activities of work and play and family and worship and sex and sleep are the holy habitats of the eternal. Thomas Merton urges us to have "unspeakable reverence for the holiness of created things."[9]

Offering our ordinary work

Foster also notes that however ordinary our job or vocation, we can pray the ordinary by offering our ordinary daily work up to the Lord. In fact, he says, "our vocation is an asset to prayer because our work becomes prayer. It is prayer in action. The artist, the novelist, the surgeon, the plumber, the secretary, the lawyer, the homemaker, the farmer, the teacher – all are praying by offering their work up to God."[10]

Foster goes further when he adds that: "each activity of daily life in which we stretch ourselves on behalf of others is a prayer of action."[11]

Ignatius Loyola notes: "Everything that one turns in the direction of God is prayer."[12]

So I celebrate that we can bring ordinary and everyday experiences of life to the Lord and imbue them with prayer. Our Lord did the same and brought together the common and the sacred in everything He did. It was true in the manner and place in which He was born. In His rejoicing in the wedding of a couple in Galilee as He added a pretty substantial slug of wine – 180 gallons actually, or 681 litres – to the sacred festivities! His way was to rub shoulders prayerfully with fishermen and tax collectors, with businessmen and rascals, soldiers and servants.

And yes, let's not forget the daily privilege of praying the ordinary when we say grace at the table and give thanks for our food. Or when our local congregation prays for good weather for the Sunday school picnic!

"Forgive us our trespasses as we forgive those who trespass against us" or "Forgive us our sins and impositions on you, as we are forgiving all who in any way offend us"

Our Lord wants us regularly to seek forgiveness for our sins. Forgiveness for sin is the primary need of all humanity. The fact is that if we are unhealed at this point of forgiveness for sin, then we bear a mortal hurt from which we cannot recover. That is why we need Christian salvation and the forgiveness of sins through receiving Jesus Christ as our Lord and Saviour. But beyond that on a daily basis we need to sweep out the dust in our souls and the smog of sin in our eyes so that we can relate uncluttered and unblocked in spirit to the Lord our God. So we need daily, because we sin daily, to ask Him to forgive us our sins, or as Dallas Willard puts it "forgive us our sins and impositions on you". And handle us with mercy.

Anglican liturgy

One of the things I love about the Anglican liturgy is that not only does it in every service require of the congregation to say the Lord's Prayer (Disciples' Prayer), but early in the service there is always place for the confession of sin. I often tease my non-conformist friends or members of newer churches by saying to them, "I love your worship and praise and preaching, but you obviously don't believe you are sinners!" This always produces a puzzled "What do you mean?"

"Well," I reply, "you never confess it!" Then comes a puzzled look. "Well," I say, as I press my case, "you never seem to make place or space in your services for the corporate confession of sin. You never confess any sins! So seemingly you guys can go week after week without sinning, and therefore without needing to confess it." A knowing look of dawning light sometimes appears on the faces of such friends, and they look at me like the wise old owl that had just declared a mighty revelation under a moonlit sky!

But in spiritual reality, it is indeed only the mercy or pity of God that makes our spiritual lives possible.

A catch in here

But, now here's the rub! The divine stipulation here is for fellowship and an absence of unforgiveness to prevail in our hearts and relationships before we can expect the Lord to forgive us. This makes anyone with whom we are out of fellowship a high priority on our spiritual agenda. Occasionally if I am driving alone on a journey, I take time out to think of anyone anywhere, wherever or whenever, past or present, who may have hurt, wounded or offended me. Then I examine my heart to see if I have forgiven that person. Then I seek to work on clearing my heart attitudes towards a place of forgiveness towards that person or persons. In fact, in my daily recitation of the Lord's Prayer, I try to use that moment to extend forgiveness in any direction where I need to. Indeed, only as I give my love and forgiveness to others am I a candidate to receive God's love and forgiveness for myself.

Sometimes this may take time, as I can testify out of my own personal experience. But we need to work on it regardless. Nor does this posture mean that we won't feel pain or hurt, or we won't forget, or we won't pretend it didn't matter and that all is the same as before. But forgiving means that the offence of the other person against us no longer separates them from us in our hearts, and nor can it then produce separation between us and the Lord.

All of this means that we live in the spiritually charged atmosphere of mercy whereby we are daily receiving it from the Lord and daily extending it to others.

So, now to the next clause.

"And lead us not into temptation" or "Please don't put us through trials"

Dallas Willard is just so good on this. Listen to him:

The final request asks our Father not to put us to the test. "Don't bring us into temptation." The "temptation" here is not primarily temptation to sin. Trials always tempt us to sin, however. And temptation to sin is always a trial, which we might fail by falling into sin. Moreover, the bad things that come upon us are always trials. And so the version in Matthew 6 elaborates this last request by saying, "spare us from bad things that might happen to us".

This request is not just for evasion of pain and of things we don't like, though it frankly is that. It expresses the understanding that we can't stand up under very much pressure, and that it is not a good thing for us to suffer. It is a vote of "no confidence" in our own abilities. As the series of requests begins with the glorification of God, it ends with acknowledgement of the feebleness of human beings.[13]

Trials to purify us

Of course it is an inescapable reality that the Lord will indeed allow us to go through considerable trials in order to purify us and to perfect our faith. Of course references to this are many and various. Listen for example to Peter: "In this you rejoice, even if now for a little while you have had to suffer various trials, so that the genuineness of your faith – being more precious than gold that, though perishable, is tested by fire – may be found to result in praise and glory and honor when Jesus Christ is revealed" (1 Peter 1:6–7, compare 1 Peter 4:12–13).

The same notion is picked up by James when he writes: "Blessed is the man who endures trial, for when he has withstood the test he will receive the crown of life which God has promised to those who love him" (James 1:12).

One does not have to be an exegetical rocket scientist to

register that this theme of the purifying effect of suffering upon the human spirit regularly occurs in Scripture, both in the Old Testament, for example with Job, as well as in the New.

So how then can we have our Lord here teaching us to pray "Lead us not into trials" while at the same time telling us in His Word that He will allow trials to come upon us so that we may be purified and made holy in character?

I am not quite sure of the answer, but I think it may lie in the next and associated petition that comes with this one, namely:

"But deliver us from evil " or "But deliver us from everything bad"

Perhaps Willard's translation here falls a bit short of the Greek word used in Matthew 6:13, *ponerou*, which means "evil" or, better, "the evil one". In other words, Satan. It is the same Greek word used in John 17:15 which in reality, and given the context, is better translated "the evil one". In 17:15, as we have noted, Jesus is praying "keep them from the evil one", in other words from the power of evil supernaturalism. This fits better with the sense of the petition in the Lord's Prayer. Our Lord does not want evil, just in the generic impersonal sense, to afflict us. More specifically He does not want the evil one, as a personal power of evil, to be allowed to touch our lives.

The fact is, that when we do go into deep trials or difficulties, we often find Satan capitalising on them in order to bring us down, or even destroy us. Thus, a person might be having a difficult time in their marriage and they and their husband or wife are in a time of real trial. But the desperate thing is that at such times the devil can climb in, capitalising on the trial, and maybe lead the man out into adultery or drive the woman out into pursuing an unnecessary divorce, with devastating consequences for the children.

Or else maybe there is an earthquake or tsunami and instead of people handling it in a stoic way (as many TV programmes reported to be the Japanese reaction to the

2011 tsunami), we see people go crazy and begin looting, or becoming irrationally violent, or using the social upheaval consequent upon the physical one to enter into acts of violence or rape. Or God may allow financially straitened circumstances in a family's life, but what if these become the grounds or pretext for fraud or theft, which lead to other awful consequences. The point is that in times of trial the devil often gets in the picture and gets active.

Given these realities, there is clearly enormous value in praying the Lord's Prayer daily and I do earnestly commend this to you, and particularly this section of it where we ask for His deliverance from evil and the evil one.

Now to the traditional ending of the prayer.

"For thine is the kingdom, the power, and the glory, for ever and ever Amen", or "Because you are the one in charge, and you have all the power, and the glory too is all yours – forever – which is just the way we want it"

It is wonderful in concluding this prayer to affirm to our heavenly Father that He is the king and the kingdom is His. In other words, He is finally in charge. He is sovereign Lord over the universe. And we register that the sovereignty of God means that in a universe of free and unprogrammed human agents, He will finally bring forth His kingdom purposes without violating human free will and our capacities for contrary choice. Humans will decide this way and that on a myriad of issues and happenings, but God, our Lord the king, will finally have His way, have His say, and bring forth His purposes. As Willard translates it, we are saying to our king, "You are the one in charge." This brings an anchor and a fundamental stability to our lives.

So by God's grace we are enabled to maintain our stability (note 2 Peter 3:7) when we can say: "thine is the kingdom", and then affirm more colloquially "because you are the one in charge".

And we know this to be true because He is the one in whom resides all power. Thus could Jesus affirm in one of His most startling claims in all the New Testament: "All authority in heaven and on earth has been given to me… And lo, I am with you always, to the close of the age" (Matthew 28:18–20, RSV). We note here also a key principle: "No Go, no Lo!"

More than that we rejoice with endless doxologies that "the glory too is all yours – forever!" This glory speaks of the character of God shining through, which it does in many places even now, but which will one day be everywhere and forever.

Which is just the way we want it!

All of which means that it only remains for us to say, Amen. And I just love Dallas's translation of that as "which is just the way we want it" – because that is what "Amen" means. This Hebrew word was originally an adjective meaning "reliable", "sure" or "true". Sometimes it was used as an adjectival verb meaning "it is reliable or true". But Amen came basically to be used as a formula meaning "surely" – or – "in very truth"! It could also mean "yes, indeed". Or, "may it be so in very truth!" In any event, the one who added the word Amen to a prayer put him or herself into the statement or petition of the prayer with all earnestness of faith and intensity of desire.

Much more is taught on prayer both by our Lord specifically and by both Old and New Testaments specifically, but what we have set forth here is at the very least a starting point both for us as individuals and also for all of us as congregations.

It has to start obviously with each one of us personally, in our own personal prayer lives.[14]

I close with Robert Coleman:

> The disciples could see the priority of prayer in Jesus' life, and knew that if they were to follow Him, they would have to live by the same rule… no other activity could substitute for this discipline of His Soul. Prayer was His way of getting things done. He never got behind in His work because He never got behind in Prayer.[15]

Chapter 13

Unity – The Seventh Mark (I)

The Unity for Which We Have Prayed

"The Holy Spirit makes us one, no matter what the diversity."

Claude Cunningham

"There is a fellowship within a fellowship – a sort of wheel in the middle of a wheel which gathers to itself all who are of its spirit in every church in every land and every age."

A. W. Tozer

"Our blessed Lord's prayer, here, is concerning those who had believed on Him, and all who shall to the end of time believe on Him through the words which He had given to His apostles, even the Word of God, 'that all may be one'…"

Marcus Rainsford, *Our Lord Prays for His Own*[1]

"Protect them in your name that you have given me, so that they may be one, as we are one."

Jesus, John 17:11

We now come to that mark of the church, namely unity, for which our Lord prayed and which for many is seen as the central and only thing for which He prayed. Possibly this is because unity is the most readily comprehensible item in the prayer. But there is much, much more we are meant to embrace. To be sure, unity is very key and it is pretty central, but it is not the *only thing* for which Jesus prayed. Thus have we noted at least *nine* other marks!

Up front we must register right away that we are not talking about unity at the expense of truth, or of holy behaviour, because there are also moral and ethical limits to those with whom we can be spiritually at one. Christian fellowship does not mean unprincipled inclusiveness.

In other words, there are both doctrinal and ethical limits to consider. For example, St John says anybody who denies the full deity and humanity of Jesus is "antichrist" (1 John 2:22) and anyone, says St Paul, who contradicts the gospel of free grace is to be anathematised (Galatians 1:8).

Likewise serious moral misconduct also disqualifies cooperation, as with anyone who is "guilty of immorality or greed" or who is "an idolater, reveller, drunkard, or robber" (1 Corinthians 6:9–10). The Apostle is clearly implying here that the sinner thus described is "impenitent".

Nor can a conscientious believer find full unity, fellowship and partnership in a congregation that does not move out in mission and lives perennially in maintenance mode.

It is notable that at the Third Assembly of the World Council of Churches in New Delhi in 1961, the then Archbishop of Canterbury, Michael Ramsey highlighted that: "The seventeenth chapter of St John describes Jesus praying not only that His disciples may be one, but also that they may become holy and that they may realise the truth. Unity, holiness and truth go together."[2]

Sadly, even he omitted here the mark of mission!

Later at that same Assembly Ramsey said: "A movement which concentrates on unity as an isolated concept can mislead the world and mislead us, as indeed would a movement

which had the exclusive label of holiness or the exclusive
label of truth."

Structural and authentic unity

John Stott has likewise noted that "the major preoccupation of
the twentieth-century church has been the search for structural
unity, but often without a comparable quest for the truth and
the life which constitute authentic unity and are the means by
which it grows."[3]

He added:

*Others have been preoccupied with truth (doctrinal
orthodoxy), sometimes becoming dry, harsh and
unloving in the process, forgetting that truth is to be
adorned with the beauty of holiness.*

*Holiness seems of paramount importance to others,
that is, the state of the church's interior life. But such
people sometimes withdraw into a self-centred piety,
forgetting that we have been called out of the world in
order to be sent back into it, which is "mission".*

*So mission becomes the obsession of a fourth
group, who, however, sometimes forget that the world
will come to believe in Jesus only when His people are
one in truth, holiness and love.*

*Truth, holiness, mission and unity belonged together
in the prayer of Jesus, and they need to be kept
together in our quest for the church's renewal today.*[4]

Our Lord prays for unity

So, let's hear Jesus' prayer on this (John 17:9, 11, 20–23):

*I am asking on their behalf; I am not asking on behalf of
the world, but on behalf of those whom you gave me...
protect them in your name that you have given me, so
that they may be one, as we are one.*

I ask not only on behalf of these, but also on behalf

of those who will believe in me through their word, that they may all be one. As you, Father, are in me and I am in you, may they also be in us, so that the world may believe that you have sent me. The glory that you have given me I have given them, so that they may be one, as we are one, I in them and you in me, that they may become completely one, so that the world may know that you have sent me and have loved them even as you have loved me.

*** ***

Well, well, well! How about that for a challenge? And what are we to make of it?

Clearly we have here a very comprehensive prayer for a very comprehensive Christian unity. It spans not only the centuries but also heaven and earth. As such, is it just a very lofty ideal, or does it hook into the here and now? How do idealism and realism intersect in this our Lord's High Priestly Prayer?

Answering this is a challenge. Let's move one step at a time.

1. Human unity

In thinking about our Lord's prayer for Christian unity, it is worth registering that this presupposes and is premised on our understanding of *human unity*. These two unities are not totally unconnected but nor are they to be confused.

First of all we would register as Christians that we all share this absolutely fundamental human unity as human beings, a unity that is not based on our common redemption in Christ, but on our common creation as humans made in the divine image (Genesis 1:27). Clearly we all share a basic unity as human beings and we have a human solidarity together as His creatures.

As human beings we all have immense value, and are

more valuable than the whole material universe because our Lord could ask, "For what profit is it to a man if he gains the whole world, and loses his own soul?" (Matthew 16:26, NKJV). So every one of us as Christians, and indeed any human anywhere on the planet, has this monumental value that we share together.

WE ALL BEAR THE DIVINE IMAGE

Beyond that we all bear the divine image in our natures – what theologians of old called the *Imago Dei.* And however defaced or damaged that divine image is, nevertheless it is there in every person – Christian or not – and is never to be destroyed or diminished.

As human beings, and Christians especially have to affirm this, we all have the power of contrary choice and we all share the rights to life, liberty, and the pursuit of happiness. Thus could the Lord say: "Be fruitful and multiply, and fill the earth and subdue it... See, I have given you every plant...", and so on (Genesis 1:28–29). In other words, the Lord says to all of us as humans, "Enjoy the world I have given you and enjoy one another, according to one another the dignity, respect and value which is intrinsic in each person." Of course this will affect us as Christians not simply in how we treat other human beings generally, but one another specifically. Thus if we deny one another our value, our divine nature, our humanness, our powers of contrary choice, or our human rights, then we deny the biblical doctrine of creation. So if Christians brutalise one another, we not only deny our gospel and its behavioural requirements, but we deny our divine createdness in the divine image.

HUMAN UNITY WIDE AND INCLUSIVE

So, by definition, this human unity includes all. It is wide and inclusive and embraces the whole human family. It is a unity shared by blacks and whites and browns, by people of different ideological or spiritual or religious persuasions, by high and low, by old and young, by educated and illiterate, by male and female.

Thus it is in stark contrast to the other narrow unities of race, nation, tribe, language, religion, denomination, or whatever. In particular it stands in strong contrast to *Christian unity*.

All of this speaks to why I like – on a daily basis in my thanksgiving time with God – to thank Him that He has created me as a *human being*. He did not create me as a dog, or a cat, or a horse, or a cow, or a camel, or a butterfly. All of those are beings. But they are not *human* beings. There is something very, very special about being a *human* being made in the image of God, able to have insights into what God is like because we know something of what we are like.

More than that, in reflecting on being a human being, we realise our human obligation to treat other human beings, whether Christian or otherwise, with the same regard, graciousness and love as we would like to be treated ourselves.

OBLIGATIONS OF HUMAN UNITY

Of course our human unity obliges us to stand with any persons, but perhaps especially with any Christians who are in any basic, fundamental human need. We stand with them not necessarily on the basis of doctrine but on the basis of common humanity. This alone if nothing else puts an obligation on us to care for other Christians as fellow human beings, even as we would care for any other *human* beings. Doctrinal or truth perception differences can never interfere here.

So grasping our human unity is something very precious and special with deep implications of all sorts, and in many directions.

2. Christian unity

This is different from, and deeper than, mere human unity, being based not primarily on *creation,* but on *redemption.* This is the fellowship of genuine believers united in Jesus Christ, sharing His regeneration and regenerating life, and bound by His received forgiveness and mercy.

Remember how Jesus said in His prayer that "this is eternal life, that they may know you, the only true God, and Jesus Christ whom you have sent" (John 17:3). Insofar then as true believers share eternal life, and partake together in knowing both the Father and the Son through the Holy Spirit, they thereby inevitably have a most profound bond, which we call Christian unity.

GOD'S OWN PEOPLE AND THEIR UNITY

Of this reality Peter spoke when he wrote: "But you are a chosen race, a royal priesthood, a holy nation, God's own people, that you may declare the wonderful deeds of him who called you out of darkness into his marvellous light. Once you were no people, *but now you are God's people*; once you had not received mercy, but now you have *received* mercy" (1 Peter 2:9–10).

Here, Peter is talking about people who were not always "God's own people", but who have now become exactly that, and people who were not always living in His marvellous light, but were previously in darkness. Now, in fact, they are bound by a glorious reality of having been called "out of darkness into his marvellous light." These are people for whom the mercy of God, as with everyone on Earth, would always have been available, but it had not yet availed for them because they had not yet received it.

So Peter is quite clear and emphatic that there was a time when they "had not received mercy", but now a time has come when they "*have* received mercy". Because of these realities they have now become a uniquely bonded people.

Indeed they have become "a chosen race, a royal priesthood, a holy nation, God's own people". And when they meet one another, they sense it, know it, and celebrate it.

And it is exactly this unity and its preservation among this "people", "God's own people", for which Jesus prays in John 17. He is also quite emphatic that He is not praying for the world or unity in the world, but in the church. He is extremely clear about this. "I am *not* praying for the world" (John 17:9). No, He is praying "on behalf of those whom you gave me, because they are yours" (verse 9). This is not to say He is uninterested in the world or unconcerned for it, because He wants the world to believe (17:21, 23). In fact He wants the world which, hates Him (15:18) and "hates" (15:19; 17:14) Christians to cease being the world and become believing Christians. He indeed wants the world to join the church to become His disciples through His witnesses.

And that witness will be most effective when it comes from people who have truly come to know Christ through repentance and faith, conversion and new birth, and who know they have become "a chosen race, a royal priesthood, a holy nation, and God's own people". There are no words adequate to describe the marvel of this happening once it has happened in people's lives along with the consequent bond and unity they then enjoy.

THIS UNITY FOR WHICH JESUS PRAYS IS ALREADY IN PLACE

This is vitally important to state because we are inclined to think that this aspect of our Lord's prayer has not been answered. But in a very real sense it has. All true and genuine believers are already one in Christ. The problem is simply that we don't manifest it. Carol and I have three wonderful children, Cathy, Debbie, and Martin, who by virtue of having been born into our family, have a unity as the Cassidy siblings born from the union of Michael and Carol. *They are then irrevocably one* as three Cassidy children in the Cassidy family.

However, it is perfectly possible that they could choose

to be separate, alienated, and out of fellowship with each other and with us. Carol and I as parents would then have to pray that the unity that they intrinsically have as part of the Cassidy family should be made manifest and that these children should come back into deep fellowship, relationship, and partnership with each other.

Thus it is with our Lord's prayer here for His children. And the prayer *has* been answered, *we are already one.*

ONCE SEPARATED NOW ONE

This the Apostle particularly makes clear in Ephesians 2 when he is speaking to both Jewish and Gentile Christians between whom there could easily have risen up a fearful disunity and alienation. But the Apostle tells them first of all to "remember that you were at that time *separated* from Christ, *alienated* from the commonwealth of Israel, and *strangers* to the covenant of promise, having *no hope* and *without God* in the world" (Ephesians 2:12). This is an extraordinary reality for us to face, but the Apostle declares it to be so. "But now," says the Apostle, "in Christ Jesus you who once were far off *have been* brought near in the blood of Christ. For he is our peace, who *has* made us both one, and *has* broken down the dividing wall of hostility" (verse 14).

In this verse there is in the Greek a series of aorist tenses whose significance is immediately evident when we register that the Greek aorist always speaks of completed action in the past. It is a once-for-all-thing. It is not something which, though begun in the past, is still happening in the present (and which would therefore require an imperfect tense in the Greek), or might just happen in the future as we await some big ecumenical breakthrough. It actually *has* happened, a completed fact of history in the past, as these Jewish and Gentile people came to Christ and thereby came to each other. As this happened Jesus created in Himself "one new man in place of the two" (Ephesians 2:15).

FELLOW CITIZENS

Paul goes on to note that once we have come to Christ we now enter into the extraordinary situation of being "fellow citizens with the saints and members of the household of God... built upon the foundation of the apostles and prophets, Christ Jesus Himself being the cornerstone" (Ephesians 2:19–20).

This unity is via a common apostolic truth foundation, and via our connectedness by new birth to Jesus Himself as the cornerstone, and via our being all together in a common structure. It enables us in unity and fellowship to "grow into a holy temple in the Lord" (verse 21). And maybe most astonishing and amazing of all, all who are true believers find themselves becoming "a dwelling place of God in the Spirit" (verse 22).

These are mind-bending truths and they thrust home to our minds and hearts the profound unity which is already there among true believers. Jesus prayed for it. And it was given. It is there. It is real. It is true.

POSITIONAL UNITY TO BECOME ACTUAL

So we grasp first of all that there is indeed a positional unity. But the issue and challenge, as I said, is whether we can and will grasp it and whether we can in fact manifest it. We celebrate the positional, but are required to work the positional into the actual.

If our Cathy, Debbie, and Martin were alienated, the challenge to them would be to demonstrate and make evident the basic unity in the Cassidy family that has already happened, as a past tense completed action, when they were born many years ago into our family.

I often tell the story of the two earthworms emerging after a rainstorm. As these two long winding creatures met each other, one earthworm said to the other: "My, but you are the most beautiful earthworm I have ever seen. Will you marry me?" To which the other earthworm replied: "Don't be stupid, I'm your other end." They might not have realised it or previously believed it, but they were already one and did not need an engagement or marriage to make it so!

DEEP ACCESS TO ONE ANOTHER

So then as both groups "have access in one Spirit to the Father" (Ephesians 2:18), so they both have access in deep unity to each other. They are one. And must now act like it.

The extraordinary consequence of that, the Apostle then points out, is that "you are no longer strangers and sojourners, [that is, distant, disunited and disconnected], but you are fellow citizens with the saints and members of the household of God" (verse 19). So then, whatever your denomination, if you are a true child of God by repentance, faith, and new birth, you are, whether you know it or not, like it or not, believe it or not, or think you can work it out or not, "fellow citizens... and members of the household of God" (verse 19).

So, then, has Jesus' prayer for unity in the body of Christ been answered? Sure it has! For we are all "joined together and grow(ing) into a holy temple in the Lord" (verse 21). That's unity. That's togetherness. More than that, and most marvellous of all, we are all as true believers in Christ being "built into it [this holy temple] for a dwelling place of God in the Spirit" (verse 22).

Just imagine if we could fully grasp this! How powerful in Christ would we be!

OUR LORD PRAYS NOW FOR A UNITY OF HIS DISCIPLES AND ALL BELIEVERS WITH THE APOSTLES

Listen to Him: "I do not pray for *these* only, but also for *those* who believe in me through their word, that they may all be one" (John 17:20–21).

This is an expanding unity, not a static one, as the church itself expands.

So our Lord is praying here for a unity which is a

combination of "these" and "those"; in other words of *these* who are here with Him at that moment with *those* who will later believe through them. So He is praying for a historical continuity and obviously a doctrinal unity between His church of the first century and that of subsequent centuries including our own. He is praying for a loyalty of the latter (us here in the twenty-first century) to the teaching of the former (those of the first century).

Our Lord here is praying for a unity in truth of His people *now* with His people *then*; it is also a unity in truth, purpose, dedication, zeal, sacrifice, commitment, and effectiveness. But we reiterate that this Christian unity is to be in truth and not at the expense of it. In fact in the very verse right before this petition we have just looked at, we find our Lord praying: "And for their sake, I consecrate myself, that they may also be consecrated *in truth*" (verse 19).

TRUE APOSTOLIC SUCCESSION

John Stott puts it this way:

> *Jesus's prayer was first and foremost that there might be a historical continuity between the apostles and the post apostolic church, that the church's faith might not change with the changing years but remain recognisably the same, and that the church of every generation might merit the epithet apostolic because of its loyalty to the message and mission of the apostles. Christian unity begins, then, as unity with the apostles (through the New Testament which makes their teaching available to us); without this, church unity would not be distinctively Christian.*[5]

This is the true so-called "apostolic succession" which is a much more doctrinal succession of loyalty to apostolic teaching than it is an organisational one via a genealogical line of bishops or popes succeeding each other organisationally.

GOING BACK 2,000 YEARS

After an evangelistic campaign, one church leader criticised Billy Graham saying he had "set the church back 100 years". When asked about this in a press conference, Billy Graham replied: "Well, I am sorry to hear that. You see, I was hoping to set the church back 2,000 years!"

Of course there were many aspects of the early church, as for example in Corinth, which we would want to avoid in our contemporary times. But the basic truth and passion of the apostles in the early church we would surely want to emulate. The fact is that by their preaching, their gospel, their passion, and their dedication, they became an overwhelming minority in the ancient world. And we could be the same in our times if we could find a true spiritual and theological unity between Jesus' apostolic group and ourselves.

Thus when certain sectors of the modern church depart from faithfulness to the apostolic first-century church they find themselves bereft of the power and effectiveness of first-century believers.

Our Lord now goes even deeper as He prays – that –

BELIEVERS WOULD HAVE WITH EACH OTHER A UNITY AS BETWEEN THE FATHER AND THE SON

The prayer here is breathtaking.

Listen to Him: **"[I pray] that they may all be one. As you, Father, are in me and I am in you, may they also be in us, so that the world may believe that you have sent me"** (verse 21). The extent and depth of what Jesus is praying for here now takes us off the dial for its extravagance. You see, He is praying that the church's internal unity may be comparable to the unity within the Godhead itself, a unity between Father, Son, and Holy Spirit. Clearly this unity is not organisational – the Godhead is not being united by a committee, but by and in a spiritual oneness. A unity of mind, purpose, relatedness, and love.

The late Archbishop of Canterbury, William Temple, put it this way: "the way to the union of Christendom does not lie through committee-rooms, though there is a task of formulation to be done there. It lies through personal union with the Lord so deep and real as to be comparable with His union with the Father."[6]

This is really a mind-blower when we reflect on the implications for daily church life. In other words, there is no pulling in opposite directions. No factions! No competition! No envy! No undermining! No criticism! No gossip! No superiority! No racism! No chasing after position!

In fact, if all the churches in any given city in the Western world related to one another like that, then that city would be blown over by the love and power of God to receive blessings beyond measure.

But our Lord now takes it a dimension deeper:

BELIEVERS WOULD KNOW A UNITY LITERALLY WITHIN THE TRINITY

So He prays that "they also *may be in us…*" (verse 21). Jesus is here praying that we, as believers, may now be drawn into the Godhead as the Father and Son are in each other. We are to be united to God in the same indissoluble tie as binds Father and Son and vice versa, and beyond that we are to be actually *inside* the Trinity with Father, Son, and Holy Spirit. There is, in other words, to be a mutual indwelling. The triune God indwells us, and we indwell Him.

US theologian Don Carson speaks powerfully of this mutual indwelling as –

> the indwelling of the Spirit in each of them and their living in God – dependent upon Him, relying upon Him, obedient to Him, maintaining the sacred Gospel entrusted to them and by which they are saved. This is at once the experience and the commitment of every true believer.[7]

Carson then adds:

> On the other hand, Christians need to grow in their unity;
> for Jesus prays, "May they be brought to complete
> unity…" (17:23). The implication is that their unity, while
> real, is not perfect. Sad to tell, too often Christians do
> not cherish deeply the things that unite them with other
> true believers: they cherish instead the divisive things.
> Even where there is some point of conscience at stake,
> there is a danger that in defending what we hold to be
> a point of truth we may endanger the integrity of this
> witness of loving unity. At the level of praxis, at the level
> of attitude, at the level of love, at the level of a growing
> grasp of true doctrine – at all of these levels the Christian
> church needs to be perfected in unity.[8]

What huge challenges all of this present to our styles of life, our prayer life, our walk with God, our abiding in Him, our fellowship, relatedness, and partnership with one another in kingdom things!

*** ***

But, in all this we hold fundamentally to the fact that the prayer was answered. We have been made basically one.

3. The purpose of unity

CREDIBLE WITNESS

Our Lord is very clear that a credible witness to the world is a major and basic purpose of Christian unity. Thus in verse 21 of the prayer He prays **"that they may all be one. As you, Father, are in me, and I am in you, may they also be in us** *so that the world may believe that you have sent me"* (my italics). So key, crucial, and central is this that He can repeat it again two verses later (verse 23), where He prays **"that they may become completely one, so that the world may know**

that you have sent me and have loved them even as you have loved me." In other words, our unity not only commends the gospel, it proclaims it. Our unity does not just support our witness, it *is* our witness. A major purpose of our unity is evangelistic.

This is why when I was International Team Leader of African Enterprise I used to have a sign put up around our South African office saying: "Before African Enterprise is a ministry, it is a testimony." That of course is a statement of an ideal and a goal. The fact is that we could have no really effective ministry as an evangelistic team unless we had a testimony of unity and fellowship together. And to the degree that that unity might be faulty or compromised, so to that degree would the ministry flowing forth from us be defective.

The hard fact is that lack of Christian unity in the church destroys our credibility in the world. This was very clear to the Apostle as he wrote to the Corinthian church to try and make them grasp – among other things – that if they were split then their evangelistic witness would be imperilled. So He rebuked them strongly for the party spirit by which some of them were saying: "'I belong to Paul', or 'I belong to Apollos', or 'I belong to Cephas', or 'I belong to Christ'" (1 Corinthians 1:12). Paul would go on to say to them, "*all* are yours" (1 Corinthians 3:22). So the Apostle puts the question "Is Christ divided?" (1 Corinthians 1:13). The truth was that if all those Christians from the different factional groups were themselves truly in Christ, then they were in a Christ who was whole, united in Himself, and not in any way divided.

THANKFUL FOR NON-DENOMINATIONAL MINISTRY

I have been very thankful in my own personal life that virtually all of my ministry, for fifty years or more, has been carried out on a non-denominational basis. Though I am a member of a denomination, I do not claim it or own it slavishly or accord it an idolatrous loyalty. Indeed, I can look at true believers whether Catholic or Protestant, Anglican, Methodist, Baptist,

Pentecostal, Lutheran, Assemblies of God or whatever, and truly say "All are mine." All of the true believers in those groupings belong to me and I belong to them. Why? Because Christ is not divided, and the Christ in them unites them to the Christ in me.

EFFECTIVE EVANGELISM

My testimony on the basis of some fifty years of interdenominational ministry in Africa is that our missions and evangelistic campaigns were at their best and most effective when both our team and the local churches of any given city had a deep unity, fellowship, and togetherness.

On the negative side, I can tell you that we have never had any of our campaigns damaged by atheists, Muslims, Hindus, Communists, free lovers, or neo-pagans. But we have had many damaged by other Christians who found fault with us in one way or another, or else assaulted the notion of cooperating with all those heretics over there who haven't got it right.

This sort of thing often damaged our evangelistic missions and campaigns. Often seriously.

I remember, for example, our mission to Monrovia, Liberia in 1985 where the initial invitation had come to us from the Liberian Council of Churches whose chairman was an Anglican archbishop who was strongly biblical and evangelical in his commitments. But the fact that the initial invitation had come to us from an Anglican made many of the evangelicals hold back! Not to be deterred, my great colleague David Richardson, then our AE Pan-African Missions Director, and a warrior and trooper for Christ if ever there was one, spent six or eight months slowly drawing together both the ecumenical and evangelical groups in the city.

Finally out of all that effort came forth an awesome united campaign that many said at the time was the best that ever happened in Liberia. But it was the unity and the newfound fellowship that had spawned the effectiveness.

ALL WHO BELIEVED WERE TOGETHER

Thus it was in the book of Acts, as we noted earlier, that Luke tells us that "All who believed were together" (Acts 2:44). But what people can easily miss is the consequence of that articulated by Luke in verse 47 when he says that "the Lord added to their number daily those who were being saved." In other words, the fellowship and togetherness which was based on their shared devotion "to the apostles' teaching and fellowship, to the breaking of bread and the prayers" (Acts 2:42) produced an effervescent, spontaneous explosion of evangelism through which new believers were daily added to the church. The extraordinary happening of verse 47 (the evangelistic explosion) was a direct consequence of verse 44 (the togetherness in the body of Christ).

Maybe that spirit is amusingly captured in the story of the West African brother applying for a job in a Christian organisation. He concluded his application saying: "You may be glad to learn that I am a retired first-class school master trained by the Basel Missionaries. I am also a Methodist, a Salvationist, a Seventh Day Adventist, and an Apostolic in order to acquire the necessary knowledge befitting a matured Protestant!"

Now that perhaps sounds like the kind of person we are after!

UNITY THE PRECONDITION OF AN EFFECTIVE MINISTRY OF RECONCILIATION

In 2 Corinthians 5:18 the Apostle points out to us the remarkable truth that "God has given to *us* the ministry of reconciliation." This is a unique ministry placed upon the Christian church. It is not placed upon the government, or the army, or academia, or the business world or anyone else. It is placed on *us*. That means on us who are Christians and whose unity transcends every divide, whether political, racial, social, gender, generation, or whatever. In reality every division in our world and in society is criss-crossed with our Lord's agents of reconciliation who, if they link hands, and work in cooperation, can pull off the most remarkable exploits of reconciliation.

I have seen this happen in our ministry and in the ministry of others many times. Thus it was in South Africa in the closing home straight of the dreadful apartheid era that it was the Christian church who participated powerfully in bringing together the different sides of South African dividedness and facilitated the emerging of our first non-racial elections in 1994. This led on to the New South Africa and the initial fulfilment of Archbishop Desmond Tutu's dream of "a rainbow nation".

And Christians have done similar things even in places such as Rwanda where the hostilities between Hutu and Tutsi were so profound. But there is no way that we can have an effective ministry of reconciliation if the church seeks to bring its contribution out of a divided community whose credibility is thereby massively compromised.

Our Blessed Lord knew this full well and therefore prayed "that they may all be one... so that the world may believe that you have sent me" (John 17:21). In short, if we do really want to have effectiveness, impact and credibility out there in the world, then we must know that it is not generated by different sections of the church doing great projects or exploits or taking great stands on social issues, it is generated by our being one and acting in cooperation as one.

This being one and acting in cooperation as one will only really come forth if we grasp afresh the profound basis of our unity.

4. The basis of unity

WHAT CHRIST HAS ALREADY DONE

I repeat and underline here what we have already said, namely that we are already one, because He "*has* made us both one, and has [past tense] broken down the middle wall of separation" (Ephesians 2:14, NKJV). And beyond that He "*has* reconciled us to Himself" (2 Corinthians 5:18, NKJV). So our task is to express and make visible the functional unity we *already* possess in Christ.

WHAT WE SHARE BECAUSE OF WHAT HE HAS ALREADY DONE

Christians need to allow themselves to marvel at and be mind-boggled by what we share because of what our Lord has done for us. It's an amazing thing, is it not, how you can get off to a flying start in a relationship with someone if you find that you have many things in common? Thus somewhere overseas I might meet a person who not only identifies themselves as a South African, but also went to the same school as me, lives in the same province, enjoys cricket as I do, has the same political views as me, has a similar sense of humour with both of us laughing at the same jokes, and who enjoys adventure books, and whose wife knew my wife at school! When you find all those things in common, away you go in a flying and wonderful experience of new friendship.

So let's just think in headline terms of some of things we share as Christians:

- The **Divine Nature**. Peter tells us that we are "partakers of the divine nature" (2 Peter 1:4). Paul tells us in similar vein that "if anyone is in Christ, there is a new creation" (2 Corinthians 5:17). Thus, as we mentioned above, if you encounter someone you have never met before, but you discover they know Christ and you share the divine nature, you are immediately and profoundly bonded.

- The **Person of Christ**. Paul says we are "created *in* Christ Jesus" (Ephesians 2:10). My late colleague Bishop Festo Kivengere who co-led African Enterprise for many years, was once asked how he as a black Ugandan could travel around the world ministering with a white South African.

Festo replied: "But Michael is my miracle brother. Because he has come to Christ, and I have come to Christ, we have come to each other. And because we share our Lord we can have deep fellowship and unity together."

- The **Person of the Holy Spirit**. Paul tells us: "you are God's temple, and… God's Spirit dwells in you" (1 Corinthians 3:16). So we share a knowledge of the Spirit and we also know that at conversion each of us was "sealed" by the Holy Spirit. Listen to the Apostle: "In him you also, who have heard the word of truth, the gospel of your salvation, and have believed in him, were *sealed* with the promised Holy Spirit, which is the guarantee of our inheritance until we acquire possession of it to the praise of his glory" (Ephesians 1:13–14).

  The experience between believers of the seal of the Holy Spirit of course is neither haphazard nor unprincipled. But rather it is on the basis of the fact that we have first of all heard the word of truth and we are no longer living in error.

- The **Gospel of our Salvation**. Beyond that, we have received the gospel of our salvation – that is a mighty happening – and we "have believed in him". In other words, we have committed our lives to Him through exercising New Testament faith. This first of all involves intellectual assent and then secondly committing one's destiny. When all that has happened, God works miraculously to put a *seal* upon us "which is a guarantee of our inheritance" and which announces to the world that we are "a purchased possession" of the living God.

  This notion comes from the early world where a wax seal was stamped onto a purchased possession in the marketplace to say that this item was no longer up for sale or purchase, because it had been bought already. As believers, we share the awesome common experience of the *seal* of the Holy Spirit given us as guarantee of what is to come in our spiritual inheritance both now and in eternity. This indicates both to the world and to all in the heavenly realm, whether good powers or bad, that we have been purchased through the shed blood of our Lord Jesus Christ to be His possession forever.

- A **divine calling**. Thus can the writer to the Hebrews say that as believers we are all people "who share in a heavenly call" (Hebrews 3:1), as "ambassadors" (2 Corinthians 5:20, as "soldiers" (2 Timothy 2:3) and as heavenly citizens (Philippians 3:20).

- **Christ's sufferings**. Sometimes it is not simply that we are tested, but we are put into experiences of real suffering. This is what the apostle Paul describes as "the fellowship of his sufferings" (Philippians 3:10, KJV). Thus can Peter tell all the recipients of his letter that they should "not be surprised at the fiery ordeal which comes upon you to prove you, as though something strange were happening to you" (1 Peter 4:12). Very few Christian believers can walk the full span of life without some experiences here and there of real suffering and very deep testing. I believe deep waters constitute the common experience of all believers somewhere along the line. And it bonds us together in unity.

- **Future glory**. Now here we speak not just of the bonding and unity that comes from things experienced together on earth in the past, but of what is to be our future destination and destiny in eternity especially in the "new heaven" and the "new earth" (2 Peter 3:13). Thus after talking about suffering, the Apostle can add: "I consider that the sufferings of this present time are not worth comparing with the glory which shall be revealed to us" (Romans 8:18). How marvellous! We are all headed into glory and will spend eternity together. All the more reason to work at getting on now!!

What a glorious reality then is Christian unity and fellowship! Nothing offered us in the music society, the book club, the local pub, the soccer or rugby team, or the sharing of a country or neighbourhood can begin to compare in any way, shape or form with real Christian unity and fellowship. It is glorious beyond the telling.

All the more reason, then, why the Scriptures urge us to work at manifesting this unity, at guarding it, and at working to make it real, which is what we must look at next.

Chapter 14

Unity – The Seventh Mark (II)

Maintaining Our Unity and its Challenges

"Dear God, I bet it is very hard for you to love all of everybody in your church all the time. There are only four people in our family, and I can never do it."

Child's prayer

"I… beg you to lead a life worthy of the calling to which you have been called, with all lowliness and meekness, with patience, forbearing one another in love, eager to maintain the unity of the Spirit in the bond of peace."

St Paul, Ephesians 4:1–3

"… protect them in your name that you have given me, so that they may be one, as we are one."

Jesus, John 17:11

"Sanctify them in the truth; your word is truth… that they also may be sanctified in truth… that they may all be one."

Jesus, John 17:17, 19, 21

Our Lord wants His people together in loving togetherness and unity in the truth. He has therefore given us a very clear mandate in this regard.

1. The mandate to Christian unity

It is clear both from our Lord's prayer here in John 17 and from many other sections of Scripture that there is a mandate to Christian unity.

Thus, for example, the apostle Paul can speak in these terms: "Only let your manner of life be worthy of the gospel of Christ so whether I come and see you or am absent, I may hear of you that you *stand firm in one spirit, with one mind striving side by side for the faith of the gospel*" (Philippians 1:27).

A few verses later he adds: "So if there is any encouragement in Christ, any incentive of love, any participation in the Spirit, any affection and sympathy, complete my joy *by being of the same mind, having the same love, being in full accord and of one mind*" (Philippians 2:1–2).

These few verses make clear that Christian unity is not only to be exhibited in fellowship but also in cooperation. There is to be a true "partnership in the gospel" (Philippians 1:5) and this will involve "striving side by side for the faith of the gospel" (Philippians 1:27). The Christian norm then is to be in cooperation rather than in competition and to be "fellow workers" (see Romans 16:3, 9, 21; 2 Corinthians 8:23; Philemon 1:24, and so on).

I. GRASP TRUTH AFRESH AS THE BASIS AND PRECONDITION OF UNITY

Perhaps we should especially note here in this scripture of 3 John 8 that John speaks specifically of "fellow workers in *the truth*." He wanted believers to be fellow workers with each other and with him, but not on an unprincipled basis. They were to be *fellow workers* in the truth. A few verses later he has commendation for another fellow worker, Demetrius, who has not only "a testimony from everyone", but also and most importantly, he has a testimony "from the truth itself" (verse 12).

In fact, so important is truth in the mandate to fellowship

that in the opening salutation of this epistle of 3 John which is sent to a colleague called Gaius, the Apostle can write: "the elder to the beloved Gaius, whom I love *in the truth*... For I greatly rejoiced when some of the brethren arrived and testified to *the truth of your life*, as indeed you do *follow the truth*. No greater joy can I have than this, that my children *follow the truth*" (verses 1, 3–4). John has four references to truth in just a couple of verses. We will elaborate on this in a few moments.

II. OUR UNITY IN CHRIST REQUIRES DEMONSTRATION

I will never forget my experience in giving one of the opening addresses at the Pan-African Christian Leadership Assembly in Nairobi in 1976. We had gathered Christian leaders from all sectors of the church and from forty-nine out of fifty-one African countries. One of the tension points in the assembly related inevitably to the race issue. But how wonderful then for me as a white person from South Africa, when I was introduced by my beloved friend and brother, Bishop Festo Kivengere, along with a great hug of affection and affirmation! This beautiful expression and manifestation of brotherly unity and fellowship across impossible barriers not only deeply touched my own heart and launched me well on my address, but it impacted hundreds within that assembly who had serious problems with white South Africans!

Or else let's suppose there is to be a major combined churches Christian mission in a given city. If this is the case the unity among the churches needs to be evident, or credibility is the casualty.

III. WE HAVE TO BE COMMITTED TO UNITY

So how then, do we maintain and demonstrate our unity and also manage the related problems and challenges integral to such an endeavour?

What is certain is that no one can achieve anything

significant without being committed to it. It must be in our sights with resolve, determination, and courage.

The reality is that without a strong commitment to unity we will not make it through all the obstacles and challenges that can obstruct our path towards that end. This would surely be why our Lord prays in John 17:15 that the Father should protect and keep His disciples "from the evil one". After all, if He wants us protected so that we may have a unity in love, purpose, holiness, truth, and mission, then it is obviously logical that the greatest dangers and obstacles will lie in those things which will seek to destroy that very same unity in love, purpose, holiness, truth, and mission.

Cataloguing all such evils would be challenging indeed, but they would include jealousy, envy, isolationism, an uncooperative spirit, self-sufficiency, arrogance, an unwillingness to learn from the other. He is clearly implying also that there will be assorted dark and satanic forces which will indeed seek to destroy the unity of His body.

Obviously then the Christian believer concerned about unity and "striving together for the faith of the gospel" (Philippians 1:27, NKJV) will require enormous commitment to press through against all the obstacles.

Personal experience

Thus it was that in all of our African Enterprise citywide missions over these last fifty years we have sought as a prerequisite to get all the churches together in order to do major citywide campaigns of evangelism together to maximise effectiveness.

One of the more ambitious of these was in Johannesburg in 1970. The struggles to get all sides together was huge. But we persevered through thick and thin. We negotiated the tangled histories of past Christian disunity in that great city. We pressed through assorted relationship hassles, personality clashes among certain church leaders, differences of political ideology, theological suspicions, racial alienations – you name it.

But we persevered until 300 churches were participating, for the best part of a year. Of course inevitably there were some who stayed out and a few who pulled out. This was always sad and damaging. One denomination pulled out because "Michael and one of his colleagues preached in the High Church Anglican cathedral where, they said, 'bells and smells' [incense] prevailed", the latter having the incidental side-effect of reducing my colleague, Abiel Thipanyane, into allergic, asphyxiating, and paralysing paroxysms of hay-fever, which totally incapacitated his sermon anyway!

Another group pulled out saying that "African Enterprise's opposition to apartheid shows clearly that they are communists", though the group in question would have been hard put to define what a communist was – ideologically I mean. But it was a convenient conservative political swear word in those days to neutralise other Christians one didn't like.

Yet another group pulled out because they read a newspaper interview that recorded, "Cassidy had declined a cigarette offer" from the interviewing columnist, from which it was concluded that "Michael smokes". No assurances from me to the contrary could prevail with my erstwhile critics, even when I told them I had given up smoking when I left school! Or shortly thereafter! So the whole denomination pulled out holus bolus, leaving the mission and me casualties of someone's theology of tobacco!

All that apart, we had nearly a full year of gospel ministry with a high percentage of Johannesburg churches combined together. This only happened because we had been *committed* to it in spite of all assaults upon our unifying endeavours. We had leapt over those theologically compelling barriers of incense, bells, tobacco, and skin pigmentation and beyond that sweetly and firmly assured all and sundry that we still held to the Resurrection and the Virgin Birth!

Yes, Christian unity requires us to make *"every effort* to maintain the unity of the Spirit in the bond of peace" (Ephesians 4:3).

IV. WORK FOR UNITY AND RECONCILIATION BY DIALOGUE AND INTERACTION

Picking up on some of the reasons groups gave in Johannesburg in 1970 for refusing to cooperate in a combined churches' outreach, we were alerted to the fact that some of the major obstructions to unity are misunderstanding, misconception, stereotyping, and living with false mythologies of one another. Or they can be rooted in a spirit of independence, building our own little empires, maintaining our *status quos,* or in our false feelings of sufficiency, even pride, which say, as the eye to the hand in Paul's illustration, "'I have no need of you', nor again the head to the feet, 'I have no need of you'" (1 Corinthians 12:21).

Many times in other African Enterprise citywide missions across Africa in these last five decades, we have come across thriving and flourishing churches who, when a combined churches outreach to the city is contemplated, declare: "We don't really need to come in on that, because we are doing it anyway. And probably better than you can." That might be true. But nowhere does it occur to them that while they may think they do not need the other city churches or believers, maybe it just might be so that the other churches and believers in the city need them! The reality is that all parts of the body of Christ need one another whether they register this or not (1 Corinthians 12:12).

Let's have a party

Anyway coming back to Mission '70, a significant consequence followed. One day an idea came to John Rees, Chairman of Mission '70, the new Secretary General of the South African Council of Churches, and myself. We had coffee together one day and were reflecting on the still existing wide gaps between the churches – not just in Johannesburg but also in the whole country. Then almost simultaneously we said to one another: "Why don't we have a party? John will invite all his ecumenical friends from South Africa, and even overseas, and Michael will invite his evangelical friends from around South Africa and overseas. Then let's get together and reflect on the challenges of mission and evangelism in South Africa at this time."

And that's exactly what we did, as African Enterprise and the South African Council of Churches sponsored that great Congress on Mission and Evangelism in Durban in March 1973. There were 800 leaders present who were accommodated on a non-racial basis in then apartheid South Africa. Virtually all denominations participated, both evangelical and ecumenical.

Similar commitments to unity were required when in 1979 we mounted the great South Africa Christian Leadership Assembly (SACLA). In that gathering we had 6,000 leaders from right across the denominational and racial spectrum together for nearly ten days in Pretoria. In that endeavour we had to weather not only theological suspicion and political assaults, but also state interference, police provocation and investigation, character assassination, and malicious Christian backstabbing from certain hyper-conservative church sectors. It was unlike anything I had ever experienced before or have experienced since. But we were committed to getting the South African church together in unity and in fellowship, and in the final event the Lord brought about exactly that with extraordinary consequences in the following years.

Consequences of fellowship

Not surprisingly, after these conferences the churches of South Africa moved forward in many ways in a much greater fellowship and unity. They were seminal experiences. And all sorts of things followed, not least new fellowship, unity, and shared endeavours and a much more united gospel witness, as well as more united Christian and biblical opposition to the injustices of apartheid. So a vast network of believers from all sides of the spectrum found itself in place and relevantly facing both the spiritual needs of South Africans for the evangelistic message and the socio-political needs of South Africans to receive the challenges of social justice.

All these togetherness and unity events began in dialogue, determination and interaction, sometimes on a costly basis, but yet they produced astonishing results. It had been worth it.

2. Limits to unity

But now we come to a crunch question. Are we obliged to be at one and strive to maintain unity with anyone and everyone who professes the name of Jesus Christ? Should all churches and denominations always be together? Is there never a case for convinced Christians with strong biblical convictions to leave a congregation in which they have hitherto worshipped, or even depart from their denomination if it seems to have lost the way and no longer clearly preaches the gospel or abides by clear biblical principles or ethics? Or should not wheat and tares grow together until the harvest? (Matthew 13:30, 39, 40). Are we not to tolerate good and bad fish in the same net? (Matthew 13:47, 48).

COMPLEX AND PAINFUL QUESTIONS

These are difficult, complex, and sometimes very painful questions.

Earlier in this chapter we noted in passing that there were indeed obvious biblical limits to cooperation and the expression of unity. Christian fellowship, we noted, does not mean unprincipled inclusiveness. Why? Because the New Testament sets forth both doctrinal and ethical limits to fellowship.

For example, the apostle John asks: "Who is the liar but he who denies that Jesus is the Christ? This is the antichrist, he who denies the Father and the Son" (1 John 2:22; compare 1 John 4:1–3). Clearly John is not exhorting believers to seek unity with them.

So too where the full deity or humanity of Jesus Christ is denied in a denomination, or congregation or even in a seminary, the latter perhaps teaching what German theologian, Helmut Thielicke called "demonic theology",[1] any unity with such is out of the question.

Likewise where the doctrine of salvation by free grace through faith is contradicted, and a religion of works substituted for it, as in sectors of the Galatian church, the apostle Paul says "let them be accursed" (Galatians 1:8). Not the most ecumenical language. Then he repeats this for emphasis in the next verse: "As we have said before, so now I say again, if anyone is preaching to you a gospel contrary to that which you received, let him be accursed" (Galatians 1:9). No unity possible there.

In fact, when the apostle Paul met with the Ephesian elders, as recorded in Acts 20, he alerted them to the fact that "fierce wolves... not sparing the flock" will come in *"from among your own selves"* (in other words other professing Christians), who will speak "perverse things, to draw away the disciples after them" (verses 29–30). Most certainly fellowship and unity with such "wolves" would be inconceivable.

SERIOUS MORAL PROBLEMS DISQUALIFY FELLOWSHIP

Interestingly enough in the letters to the seven churches in the book of Revelation (chapters 2–3), it was not just truth issues on which they were challenged, but also moral and behavioural ones. Likewise with the Corinthians. Thus it was that serious moral misconduct would disqualify cooperation and unity, and the Apostle therefore told them that they "are not to associate *with anyone who bears the name of brother* if he is guilty of immorality or greed, or is an idolater, reviler, drunkard, or robber" (1 Corinthians 5:11).

Of course he has to be speaking of people for whom this is an impenitent lifestyle. But noting that "such were some of you" he of course makes welcome those who had changed and turned from those behaviours and lifestyles (1 Corinthians 6:11).

TRUE UNITY POSSIBLE

On the other hand, true unity is both possible and required where the moral and ethical norms of Christian faith are embraced and obeyed and where there is a true and deep intellectual and theological embrace of the deity and humanity of Jesus.

If those two major criteria are operative, we have a basis – and indeed obligation – to seek unity and fellowship with other believers, groups, or denominations.

This raises on the macro level the whole so-called ecumenical challenge of modern times, as well as the practical personal and individual challenge on the micro level of the struggles of many believers who seek to be biblically faithful in certain denominations or local congregations.

3. The ecumenical challenge

My old dad, who was brought up in Scotland, was a great raconteur with a wicked sense of humour. The combination of these two accidents of history produced an encyclopedic galaxy of Scottish stories. One such story was about old Jock McGregor, who, in Glasgow in a thorough state of inebriation, woke his minister at two in the morning, and shouted for attention.

"What is it, Jock?" said the woken minister in bleary-eyed irritation.

"Ministerrr, I want to talk to yew about churrrch unity."

"Go home, Jock. I can't talk to yew about churrrrch unity at two a.m. Go home. And besides, Jock, yew're drunk."

"But, ministerrr," remonstrated Jock, "it's only when I'm drunk that I want to talk about churrrch unity!"

At which my dad, an old-time, unreconstructed Anglican

roared with sympathetic laughter, as if to say: "I think old Jock's got a point."

Many others might despairingly agree, not least those in many mainline denominations which have become ever more theologically heterogeneous.

OIKOUMENE

The word *oikoumene* in the original Greek meant "the inhabited world". That was its meaning in Luke 2:1 where the great New Testament historian records: "In those days a decree went out from Caesar Augustus that all the world [*oikoumene*] should be enrolled." Our word here derives from the Greek verb *oikeo* meaning "I dwell". From this concept came the notion in the early years of Christian history of a place where all Christians in the inhabited world *dwelt*.

It was not a long step thereafter to the notion of ecumenical councils such as those that were established in the fourth and fifth centuries. The understanding here was that in these councils the bishops of the "whole inhabited world" were present.

Not surprisingly in the sixteenth century, after the Roman Catholic Church had convened what they called the Ecumenical Council of Trent, the English Reformer Thomas Cranmer wrote from England to John Calvin in Switzerland that the Protestant churches should arrange their own council which could come together, and if need be oppose the findings, theology, and claims of Trent.

ECUMENICAL MOVEMENT

So from these kinds of beginnings and genesis came the twentieth-century developments where the term "ecumenical" came to mean that which unites or brings together – not just Christians from different areas but also Christians from different backgrounds and persuasions.

As to what we now call the Ecumenical Movement,

this is normally considered to have arisen out of the great Edinburgh Missionary Conference in 1910, which was in many ways the first really international conference of a multi-denominational nature. The theme and aim of that conference, interestingly enough, was basically mission, and what John R. Mott, one of the great visionaries of that gathering, declared as "the evangelisation of the world in this generation". In that vision there was a strong notion of the possibility of various churches and bodies coming together in order to fulfil this missionary task.

Unfortunately, what started with very clear purposes of mission and evangelism as well as a very clear theology, began, in due course, to be watered down in different ways until the emphasis on both biblical evangelism and biblical truth became, in the view of many, significantly muted.

ECUMENISM AND THEOLOGICAL CONFUSION

The consequence of this, as the years have rolled by, has been the notion of ecumenism becoming a source of both theological confusion and indeed theological division. Thus different denominations around the world had assorted groups within themselves who either strongly supported or strongly opposed the Ecumenical Movement generally and the World Council of Churches specifically.

That's why, for example, at the Lausanne Congress on World Evangelization held in Cape Town in October 2010, evangelicals with their strong biblical emphases gathered from close on 200 countries to look at the task of world evangelization, while the World Council of Churches representatives were only present in an observer capacity.

Clearly there are major divisions here. What are we to say?

THE BASIC ECUMENICAL IMPULSE IS LAUDABLE

There is little doubt that the basic, unifying, and underlying impulse of the Ecumenical Movement generally and the World Council of Churches specifically is laudable. The spiritual and theological instinct is sound. It would broadly speaking seem to be in line with our Lord's prayer in John 17.

Likewise, dialogue between Protestants and Catholics aims for better understanding, cooperation, and fellowship. Some even believe the great Reformation schism could one day be healed and the chasm bridged.

In any event, Christian fellowship and unity of purpose across these endless barriers are goals all true believers in Christ should work and pray for.

ANSWERS VARY

But such impulses do raise immediate questions about what *sort of unity* we are after and on what basis – as well as how this could be achievable. The answers vary of course from different sectors of the church as well as from different individual believers. For some ecumenism is a term of delight. Angel voices sing all around it. For others it is synonymous with theological compromise, feebleness in world missions, and perilous acts of flirting with interfaith's watering down of the gospel.

Such sceptics cannot see how such interfaith unity could ever serve as a witness of anything to the world.

PERTINENT QUESTION

In any event we do have to ask the pertinent question:

What does the text of John 17 say? Clearly it is speaking of a spiritual unity of all true believers, which though positional nevertheless has to be made real and evident. But the prayer itself is not about organisational oneness per se, the Godhead not being held together by a committee but in spiritual oneness.

THE PROBLEM OF DEFINING A CHRISTIAN

Of course, part of the problem here – if we are seeking for a so-called "compelling witness" – is that our modern context reveals a plethora of differing understandings even to what a Christian actually is. Some see a Christian as someone raised and educated in the West – somehow or other a late child of what used to be called Christendom, but which is now largely defunct. Even if you come from a pseudo-Christian culture you are held by some to be a Christian.

For others a Christian is one who is basically a theist and roughly lives by traditional Christian moral principles.

Others see a Christian as a baptised person who is also a church member, either nominal or actual.

For yet others a Christian can be defined only as one who professes to have been "born again" and become committed to Christ.

Another category would say a Christian is anyone who is a jolly good fellow and attends their Anglican church at Easter and Christmas!

A final category could be the "sprinkler Christian", you know – sprinkled with water at baptism, confetti at their wedding, and earth at their funeral!

So right here there are serious and very complicating definitional differences and problems.

And there are still others.

THE ADDITIONAL PROBLEM OF AUTHORITY

The unity, fellowship, and definitional problem is further compounded for us with the current different understandings of spiritual authority. For the Roman Catholic, it is the Bible interpreted by tradition and the teaching authority of the church (the Magisterium) over which the Pope presides. The Bible and tradition were placed on a par with each other at the Roman Catholic Council of Trent, which met in three stages from 1545 to 1563.

For the Anglican, according to the church's "Thirty-nine Articles", authority is supposed to reside in Scripture alone (clauses 6, 8, and 20), but over time this has been muddled by other claims for authority in other areas such as tradition, reason, culture or the Lambeth Quadrilateral (as revised in 1888 from an Episcopalian Quadrilateral formulated in Chicago in 1886). The Lambeth Quadrilateral articulates Anglican identity as being the acceptance of the Holy Scriptures, the creeds, the sacraments of baptism and Holy Communion and the historic episcopacy.

For the sixteenth-century Reformers, as for modern so-called evangelicals and Pentecostals, it was, and is, *sola scriptura* (the Bible alone) that formed the basis for authority.

Ouch, folks! There it is. We gotta problem!

To navigate all these differences and complexities is a challenge indeed.

THE BIBLE AS COMMON DENOMINATOR

Perhaps fortuitously, in all these positions on the nature of authority, it is the Bible that is the common denominator, and therefore surely the best place to find guidance – at least initially – for bridging the assorted chasms, or at least understanding why the chasms exist.

So let's try riding for a while with John Wesley who said: "I began not only to read, but to study the Bible, as the one, the only, standard of truth, and the only model of pure religion."[2]

The Roman Catholic theologian, Hans Küng, conveyed the same conviction when he wrote: "The Church must ever and again wander through the desert, through the darkness of sin and error... There is, however, one guiding light it is never without, just as God's people in the desert always had a guide: *God's word is always there to lead the Church*" (my italics).[3]

Perhaps then there are a few pointers in Scripture itself to help us through.

i. The Jew outwardly and the Jew inwardly

In the Bible there is an instructive distinction effectively brought between the one who is a "Jew outwardly and a Jew inwardly" (Romans 2:28–29). The statement implies that some Israelites were genuine believers in Jehovah, real followers of Him, but that some were not. Commenting retrospectively on this from the New Testament perspective, the writer to the Hebrews can bring the divine words about those Old Testament Israelites who rebelled in the wilderness: "Therefore I was angry with that generation, and I said, 'They always go astray in their hearts, and they have not known my ways.' As in my anger I swore, 'They will not enter my rest.'" (Hebrews 3:10–11). The notion is clear here of the authentic and the inauthentic being among the people of God.

This is further underlined in the apostle Paul's warning in 1 Corinthians 10:1–8, where some professed Old Testament believers had God's approval, while others did not.

As we have seen, Paul makes the same point in Romans 2:28–29: "For a person is not a Jew who is one outwardly, nor is true circumcision something external and physical. Rather, a person is a Jew who is one inwardly, and real circumcision is a matter of the heart – it is spiritual and not literal. Such a person receives praise not from others but from God."

So among both the Jewish and the Christian believers there were the spiritually good guys and the spiritually bad guys, all wrapped up in one company.

This also ties up with the biblical picture of the "faithful remnant" of Israel as a minority group of faithful believers within the wider nation (see, for example, Isaiah 10:20; 46:3; Jeremiah 6:9, and so on).

Clearly the apostle is carrying into the church these warnings of the authentic and the inauthentic in the visible life of God's so-called people.

ii. Wheat and tares

This concept is also picked up in Matthew 13 where our Lord tells a parable of a field in which seeds of wheat and tares – which when blossomed look very similar – are both sown in one field. The wheat seeds, sown by "the Son of Man" (verse 37) are the "sons of the kingdom" (verse 38a), and "the weeds are the sons of the evil one" (verse 38b); "the enemy who sowed them is the devil" (verse 39).

The thrust in this parable of "both growing together until the harvest" (verse 30) clearly conveys that in the church, side by side, there will be an admixture of genuine and phoney and of true and false believers, both of whom profess to belong to God. However, the parable conveys that it is not always possible to distinguish true from false, as wheat and tares look so alike. Beyond that, great harm may come from premature human efforts to separate the false from the true – "lest in gathering the weeds you root up the wheat along with them" (verse 29). No, our Lord seems to be saying, leave the final identification and separation of true and false to me, the "Son of Man" (verse 41), and the ultimate judge of all.

iii. True and false teaching

But in the meantime we are most unwise if we think there is no difference between wheat and tares, because clearly the one can strangle the other. Hence Paul's warning to the Ephesian elders to be on guard against "the fierce wolves… *among your own selves*" who "will arise speaking perverse things" (Acts 20:29, 30). In other words, within the church, false and perverse teaching can arise which can imperil the true.

Paul can likewise warn of people "holding… a form of religion, but denying its power" (2 Timothy 3:5a). His succinct advice: "Avoid such people" (verse 5b). He does not say "cling to them in fellowship, regardless". In the next breath he likewise warns of "men of corrupt mind and *counterfeit* faith" (2 Timothy 3:8) who "oppose the truth" (verse 8).

So here "counterfeit faith" and "the truth" are clearly

juxtaposed. They are a reality inside the church. Moments later he warns Timothy to "beware" (2 Timothy 4:15) of Alexander the Coppersmith who "strongly *opposed* our message" (verse 15b). So in the church there are even opponents of the truth bringing messages that are "counterfeit".

Don't teach any different doctrine

Very instructive is Paul's urging Timothy and all his colleagues in leadership "not to teach any *different* doctrine" (1 Timothy 1:3) than what they have learned from him, nor be like those who have "swerved" – a very vivid image – from his teachings (1 Timothy 1:6), and are "without understanding [in] either what they are saying or the things about which they make assertions" (1 Timothy 1:7).

Indeed, says the Apostle, "Pay close attention to yourself and to your *teaching*; continue in these things" (1 Timothy 4:16). A sound personal life and sound teaching are two key twins in the life of the Christian – especially in the life of the Christian leader or minister.

Deep concern for truth

Clearly, throughout Paul's letters – as here with Timothy – his deep concern is for truth to be preserved and error to be confuted. That's why he can tell Titus of one of the requirements of an elder being that "He must have a firm grasp of the word that is trustworthy in accordance with the teaching, so that he may be able both to preach with sound doctrine and to refute those who contradict it" (Titus 1:9). Again here in juxtaposition in the church are teachers of "sound doctrine" and "those who contradict it".

Likewise Jude, in his single chapter letter to unidentified readers, can appeal to them "I... appeal to you to contend for the faith that was once for all entrusted to the saints" (Jude 1:3). Why? Because "certain intruders have stolen in among you, people who long ago were designated for this condemnation as ungodly, who *pervert* the grace of our God into licentiousness and deny our only Master and Lord, Jesus Christ" (verse 4).

So here again we learn of the possibility of there being church people who will "pervert the message of grace", even getting into licentiousness and then going beyond that to "deny" our Lord Jesus Christ. It is a chilling warning. So there is no sense here that it doesn't really matter what is taught in church, so long as we are all nice gals and guys and jolly sincere!

Meaning does matter

For all the New Testament writers, the meaning clearly *does* matter, and the concern to guard and protect the truth of the gospel message against false or erroneous teachings is all-pervasive. And, as earlier noted, in our Lord's letters rebuking the seven churches in the book of Revelation, His concern about false teachings is everywhere.

Returning to the words of Don Carson, we note his observation that: "It does not take much knowledge of the current ecclesiastical and theological scene to recognize that, if basic New Testament tests are preserved and applied to the sweep of modern Christendom, not everything that calls itself Christian truly qualifies."[4]

Uniting wheat and tares?

So, Carson adds,

> if ecumenists seek to join together into one organization all branches of "churchianity" known to Christendom, then they are trying to unite wheat and tares... Whoever cites John 17 to justify a unity that embraces believer and apostate, disciple and renegade, regenerate and unregenerate, abuses this passage. Such ecumenism has its roots not in Scripture but in misguided (if well-intentioned) notions of what New Testament Christianity is all about.[5]

Part of the problem is that there are some whose so-called charity, broad-mindedness, and tolerance want to include and embrace pretty well everyone, so long as they sincerely profess some species of spirituality, or religiosity. This vision in fact reflects secular liberalism more than Scripture.

Thus can Chris Sugden of the Oxford Centre for World Mission note: "Secular liberalism places the value of inclusion over against faithfulness and faith. The claim to speak from the centre must face the challenge of whether the faith that defines the centre is the centre of faith or the centre of the secular vision of inclusion."[6]

Don't separate from the visible church but reform it

That said, most scholars seem agreed that when the Reformers spoke of the visible and invisible church, it was not with a view to separating from the visible church but to reforming it. Because the real and true church of Christ consists of real people, it can never in reality be exclusively invisible! The point is to make the invisible church visible, real, and active in a desperately needy world. The challenge is to avoid a hair-trigger readiness to split away into splinter groups.

In fact, although the Reformers did ultimately split from Rome, that was not their original intention, and they were against what the late David Watson, a great British churchman and evangelist, called

> the constant tendency to cream off from the visible
> church a spiritual élite to form a "pure" fellowship
> consisting only of members of the invisible church.
> Although the hidden and spiritual aspects of the church
> are of prime importance, its visible form, complete with
> inevitable mixture and impurities, is part of its essential
> nature.[7]

Noted Karl Barth once: "If we say with the creed, *credo ecclesiam* (I believe in the church), we do not proudly overlook its concrete form…"[8]

Incidentally, this notion of the invisible and visible church is present also in St Augustine's writings and habitually employed by John Wycliffe, and the Reformers.[9]

iv. Seek a principled ecumenism

In the light of all this, what then should we be seeking when thinking about how we find unity with other groups, churches, or clusters of churches? I believe the answer lies in lovingly and graciously seeking what some have called a "principled ecumenism". Or if you like, "a biblical ecumenism", which John 17 could affirm. It would have, as I see it, several commitments:

- **A commitment to walk the way of love**, especially with all who profess to be Jesus followers. "I made your name known to them [meaning, character] and I will make it known, so that the *love* with which you have loved me may be in them, and I in them" (17:26).

- **A commitment to pursue that posture of conviction on essentials, liberty on non-essentials and love over all.**

- **A commitment to pursue biblical truth** in dialogue, and even shared worship and study, accepting our need, as the Lord prayed to be "sanctified in the truth" (verse 17a). Why? Because "your word is truth" (John 17:17b). The prerequisite for this pursuit of truth has to be not so much an identical view of Scripture's nature and inspiration, but rather a willingness "to take the Bible seriously" and seek to discern what the text (the Word) actually says via the historico-grammatical method. This allows the grammar, vocabulary, and syntax of a passage to tell us firstly what it is saying in its natural and obvious sense, *but also* to open up to us what it meant in the historical context in which it was first written. From that can be made a transposition to what it means for us now. So we ask: "What does the text say? What did it mean then? What does it mean now? What does it mean for me?" We are thus looking at the two horizons of the text. Then and now.

- **A commitment to pursue the early church commitment,** which enabled them so effectively, to continue "steadfastly in the *apostles' doctrine* [truth], *fellowship* [the outworking of love], in the *breaking of bread* [sacramental life], and in *prayers* [worship and petition]" (Acts 2:42, NKJV). This was unquestionably the inner key and secret to the early church's explosive growth and dynamic power.

- **A commitment to keep in mind that within almost any Christian fellowship, denomination, congregation, or denominational cluster** (such as the World Council of Churches, World Evangelical Fellowship, and so on), **there will inevitably be an admixture of wheat and tares,** of authentic and inauthentic, of truth and error, of the church visible and the church invisible, and of the New Testament equivalent of "Israel after the flesh and Israel after the heart" (see Romans 9:1–8) and it is not our task judgmentally to sort out which is which. That is God's ultimate task. Nor ultimately will He finally avoid it or evade it (see Matthew 13:41–42; 7:21–23; 2 Thessalonians 1:5–10; John 5:22–29). At the final judgment there will be a separating and a sorting out of which is which (Matthew 25:31-46; Revelation 20:11–15). Let's be very clear on that.

- **A commitment to seek out fellowship, understanding, and cooperation with genuinely Christian churches, groups and individuals, and** *"If it is possible,* so far as it depends on you, *live peaceably with all"* (Romans 12:18). And we withdraw from such efforts only if there is a clear denial of Christ, or of the Word of God, or the gospel of grace, or of proper Christian behaviour.

So then:

4. Can a Christian believer concerned for both unity and truth ever leave his or her denomination or congregation?

My dear Professor of Church History at Fuller Seminary, the late Geoffrey Bromiley, one of the greatest church historians of the twentieth century, used to give us students his take on the question heading this section.

His answer was: "You should not leave the Christian fellowship, group or denomination in which you were raised unless it either becomes apostate or throws you out." As he was both Anglican and English, as well as a Cambridge man, he had a head start in my taking his voice more seriously than other voices!

Funny how a word like his can stick in one's mind so that it becomes a settled life-conviction.

Bromiley used to say, with the perspective of a deep grasp of twenty centuries of church history, that these breaks or hair-trigger and over-eager departures from one's denomination usually bring "short-term gains, but long-term losses". A penetrating thought.

JOHN WESLEY

While Wesley never declared the Anglican Church apostate, he did with his converts fear "putting live chicks under dead hens", hence his formation of the first-class meetings and then the "societies". But, he affirmed, in 1776, "We will not, dare not separate from the church. We are not Seceders, nor do we bear any resemblance to them."[10]

However, the Anglican Church so opposed, sidelined, marginalised, and finally excluded John Wesley from their pulpits that he was effectively thrown out. This is very clear when one reads his journals where he discusses these issues and problems endlessly. They are highly instructive and illuminating. I commend them to you.

Wrote Wesley:

It was still my desire to preach in a church, rather than in any other place; but many obstructions were now laid in the way... Being thus excluded from the churches, and not daring to be silent, it remained only to preach in the open air; which I did at first, not out of choice, but out of necessity.[11]

THREE OPTIONS

In the case of denominations that are theologically heterogeneous, or ones that seemingly have got into theological compromise, John Stott says he sees three options.

Firstly, "separation or secession". Some form of doctrinal purity may be secured, but unity is lost. And love is betrayed.

A second option is "compromise and even conformity". This means staying put where we are and just going happily with the flow, keeping one's head down and maintaining a species of peace or truce. This time love is not compromised, but truth is. And so is courage.

The third option is

comprehensiveness without compromise, that is staying in without caving in. Frankly it is the most painful of the three options. The other two options are easier because they are ways of cutting the Gordian knot. The first is to separate from everybody you disagree with, and so enjoy fellowship only with like-minded Christians. The second is to decline to maintain a distinctive testimony, and so regard all viewpoints as equally legitimate. These are opposite options (separation and compromise). But they have this in common: they are both ways of easing tension and escaping conflict. You either get out or you give in. The harder way, which involves walking a tightrope, is to stay in, while at the same time refusing to give in. This means living in a permanent state of tension, declining either to compromise or to secede.[12]

PURSUE TRUTH AND UNITY

Summing up, Stott observes that

> *the way of separation is to pursue truth at the expense
> of unity. The way of compromise is to pursue unity at the
> expense of truth. The way of comprehensiveness is to
> pursue truth and unity simultaneously, that is, to pursue
> the kind of unity commended by Christ and his apostles,
> namely unity in truth.*[13]

This seems to me to be right and, ultimately, the best way to go, without any of us in our churches feeling that we are the sole repositories of truth, or that we have nothing to learn from those of contrary viewpoints. Often our theological Samaritan will have useful insights for us!

In the meantime, believers who are in theologically heterogeneous denominations and who are also concerned for both truth and unity, will seek lovingly to remind their leaders – whether archbishops, bishops, or ministers – that "there are in fact limits to the principle of comprehensiveness in the church... The truth of God revealed in Christ may be flexible, but it is not infinitely flexible."[14]

Even so, we are not to be factious. Thus Paul can tell Titus pretty crisply: "After a first and second admonition, have nothing more to do with anyone who causes divisions" (Titus 3:10).

NO REUNION ALL ROUND!

But nor are we willing to go to the other extreme and sit idly by if our denominations or congregations risk fulfilling what Anglican-turned-Catholic Ronald Knox (1888–1957), tongue in cheek, lampooned as "reunion all round" and which appeared in his *Essays in Satire*. Its subtitle was "A plea for the inclusion within the Church of England of all Mahommedans, Jews, Buddhists, Brahmins, Papists and Atheists". In the new and universal church that he saw emerging, "nobody will be expected to recite the whole Creed", he wrote, "but only such clauses as he finds relish in; it being anticipated that, with good fortune, a large congregation will usually manage in this way to recite the whole Formula between them."[15]

Nossir! That kind of thing gives grounds to biblically concerned believers to leave churches, as Knox did.

"The muddle of the middle", as Dr Calvin Cook, another of my greatest mentors, and now with the Lord, used to call it, is not where we are required to live.

WHAT'S YOUR COUNSEL?

So then, what counsel would you give to a minister friend of mine whose homosexual bishop told him: "I forbid you to preach conversion to any baptised Anglican"?

And what of another missionary doctor friend of mine who was a deacon in the leadership of a cathedral and who ran the cathedral's Bible studies. Then along came a new dean, much less sympathetic to biblical things, who told my friend: "I don't want you to talk about the new birth or the Holy Spirit in the Bible studies." As he had no hyper-Pentecostal or extreme views of the Spirit's work, my friend was very perplexed and startled. So he remonstrated with the dean, who then removed him from being a deacon, and from leading the Bible studies, which he then closed down, and told my friend and his wife they must "just sit in the congregation".

But as my friend received no spiritual food from the preaching, and his ministry offerings were spurned, and his soul was starving and shrivelling, he finally decided to call it a day. He is now a key layperson, and a significant leader in a Baptist church. So were he and his wife right to leave their denomination? Effectively they had been told: "[We] have no need of you" (1 Corinthians 12:21). Was rejection ejection, as per historian Geoffrey Bromiley's second criterion for validly leaving your church – namely if you are thrown out or ejected? Comes pretty close. They could neither bury their gifting, nor offer their contribution. And they *were* people with a valid and recognised ministry. They had gifts of leadership also. Orthodox in doctrine. Dedicated for service. Willing to contribute. But, "No, you just sit in the congregation."

Were they right to leave that cathedral?

You tell me.

BREAKING FOR CULTURAL REASONS

Of course some, especially the young, for basically cultural reasons, break fellowship and leave churches or denominations especially older ones, because they don't like the dreary preaching style, or the music is not "Ancient and Modern", but "Ancient and Obsolete"! Or the organ too lugubrious. Or the ethos too this or too that. And many young sort of "surf the churches", searching out both preaching and worship styles which culturally fit who they are, until finally they find a place that is "cool".

There are few theological issues here, one would imagine, except that they *do* want to be where the gospel is faithfully and recognisably preached and where effective discipling takes place. This has to be seen as a real challenge to all pastors. Of course people do want spiritual food, and if it is too long denied in one place, they will seek it elsewhere. As I've pointed out to a few pastors who have complained to me of other pastors sheep-stealing their people, sheep go where there's grass!

And even to those inclined to search around, the challenge of these chapters remains valid – namely to walk the road of both truth and love, with the twin commitments of both biblical faithfulness and Christian unity held in creative tension, even if it's pretty painful at times!

DOUBLE ORTHODOXY OF DOCTRINE AND COMMUNITY

In conclusion and summary, we register afresh that our heavenly Father *loves* the world, and so desperately wants His church to reach those in it; for it to be credible to the world; and for its message to be believed by the world that His Son, just hours before His agonising death, could so have us on His heart as to pray this impassioned prayer that we live together and minister to the world together, not only in love and unity, but in what Francis Schaeffer used to call "true truth".[16] Schaeffer's insistence, which neatly captures that of John 17, is that we need two orthodoxies – a double orthodoxy in fact. "Just as there needs to be an orthodoxy of doctrine, there needs to be an orthodoxy of community."[17] That way we will certainly be able, credibly, to reach the world, "so that the world may believe" (John 17:21).

A prayer in the Anglican Prayer Book rightly puts it this way: "Give your church power to preach the Gospel of Christ, and grant that we and all Christian people may be *united in truth, live together in your love, and reveal your glory in the world*" (my italics).

That's what our Lord wanted. Clearly, it was not just the church that was on His heart, but the world.

Likewise must both be on ours.

Chapter 15

Love – The Eighth Mark

"Without true Christians loving one another, Christ says, the world cannot be expected to listen, even when we give proper answers... (so) after we have done our best to communicate to a lost world, still we must never forget that the final apologetic which Jesus gives is the observable love of true Christians for true Christians. As with the Early Church, so with us, people should say above all 'Behold how they love one another.'"

Francis Schaeffer, *The Mark of the Christian*[1]

"Love is the primary word given to guide us into the best we can ever hope to receive or give."

Eugene Peterson[2]

"A new commandment I give to you, that you love one another."

Jesus, John 13:34a

"I ask... that the world may know that you have sent me, and have loved them, even as you have loved me."

Jesus, John 17:20, 23

"I have made your name known to them, and I will make it known, so that the love with which you have loved me may be in them...".

Jesus, John 17:26

We spoke much of unity in our last two chapters. But now our Lord prays the almost unthinkable: *"that the love with which you have loved me may be in them..."* (verse 26). Without question, the primary key in achieving anything Christian lies in rising to the exacting and beautiful demands of love.

In fact, in my view, and based on my own struggles to love unconditionally, I would say that the command to love is the single most gutsy and difficult challenge of all the Bible. It sounds so easy, so romantic, so deliciously sentimental, so dreadfully prosaic, one might almost say, that we dismiss what it asks of us as if it were some light thing.

But it isn't. It is blood and guts hard.

In fact, it's the hardest thing in the Christian life. Ask me to preach? Fine. Or teach? OK. Or lead a Bible study? Can do. Sing a hymn? Sure, I can hold a tune. Chair a committee? Piece of cake. Help an old lady over the road? No problem, so long as she walks slowly! Give a tithe? Done it for ever. Help someone I like? That's fun. Share a word of witness? Not too difficult. Go to church? My folks got me into it as a kid. Been at it ever since.

But love? All the time? Everybody? My neighbours? All of them? Even as myself? Good, bad, and ugly? Heretics too? Those who stab me in the back? Or assassinate my character?

Hey, come on! That's something different! That is tough. Very tough indeed. Impossibly so, one might say.

But where such unconditional, indiscriminate love does truly operate, not just for those congenial or lovable to us, but for those who are unlovely, unappealing, plain objectionable, even hostile to us, then the world stops and takes note. People sit up and register something special.

Different symbols

In reality, down through the centuries of the church's life, people have displayed different symbols to show they are Christians. Some adorn themselves with a necklace with a cross or pendant. Or a bracelet. WWJD, it asks. What Would Jesus Do? One friend of mine wore a lapel badge – 70 x 7. Yes, the 490 times we are meant to forgive. He was on about 489 then! Still others put a fish symbol on their car. Some like a bumper sticker: "The Messiah is the Message." "Smile, God loves you." "Love your enemy. It will drive him crazy."

Of course, we don't really object to all the symbols. But there is one mark which makes the final difference, which constitutes the final apologetic when all pleading, arguing, and preaching have run their course and failed – one mark which will stand when time becomes eternity – one mark which lasts when all else has passed away.

And it is the mark of love. "So faith, hope and love abide, these three; but the greatest of these is love" (1 Corinthians 13:13).

A new commandment

As our Lord prepares to end His earthly ministry and to face the agonising and wrenching ordeal of the Cross, and manifest to the world the ultimate expression of divine, forgiving love, He presents to His little panting band of perplexed followers what it was that He wanted as their distinguishing mark, as the mark of the Christian: "A new commandment I give to you, that you love one another; even as I have loved you, that you also love one another. By this will all men know that you are my disciples, if you have love for one another" (John 13:34–35).

And Jesus seems to be saying: "Let this be the badge by which you will be known, and the dynamic by which you will prevail in taking my message to the uttermost parts of the earth."

To be sure, the world would in due course get the message and its import when after the frantic bewilderment of the Cross, the breathtaking, universe-changing happening of the resurrection, and the overwhelming Pentecostal outpouring of the Spirit, the disciples of Jesus then took to the streets as followers of a leader who had been judicially murdered, and preached forgiveness. Yes, they preached forgiveness!

That had never happened before. That was different. For history knew no precedent. No violent protests. No street marches. No taking up weapons against the wicked perpetrators of that crime. No strikes bringing Palestine and its Roman rulers to their knees. No assassination of the Sanhedrin! No! Just the manifestation of their Saviour's love. At Pentecost. As they preached forgiveness and set forth the Cross.

And was not all this the first fruits of what our Lord had prayed for? So that the secular state in due time would say – "See how they loved one another."

What we do know most certainly is that it was not only precept and practice, and then prayer, but also love and its demonstration that our Lord was talking about in those closing and climactic hours of His earthly life.

The closing drama of course began in that Upper Room as the Feast of the Passover got underway, and John observes that "Having *loved* His own who were in the world, He *loved* them to the end" (John 13:1).

Then He does the unimaginable. He washes His disciples' feet (John 13:5). And sets them an unforgettable example which would be burned for ever upon their minds and hearts.

And then broke bread with them.

And even let one of them betray Him.

Then He taught them.

About lots of things.

One of these was love.

And He prayed about it too: "that the love with which you loved me may be in them" (17:26).

What He taught about love in those final hours

This new commandment (John 13:34), its parameters, shape, and extent, went surely higher than their benumbed minds could register. It was to be *"even as I have loved you"*. His love for them was to be the yardstick, plumb line and standard for them to each other. And this was before love's ultimate display on Calvary's tree.

Then they learned the missionary consequences of this love: "All men will know you are my disciples, *if* you have love for one another" (John 13:35).

More than that: "If you love me, you will keep my commandments" (John 14:15). But now the mighty word about another major consequence if they were thus obedient – He would pray the Father for the release into their lives of the Holy Spirit. And the Father would give "another Counselor, to be with you forever, even the Spirit of truth... he dwells with you and will be in you" (John 14:17). Their own internal instructor would "teach" (John 14:26) and "guide" (John 16:13) into this vitally important Christian component, which of course we've been talking much about, called truth.

Hard to take in

Now something hard to take in. Both Father and Son will love us and Jesus will manifest or make Himself and His love real and present to us, if having His commandments and keeping them, we show thereby that we love Him. Yes. Those who in obedience "love me will be loved by my Father, and I will love him and manifest myself to him" (John 14:21).

The image is further enriched as our Lord promises not only that Father and Son will "love" us, but that they will "come" to us, and make their "home" with us if we love Jesus and "keep [His] word" (John 14:23).

Now again He presses the point further. "This is my commandment, that you love one another as I have loved you" (John 15:12). And it is the sacrificial Calvary self-giving that is the measure of the love required, because "Greater love has no man than this that a man lay down his life for his friends" (John 15:13). At which He affirms He will call them His friends, "if you do what I command you" (John 15:14)

– and – so He implies, live and love sacrificially, even to the laying down of your lives for each other.

We hear such a word.

And tremble.

Who is adequate for these things? Not this sinner who is writing. That's for sure.

Now they hear more. "The Father Himself loves you, because you have loved me and have believed that I came from the Father" (John 16:27).

As it was too much for them to take in, so it is too much for us. It is a high goal, we cannot attain to it.

Surely our Lord knew just that. That was why it now had to be prayed about.

How our Lord prayed about love

Note what we highlight in chapter 17 verses 22–26:

> The glory that you have given me I have given them, so that they may be one, as we are one, I in them and you in me, that they may become completely one, so that the world may know that you have sent me and have **loved** them even as you have **loved** me. Father, I desire that those also, whom you have given me, may be with me where I am, to see my glory, which you have given me because you **loved** me before the foundation of the world.
>
> Righteous Father, the world does not know you, but I know you; and these know that you have sent me. I made your name known to them, and I will make it known, so that the **love** with which you have loved me may be in them, and I in them.

So what have we here? We have a climactic crescendo of intercession making us soar into realms unknown. It not only includes as He prays to the Father "the glory that I had in your presence before the world existed" (verse 5), and "the glory that you have given me" (verse 22), and the unity in the Godhead ("one, as as we are one", verse 22), but also into the unfathomable and mysterious depths and heights of Trinitarian love between Father, Son, and Holy Spirit. Now this is mystery. We may know a bit of our own love relationship with a spouse, child, friend, or colleague, but we can scarcely touch the hem of the garment of love existing within the Godhead.

Not in that Trinitarian bond are there any slips of love. Any little betrayals of love. Any discourtesies. Any conflicts of purpose. Any rivalries. Any jealousies. Any disconnects of communication.

No! All is perfection. All is understanding. All is unity of agenda and purpose. All is love. Perfect love. This is the glory and this the love, He reminds the Father, which the Father gave Him, "before the foundation of the world" (verse 24).

The character of God shining through

And note, the glory of God is there too – that glory that is the character of God shining through. A character whose primacy is love. For, yes, Father, He is saying, "I made your name known to them [character], and I will make it known [remember, the Cross was still to come], so that the love with which you have loved *may be in them* and I in them" (verse 26).

So, here's the bombshell. Here's the word of dynamite. Here's the inexpressible. He wants that internal, matchless, and Trinitarian Godhead love to be in us, His disciples. Yes, in us. Actually and truly in us.

But how can this be? How can it possibly be?

Only one way.

One solitary way.

Namely, if He – is – in – us.

Not through our being church members.

Or baptised.

Or confirmed.

Or attending a Bible study.

Or occasional communion.

But only if He is actually *in* us. "I in them," He says (verse 23), and gives that notion pride of place as He terminates the prayer: "I in them" (verse 26).

The vital clue

Here now is the amazing secret, the inner key, the vital clue, Jesus actually indwelling us.

My dear late friend, Bill Bright, distinguished founder of Campus Crusade, once said to me: "Michael, the Christian life is not just difficult to lead. It's impossible. And the only person who can live it is Jesus Christ, so we have to have Him in our hearts. Otherwise we can only fail."

St Paul understood this as He spoke to the Colossians about the riches of the glory of this mystery, which is "Christ *in* you, the hope of glory" (Colossians 1:27). To the Corinthians he put it this way: "Do you not know this, you are God's temple and that God's Spirit dwells *in* you?" (1 Corinthians 3:16). To the Ephesians it came thus: "you also are built into it [the holy temple of the Lord] for a *dwelling place of God* in the Spirit" (Ephesians 2:22). For the Galatians, the Apostle put it unmistakably clearly: "I have been crucified with Christ; it is no longer I who live, but Christ who lives *in me*" (Galatians 2:20).

The hymnwriter Charles Wesley sang and prayed it right:

> *Love divine all loves excelling,*
> *Joy of Heaven to Earth come down.*
> *Fix in us thy humble dwelling*
> *All thy faithful mercies crown.*[3]

So this love is not ours. It is derived. And it comes forth as we allow the Son to reveal to us "the name" (character) of the Father (verse 26). It is that character – if we can truly register and absorb it – that will in measure beget that love of God in us for others.

Noted George Newton: "Love is originally, primitively and essentially in the Lord, and from Him it is given down into the hearts of true believers."[4]

So it all becomes possible only as we literally "partake of the divine nature" (2 Peter 1:5). There is no other way.

Love unpacked

Of course our Lord here in His High Priestly Prayer speaks of love in this very general and generic way. But it is not unpacked for us. There is no elaboration. The Cross of course is still to come, where all the "unpacking" will be supremely displayed.

But there are two places in Scripture where teaching on love is substantially unpacked: 1 Corinthians 13 and Romans 12.

Let's major then into Paul's great hymn of love in 1 Corinthians 13. He is noting here that three things fail – prophecies, tongues, and knowledge (verse 8).

But three things last – faith, hope, and love. And the greatest of these is love.

Commenting on this grand chapter in general terms, Henry Drummond in his legendary little classic *The Greatest Thing in the World* wrote as follows:

> *Can you tell me anything that is going to last? Many things Paul did not condescend to name. He did not mention money, fortune, fame; but he picked out the great things of his time, the things the best people thought had something in them, and brushed them peremptorily aside. Paul had no charge against these things in themselves. All he said about them was that they would not last. They were great things, but not supreme things. There were things beyond them. What we are stretches past what we do, beyond what we possess.*

*There is a great deal in the world that is delightful
and beautiful; there is a great deal in it that is great and
engrossing; but it will not last.*[5]

Three zeroes

In my book of yesteryear, *The Politics of Love,* I paraphrased
the Apostle's notion this way:

*When we do noble things, but without love, we don't
score 50 per cent or 33 per cent or 10 per cent before
God. We get zero. Our grand egos reel. Our self-
righteousness protests. Our political zeal rebels.*

*First, the apostle takes up human speech. Whether
it be the mighty eloquence of political orators or the
charismatic utterings of the Christian faithful, if not done
in love, the score is zero. To God's ears it is all simply a
noisy gong or a clanging cymbal.*

*Second, if we have great prophetic gifts and can
challenge both Church and State, and if we have huge
intellectual or spiritual prowess or indeed mighty religious
faith, nevertheless if it operates without love, it scores
zero.*

*Third, if we have social concern and generosity or
passionate political love for justice so that we would give
our bodies to be burned, if we do it without love, our
score again is zero.*

*In South Africa (for example), where there are causes
on every corner and in every second cluster of people,
this Pauline word speaks to us with terrifying directness.
If we are doing these things without love, God's **agape**
love, they score zero and count in his sight as "wood,
hay or straw" (1 Corinthians 3:12).*[6]

So let's look then at Paul's ninefold anatomy of love to see what
is required if we would score differently and attain that love
which William Barclay called "unconquerable benevolence

and invincible good will". **Agape** love is God's "in spite of" love for us. It is God's unmerited love that is bestowed upon undeserving people.

Patience: Love is patient.

Kindness: Love is kind.

Contentment: Love is not jealous.

Humility: Love is not boastful or arrogant.

Courtesy: Love is not rude.

Unselfishness: Love does not insist on its own way.

Good temper: Love is not irritable or resentful.

Guilelessness: Love does not rejoice at wrong but rejoices in the right.

Fortitude: Love bears, believes, hopes, endures all things.

THE NINEFOLD ANATOMY OF AGAPÉ LOVE:

1. Patience

The Apostle states simply and clearly that "Love is patient" (1 Corinthians 13:4a). Patience is that capacity to endure difficult circumstances, situations, or people without becoming provoked or responding in an inappropriately negative way. It is that quality that some people are able to exhibit when they show forbearance under strain or when provoked by tiresome people with tiresome attitudes or tiresome manners of operating.

Paul urges in 1 Thessalonians 5:14–15 (NAB): "be patient with all. See that no one returns evil for evil; rather always seek what is good for each other and for all." Of course Paul also lists it in Galatians 5:22 as one characteristic of the fruit of the Spirit "against which there is no law". It is manifested also when there is always a ready grace to forgive or to show mercy or to manifest understanding and restraint when one is aggressively attacked or unnecessarily provoked.

I often think back into the apartheid years of the amazing patience that the African people manifested for so many decades under multiple provocations from that inhuman system. It is that ability not to go pop when one's fuse has burned to the very end! St Augustine once said that, "Patience is the companion of wisdom." And there are almost always positive outcomes when wisdom and restraint have prevented one blowing one's fuse. A Chinese proverb highlights the wisdom of patience: "One moment of patience may ward off great disaster, one moment of impatience may ruin a whole life."

2. Kindness

"Love is kind" (1 Corinthians 13:4a).

I think "kind" is one of the loveliest adjectives to describe any person. And the Bible is full of praise for this special characteristic. "An anxious heart weighs a man down, but a *kind* word cheers him up" (Proverbs 12:25, NIV). "He who is *kind* to the poor lends to the Lord, and he will reward him for what he has done" (Proverbs 19:17, NIV). And Scripture's other exhortations to this are numerous. Thus, "be kind and compassionate to one another, forgiving each other, just as in Christ God forgave you" (Ephesians 4:32, NIV). And of course the kindness required of us is basically a reflection of what the Lord manifests in His own nature so that He can affirm: "'I am the Lord, who exercises *kindness*, justice and righteousness on earth, for in these I delight', declares the Lord" (Jeremiah 9:24, NIV). Naturally it is again listed as one characteristic of the fruit of the Spirit in Galatians 5:22.

Our Lord was incredibly kind

Our Lord was incredibly kind to people and the totality of those multiple kindnesses has drawn people powerfully to Him for over twenty-one centuries. The fact is, as Mark Twain, once said: "Kindness is the language which the deaf can hear and the blind can see." I suspect it is true that at different stages of life we admire other people for different qualities in them. When we are young, I guess we admire people for being pretty or well built or impressive in appearance. As we get older we admire people for being clever and smart. Later on we admire people who seem to be successful and achieving great things. But I think as one reaches old age – and I am now in that category – one admires people most who are kind and who manifest kindnesses, even when situations do not require it. They just seem to go the extra mile to be kind and to bless. Such people find both a special place in my heart and gratitude. Perhaps in our commitment to show love we should aim to manifest a stream of nameless, uncatalogued, and unremembered acts of kindness.

I love that lovely Quaker statement: "I will pass through this world but once. Any good thing that I can do, or any *kindness* that I can show to any human being, let me do it now. Let me not defer it nor neglect it, for I shall not pass this way again."[7]

3. Contentment

"Love is not jealous" (1 Corinthians 13:4b).

In my book *The Politics of Love*, I noted that

> *the apostle's reference here is not to a crude condoning of an immoral status quo, nor to a wimpish acceptance of injustice, nor to a passive acceptance of wrong. He is speaking of a love that is not jealous. It does not fall prey to the tyranny of envy. It does not want what other people have. It does not manifest ill will to those more gifted than ourselves, more capable than ourselves, more powerful than ourselves, or more comfortable than ourselves. This generous-spirited love will not want someone else's position or prominence. It will not clamber over precept and principle to reach power. It will not demean, detract, belittle or diminish. This love puts its ambitions under God's control. How far we all are from this!*[8]

Contentment, it seems to me, means being able to be satisfied with what is in one's life and not always thinking that the grass is greener on the other side. There are many ways this can apply to us. It may relate to our finances, our station and place in life, the way we are perceived in society, or where we stand in the seniority stakes of life. I am always struck by the psalmist's word, particularly when it comes to positions of power and prominence: "For exaltation comes neither from the east Nor the west... but God... puts down one, And exalts another" (Psalm 75:6–7, NKJV). One of the negative sides of this coin is uncontrolled ambition. We have noted how this gripped Julius Caesar when he said: "I would rather be first at Brundisium than second at Rome." His ambition required him to be number one wherever he was. The notion of being number two was unthinkable. And as for the biblical idea of servant leadership, that was nowhere in the motivational universe of Julius Caesar.

But St Paul for his part can affirm that "Godliness with contentment is great gain" (1 Timothy 6:6, NIV).

In a sense, real Christian contentment requires us to find in our inward being a full satisfaction with our Lord in who He is to us, in the promises and assurances of His Word, and in being assured that His will and providences are prevailing in our lives.

4. Humility

"Love is not... boastful or arrogant," states the Apostle (1 Corinthians 13:4b).

Two of my very great heroes in ministry, as this book has already substantially revealed, are Billy Graham and John Stott. In both cases, one of the most striking characteristics and qualities about them is their humility. They just never saw themselves as big shots, but rather as servants of Christ trying to do faithfully that to which they had been assigned. Malcolm Muggeridge was overwhelmed by this particular quality when he met the legendary Mother Teresa in Calcutta.

The thing is that in such people there is no patting oneself on the back, no self-congratulation, no sense of superiority, no giving oneself airs, no pretension of being better than others.

As for our Lord, He was the ultimate example and, notes the Apostle in his famous passage on *kenosis*, or self-emptying, "though he was in the form of God, did not count equality with God a thing to be grasped, but emptied himself, taking the form of a servant, being born in the likeness of men. And being found in human form *he humbled himself* and became obedient unto death, even death on a cross" (Philippians 2:6–8).

This was the final and ultimate example. Thus likewise could He enter the houses of sinners, tax gatherers, the poor, the destitute, and the marginalised. He could commend a little child for its humility. He could wash the feet of His disciples.

The Lord approves humility

So small wonder that the Bible endlessly commends this quality and speaks of how the Lord approves of it. For example, "He does not forget the cry of the *humble*" (Psalm 9:12, NKJV). "Lord, You have heard the desire of the *humble*" (Psalm 10:17, NKJV). Said Jesus: "But he who is greatest among you shall be your servant. And whoever exalts himself will be humbled, and he who humbles himself will be exalted" (Matthew 23:11–12, NKJV).

Joseph Lamb, an astute observer of life once said: "The road to success leads through the valley of humility, and the path is up the ladder of patience and across the wide barren plains of perseverance. As yet, no shortcut has been discovered."[9]

Perhaps what is required of us is to pray that the Lord would "grant each of us that wholesome feeling of being extraordinarily small and incredibly unimportant."[10]

I conclude this little section on a lighter note with the lovely story of the reporter commenting to Winston Churchill about Mr Attlee, then leader of the Labour opposition in the

UK: "Well, Mr Churchill, at least Mr Attlee is a humble man." To which Churchill, with his unerring instinct for devastating repartee, replied: "Yes, Mr Attlee has a lot to be humble about!" Well, perhaps we can refrain from commenting on Churchill, but at least we all know that, like Mr Attlee, we too have "a lot to be humble about"!

5. Courtesy

Writes St Paul: "Love is not... rude" (1 Corinthians 13:5).

I am always profoundly challenged when I re-read and seek to grasp the implications of Paul's word to his disciple Titus when he told him always "to show perfect courtesy toward all people" (Titus 3:2, ESV). Any one of us reading these words has to feel convicted of our multiple failures in this regard, whether at home or in the workplace, or wherever we seek to contribute. And we can all think of people, whether high or low, rich or poor, prominent or obscure, who deep down could tell you of having been deeply wounded, alienated, or made intransigent by the cruel pricks of discourtesy. Of course it is easy to be polite to those we like or respect, or perhaps in utilitarian terms those from whom we want something, but the biblical exhortation is perfect courtesy always to all. Every one of us stands condemned.

Henry Drummond, commenting on this quality, could say, "Politeness has been defined as love in trifles. Courtesy is said to be love in little things. And the one secret of politeness is to love. Love cannot behave itself unseemly."[11]

Relationships oiled by courtesy

The hard fact is – and it's a beautiful one – that the wheels of interpersonal relationships and day-to-day life are most wonderfully oiled by courtesy. And surely it is a quality that comes from the Lord Himself. Thus could St Francis of Assisi once affirm: "Know... that courtesy is one of the properties of God."[12] I'm told Julian of Norwich used to speak of Jesus as "My Courteous Lord". That was her personal experience.

And even the tough, though eloquent, Roman orator Cicero could recognise that "Nothing is more becoming in a great man than courtesy and forbearance."

I well remember the first encounter I ever had with Harry Oppenheimer back in 1970. I was seeking support from him for our ambitious, year long, Mission '70 Project to Johannesburg with some 300 churches anticipated to participate. In trepidation I entered his inner sanctum at 44, Main Street. Oppenheimer rose and greeted this young, pip-squeak evangelist with the greatest courtesy, a warm smile, and an outstretched hand. He sat me down at a long table, offered me tea, and then, holding a sharpened pencil at the ready over a blank pad, he enquired graciously, "What can I do for you?" I guess he could have guessed! Anyway, his gentle eyes fixed me intently in his gaze as he listened to my errand. No impatience. No irritation that he'd done this sort of thing a thousand times before. Just courtesy. And real listening.

Our conversation over, he walked me to the door of his office, opened it, ushered me through, and followed me out. I was staggered. Then blow me down, he walked me along the corridors of his financial empire, chatting merrily all the way. Finally we were at the lift. With courtesy going beyond every call of duty, he pushed the button, waited for the elevator, shook my hand, again graciously waiting, and then said his au revoirs.

I left feeling like a million dollars and bathed in the warm glow of the matchless courtesy of a true Christian gentleman. No! I didn't get a million dollars! Though Mission '70 did receive a very handsome cheque!

However, I had seen courtesy exemplified. Perhaps that was more important.

So, affirms the Apostle, "Love is not rude." It does not have to resort to this poor imitation of strength.

6. Unselfishness

Notes the Apostle: "Love does not insist on its own way" (1 Corinthians 13:5). The King James version translates that: "Love… seeketh not her own." Two scriptures particularly – one from the Old Testament, and one from the New – have down the years challenged me in this regard. One is the divine word through the prophet Jeremiah: "Should you then seek great things for yourself? Seek them not" (Jeremiah 45:5, NIV). I suppose the most compelling reason for this divine injunction is that such things – whether power, or wealth, or position or whatever – if sought for selfishly for oneself, or as a dimension of our overweening ambition, are not worth anything anyway. Nor can the Lord readily trust us with such things if we are bent and resolved on seeking them for ourselves.

A powerful New Testament word on this is that of the Apostle in Philippians 2:4: "Each of you should look not only to your own interests, but also to the interests of others" (NIV).

If I think back to the bad old days of apartheid, the major problem with that policy was that whites were seeking after their own interests at the expense of those of black people. The dreadful policy of apartheid was the baleful consequence.

The Cross of Jesus properly embraced crosses out our self life and replaces it with Calvary love which wants the best things for other people, even before ourselves.

Perhaps the most endless supply of unselfishness with which our planet is blessed comes from the hearts and lives of so many mothers of this world. Even the discomforts of pregnancy and the pain of childbirth are normally bathed with the endlessly patient, unselfish concern of the mother for her child. Then think past all that to the myriad moments of selfless maternal caring, midst exhaustion, in the night risings to feed her squawking, impatient, demanding junior. Then the childhood years. Mum scarcely has a life of her own. It's fetching, carrying, cooking, sewing, picking up the pieces, wiping tears, and saying "there, there" over the millionth grazed knee or the billionth tumble. And if there's sickness, then morning, noon, or dead of night, Mum will be there regardless of fatigues or personal needs, to comfort, nurture, muse, console, provide, make comfortable. And then for the teenager, day and night demanding the earth, Mum will be there. Selfless, caring, giving, giving, giving. Unselfish.

Yes I thank my mum for this, and thank you to so many Mums in every corner of God's earth for showing your children that maternal incarnation of Jesus' unselfish self-giving. "Unselfishness personified" is a label many a grown man or woman would want retrospectively to attach to their mothers.

And was not Mary, the mother of our Lord, the supreme precedent?

7. Good temper

Again, with devastating simplicity and massive challenge, the apostle writes: "Love… is not irritable or resentful" (1 Corinthians 13:5). This is love that is not easily provoked. It can keep its cool and not react with intemperate words, almost always regretted, or hot-headed impetuosity. This is love that shows calmness of mind, steady emotions, and controlled composure. Probably most of us know times or seasons in our lives when anger or temper are hovering just beneath the surface, like a volcano about to erupt. Then all it needs is a provocative word from someone and we explode. Heat comes in and light goes out. Anger wins. Love loses.

Of course the worst manifestation of this is when we so-called "lose our temper". Some call it boiling over, or blowing one's top. Others speak of losing one's cool, or flying off the handle, or going ballistic.

Blessed are the self-controlled

Whatever language one uses, it speaks about a response that is out of control. So if "self-control" is one characteristic of the fruit of the Spirit, then at this point and in that regard, we are scoring a big zero. Interestingly enough when our

Lord in the Beatitudes promises: "Blessed are the meek, for they will inherit the earth" (Matthew 5:5), He is describing not the caricatured quality of "meek and mild" which speaks almost of passivity or even weakness, he is rather describing the quality of a God-controlled life. The Greek word for this, *praus*, was one of the great Greek ethical words. It was not speaking of spinelessness or feeble subservience, but of one who has exactly the right reactions in any given situation.

Thus, for example, could the ancients speak about the quality of meekness (Greek *praotes*) as defining every virtue as the mean between two extremes. So there could be, for example, the one extreme of the spendthrift or the other extreme of the miser. But in-between there is the generous person. The great commentator William Barclay writes: "*Praotes*, meekness… is the happy medium between too much and too little anger. So the first possible translation of this beatitude is: *Blessed is the man who is always angry at the right time, and never angry at the wrong time.*"[13]

The control of the Holy Spirit

Another regular Greek usage of the word *praus* speaks about an animal trained to obey the word of command and respond exactly as appropriate, for example a horse, to the touch of the reins on its neck, or the pull of the bridle in its mouth. In other words, the animal is under perfect control. Its responses are exactly appropriate to the stimulus. So Barclay can offer another and complementary translation of this beatitude as follows: "Blessed is the man who has every instinct, every impulse, every passion under control. Blessed is the man who is entirely self-controlled."[14]

That self-control of course does not come naturally to us but it is a control that emanates from the Holy Spirit and is given as one of His gifts.

Of course we have to note here that Scripture is not saying we should never be angry. And the New Testament records some occasions when our Lord was extremely angry and on one occasion even made "a whip of cords" so that he could drive out both animals and money-changers from the temple while overthrowing the tables at which they were plying their trade (John 2:15). The apostle Paul can even exhort the expression of appropriate anger but which does not transgress appropriate boundaries. "Be angry, but do not sin" (Ephesians 4:26).

Resentment and bitterness

And of course, the first cousin to inappropriate anger and irritability is resentment. We harbour some bitterness within us and hold onto it in our minds as a subject of angry inner contemplation. This can happen when we feel real or imagined grievances and don't quickly let them go or forgive them. Sometimes I have found it a useful exercise to try and think of any people anywhere in the world whom I resent or feel bad towards for any reason. Then I forgive them. This can be a deep challenge. But it is worthwhile working it through because once we do, and once we forgive, we are freed up and able to move on with our emotions uncluttered by damaging internal dynamics that do nothing but slow us down and incapacitate us for dealing in a controlled way with the real situation before us.

And the Apostle is saying that this basically is what love requires of us.

8. Guilelessness

This basically is Henry Drummond's one-word summary of Paul's affirmation that "Love... does not rejoice at wrong, but rejoices in the right" (1 Corinthians 13:6)

As I have written elsewhere about my own country of South Africa:

> *it is a curious thing, especially in this land where so much is wrong, to discover the astonishing degree in which many rejoice in the wrong. In seeming to lament it, they in fact wallow in it and love to narrate the latest*

horror as if basking in its beastliness. It is in most of us
a pervasive habit of mind. Sometimes self-righteous to
a degree, but birthed by an evil system (thankfully now
behind us), it can so lay hold upon us that no good or
right thing can be rejoiced over. No credit for anything
good or positive can be given to the enemy or the other
side. Everyone is made to walk small and no one but
I dare walk tall. It is the working of shrivelled spirits,
void of largeness of heart and of the luminous, positive
guilelessness of which the apostle here writes. So, God
give us the grace to be guileless, not rejoicing in the
wrong, but in the right, and knowing also that right is
right, even if everyone rejects it, and wrong is wrong
even if everyone accepts it.[15]

But love will rejoice in the right

On the other side of the coin of rejoicing in wrong is the
possibility of "rejoicing in the right" when we hear something
good or beautiful or wonderful that someone else has said
or done. We should be saying "that's a wonderful thing to
share", even though there may be a little niggling feeling of
reluctance inside because of secret jealousy or envy. But love
will rejoice in the right as much as it will decline to rejoice in
the wrong.

In fact, if we find it in any way difficult to rejoice in the
right or celebrate someone else's triumph because of those
tinges of envy, we should there and then sit down and write
to that person or phone them; perhaps send them a text
message or an email and commend them for their success or
triumph. Then pray for them for the Lord to continue to bless
their endeavours. There is nothing quite like that to kill off
any vestiges of envy which might remain within us or any
diminished capacities to rejoice in the right while genuinely
lamenting in our secret souls some moral lapse in the life of
someone we know.

Curiously enough, I have found genuine blessings coming

my way when I have sought to minister to, or commiserate with, some brother who has had a serious moral lapse. We do not excuse such things. But we refrain from the mechanisms of judgment lest we ourselves "should be a castaway" (1 Corinthians 9:27, KJV).

9. Fortitude

"Love… bears all things, believes all things, hopes all things, endures all things" (1 Corinthians 13:7).

This is a very distinctively Christian capacity that flies on the wings of love.

I just love the prayers of the apostle Paul. One of them that is exceedingly special to me is found in Colossians 1:3–14. One section is particularly potent where the Apostle prays: "May you be strengthened with all power, according to his glorious might, for all endurance and patience with joy" (verse 11). The two words "endurance" and "patience" are the translations of two fascinating Greek words. The first is *hupomone*. This means "fortitude", as being able to cope with, manage and endure difficult circumstances.

The second word is *makrothumia*, translated as "patience", as a capacity to cope with and manage difficult people. In a sense both words speak of Christian fortitude – on the one hand to cope with difficult circumstances – and on the other to cope with difficult people. Not only to cope with them, but to do so, the Apostle encourages us "with joy"! But he is careful to premise this by saying it requires our forsaking our own capacity to achieve this by ourselves, but in order to "be strengthened with all power, according to *his* glorious might" (Colossians 1:11). We can manifest this kind of endurance and patience only if we are plugged into and receptive of the power and glorious might of the living God Himself through the Holy Spirit.

Circumstances and people

These two qualities address the way all life divides out for all of us, namely into *circumstances* we live in and *people* we live with. Paul is here saying that love will enable us to bear whatever comes to us through either circumstances or people, to believe the best in all circumstances, to hope positively in every situation, and to persevere regardless of what we are facing.

Fortitude is the capacity to cope steadfastly with fear, pain, danger, as well as uncertain, complex, or intimidating contexts or intimidation. In fact, courage is perhaps the key virtue because it enables and equips us to carry out and guarantee all others.

C. S. Lewis cast this in a slightly different form in the oft-quoted "Courage is not simply one of the virtues, but the form of every virtue at its testing point."

De Klerk and Mandela

If I reflect back into my own South African context, I think former President F. W. De Klerk manifested enormous *political courage* in 1990 when he made the decision to release Dr Nelson Mandela from prison, unban the liberation movements, and pave the way for open, free, and democratic elections. He would obviously have known that in personal and political terms this was a suicidal act. But he finally came to the realisation that it was the right one. However it took courage and fortitude to embrace it.

Likewise on the other side, Dr Nelson Mandela manifested astonishing courage and political fortitude when he chose, in coming out of prison, to have an attitude of forgiveness and to seek reconciliation. That too, at one level, could have been an act of political suicide if the whole black population had rejected the road of reconciliation and forgiveness. But the black population of South Africa, which by that time had already manifested extraordinary fortitude and political patience, once again rose to the occasion to take the "road less travelled".

In the last analysis it was love that at the bottom of things was working in the minds and souls of both De Klerk and Mandela.

In embracing love's way of walking, bearing, believing, hoping, and enduring all things, we will find through the strengthening power and might of our Lord that neither circumstances nor people will finally get us down. Rather, we will find ourselves enduring, yes, to the very End of the Day.

*** ***

So there we have it. The ninefold anatomy of love. Clearly, love is not just a pleasant feeling or a happy emotion. As we said at the beginning, it is gutsy, tough, incredibly demanding, and surely the most exacting but rewarding requirement which Scripture could possibly put upon us.

Love from the centre of who you are

The apostle Paul summarises this practical love in his epistle to the Romans: "Let love be genuine", he implores (Romans 12:9).

Let's look at Eugene Peterson's translation of Romans 12:9–21 in *The Message*:

> Love from the center of who you are; don't fake it.
> Run for dear life from evil; hold on for dear life to good.
> Be good friends who love deeply; practice playing
> second fiddle. Don't burn out; keep yourselves fuelled
> and aflame. Be alert servants of the Master, cheerfully
> expectant. Don't quit in hard times; pray all the harder.
> Help needy Christians; be inventive in hospitality. Bless
> your enemies; no cursing under your breath. Laugh
> with your happy friends when they are happy; share
> tears when they are down. Get along with each other;
> don't be stuck-up. Make friends with nobodies; don't
> be the great somebody. Don't hit back; discover beauty
> in everyone. If you've got it in you, get along with

*everybody. Don't insist on getting even; that's not for you
to do. 'I'll do the judging', says God. 'I'll take care of it.'
Our scriptures tell us that if you see your enemy hungry,
go buy that person lunch, or if he is thirsty, get him a
drink. Your generosity will surprise him with goodness.
Don't let evil get the best of you; get the best of evil by
doing good.*

*** ***

So our Lord prays in the last sentence of His High Priestly
Prayer: "I made your name known to them, and I will make
it known, so that *the love with which you have loved me may be in
them, and I in them*" (John 17:26).

And perhaps the most compelling reason of all why we
should seek to walk this way of love is that this love is eternal.
Pope John Paul II once said: "Only love lasts forever. Alone it
constructs the shape of eternity in the earthly and short lived
dimensions of the history of man on earth."[16]

How do we attain it?

It is all so awesome, magnificent, and huge that we have to ask
ourselves again, and be forever repeating the question: How
do we reach to this love and or even begin to attain it? This
requires us to repeat again and reiterate the last two verses
of our Lord's prayer: "Righteous Father, the world does not
know you, but I know you; and these know that you have
sent me. I made your name known to them, and I will make it
known, so that the love with which you have loved me may
be in them, *and I in them*" (my italics).

The last four words "and I in them" can only mean
that this capacity for love, along with our Lord's intended
programme of continuing to make Himself known, can only
be enabled and made possible by the indwelling Jesus Christ
through the power of the Holy Spirit.

It all hangs on the enabling Holy Spirit. And so it is to

that matchless ministry that becomes the gateway to glory – both God's and ours – that we now turn.

Yes, "For yours is the kingdom, the *power* and the glory, for ever and ever. Amen."

But to love each other, Lord, as you and the Father love each other? Ouch, Lord. Help!

Chapter 16

Power – The Ninth Mark

"You shall receive power when the Holy Spirit has come upon you; and you shall be my witnesses in Jerusalem and in all Judea and Samaria and to the end of the earth."

Jesus, Acts 1:8

"Not by might nor by power, but by my Spirit, says the Lord…"

Zechariah 4:6

"Before Christ sent the church into the world He sent the Spirit into the church. The same order must be observed today."

John Stott[1]

"The power of God… is never an impersonal application of force from without… The Holy Spirit is God's way of being present with us, making us participants in His being and work."

Eugene Peterson[2]

"My speech and my message were not in plausible words of wisdom, but in demonstration of the Spirit and of power."

The apostle Paul, 1 Corinthians 2:4

"I made your name known to them, and I will make it known, so that the love with which you have loved me may be in them, and I in them."

Jesus, John 17:26

I remember the exact place, time, and setting when I saw it. Yes, when I saw that Jesus also prayed about the power of the Holy Spirit as one of the marks and characteristics He wanted in His church.

This bit of remembrance takes me right back to when I first put pen to paper on this volume, as referred to in my initial Preface. It was early in 1999, as you may remember if you read the Preface (!), and Carol was with me for a time of sabbatical rest and study at Trinity Western University near Vancouver, British Columbia. I had gone out for a retreat time with the Lord in David and Lesley Richardson's lovely Jabulani Cabin in the Rockies. It was to be some days of solitude before Carol joined me. The cold, bracing, bleak, and snowy weather outside made the little cabin all that much more warm, inviting, cosy, and comforting.

I was deep into my John 17 reflections when I found myself, as I had found myself many times before, wondering how and why it was that Our Lord could pray for His church both then and in subsequent centuries without referring to its need for the power of the Holy Spirit.

Suddenly I saw it! Then in the manner of Archimedes making his big discovery and yelling out: "Eureka!", I let out a great shout of doxology: "Yes, Lord, it is there! Halleluiah! Praise your Name!" Plain as daylight! And so powerfully. Indeed, Lord, how could it be more powerful because you locked this great truth into the closing four words of your prayer: **"and I in them."**

The truth I was looking for was climactically there. In many ways as plain as daylight for anyone to see other than a spiritual dumb cluck like me!

And so we look again at the very final words of the prayer: "I made your name known to them, and I will make it known, so that the love with which you have loved me may be in them, *and I in them*" (verse 26). That had to speak of the Holy Spirit.

After all, how in reality would Jesus be in them? By the Holy Spirit of course. And this He had made as plain as He possibly could in His Final Discourse (John chapters 14, 15, and 16). Indeed, as we have noted numbers of times before in this volume, the Final Discourse has all the clues to any meanings of mystery in the prayer. In a sense we are taking the theology of the Spirit in the Final Discourse and seeing it impregnated in those final words of the prayer. **"And I in them."**

So:

Who is the Holy Spirit?

THE HOLY SPIRIT IS THE SPIRIT OF GOD

Of course, by the time we reach the Final Discourse of Jesus, this is a basic teaching and assumption of Scripture. The assumption and teaching could scarcely be more basic and fundamental to the whole Bible, appearing as it does already in verse 2 of Genesis 1. Observed the Genesis writer: "In the beginning God created the heavens and the earth. The earth was without form and void, and darkness was upon the face of the deep; and the *Spirit of God* was moving over the face of the waters" (Genesis 1:1–2).

Both the Hebrew and the Greek words *(ruach* and *pneuma)*, translated as "Spirit" in our Bibles, carry the notion of spiritual energy creatively let loose as an executive spiritual force invading a person or situation, as power being exercised, or as supernatural spiritual life being demonstrated by action. Power in action is the basic idea in just under 100 Old Testament references to the "the Spirit of God".

And it is exactly this "Spirit of God" who comes in an empowering and enabling manner on assorted characters in the Old Testament. For example, even Pharaoh could acknowledge as he came face to face with Joseph that this was one "in whom was the *Spirit of God*" (Genesis 41:38).

The New Testament also uses this appellation in numbers of places, as when St Paul writes: "All who are led by the *Spirit of God* are sons of God" (Romans 8:14).

So what God does, the Spirit does. What God wants, the

Spirit wants. This understanding would already have been in the disciples as they heard Jesus' Final Discourse.

Then:

THE HOLY SPIRIT IS THE SPIRIT OF JESUS

Said historian Luke describing the missionary journeys of Paul and Timothy, "they attempted to go into Bithynia, but the *Spirit of Jesus* did not allow them" (Acts 16:7). Now this matured understanding, as described by Luke, was almost certainly not yet fully in the disciples as Jesus spoke to them in the Final Discourse. It was, however, something they were being forced to grapple with, just as when Jesus said: "When the Counselor comes, whom I shall send to you from the Father, even the Spirit of truth, who proceeds from the Father, *he will bear witness to me*" (John 15:26).

They were hearing of the one who seemingly would represent Jesus, guide them more fully into the truth of Jesus (John 16:13), and who would be to them Jesus in Spirit form internalised *in* them, as against Jesus in physical form standing *in front* of them. This Counsellor, He said, this Spirit of truth, not only will "dwell *with* you", as He put it (14:17) but "will be *in* you" (14:17).

I remember many years ago, when our children were small, Debbie and one of her little friends were sitting in the back of our car and going into town with Carol. As children in their simple loveliness can do, they began to talk about God. At which Debbie, the budding theologian, announced like the wise old owl with some finality that "You know, God is Jesus' surname!"

"Well," I figured chuckling, when a much-amused Carol told me this tale, "that's pretty good theology!"

THE MAN BEHIND THE PROJECTOR

But we must certainly note here that the Holy Spirit is the one whose role fundamentally includes glorifying Christ. Said our Lord: "He will glorify me, for He will take what is mine and declare it to you. All that the Father has is mine; therefore I said He will take what is mine and declare it to you" (John 16:14–15). This "Spirit of truth," said Jesus, "will bear witness to me" (John 15:26). The Holy Spirit, as it were, projects Jesus to us and to the world. He is like the man behind the projector, with the picture emerging from the projector being Jesus.

So every so-called "Holy Spirit revival", if it's authentic, will be a Jesus revival. Likewise every so-called charismatic movement of the Holy Spirit will be a Jesus movement. If therefore in a church you hear nothing talked about but the Holy Spirit, then you know there is something wrong, because the Holy Spirit will always project and glorify not Himself, but Jesus.

Canadian theologian Jim Packer puts it this way:

> In his new covenant ministry (for this is what Jesus was talking about) the Spirit would be self-effacing, directing all attention away from Himself to Christ and drawing folk into the faith, hope, love, obedience, adoration, and dedication which constitute communion with Christ. This, be it said, remains the criterion by which the authenticity of supposedly "spiritual" movements... may be gauged.[3]

THE SPIRIT AS FLOODLIGHT

Still with Packer, he has a lovely illustration of going to a church one winter evening in Canada when he was about to preach on the words "He shall glorify Me". As he got to the church, he saw the building floodlit and saw in that image exactly the illustration needed for his message. He commented in these terms:

> When floodlighting is well done, the floodlights are so placed that you do not see them; you are not really supposed to see where the light is coming from; what you are meant to see is just the building on which the

floodlights are trained… This perfectly illustrates the Spirit's new covenant role. The Spirit, so to speak, is the hidden floodlight shining on the Saviour.[4]

As the Holy Spirit, He is also –

THE SPIRIT OF HOLINESS AND SPIRITUAL FRUIT

Said Jesus: "But the Counselor, the Holy Spirit, whom the Father will send in my name, he will teach you all things" (John 14:26). If He is the *Holy* Spirit, then manifestly He is going to be concerned for our holiness. Or we could say that His major concern is our sanctification. This is tough, because most of the time we resist the challenge to holiness and shrink from the notion of being purified into the likeness of Christ. That can indeed be pretty painful and desperately challenging. Thus could Augustine once cry out: "Oh God, make me holy, but not too quickly!"

Of course we also all like the idea of Jesus baptising us with the Holy Spirit, but we are not sure at all about John the Baptist's words that Jesus "will baptize you with the Holy Spirit *and with fire*" (Matthew 3:11). The thing is that we realise fire to be about purging, purifying, cleansing, burning up dross, and incinerating garbage.

But the Bible is clear and unequivocal on this: "This is the will of God, even your sanctification" (1 Thessalonians 4:3, KJV). So the Spirit of God is much more interested in our characters than in our happiness and in the kind of people we are and are becoming than in what we accomplish. What the Holy Spirit will not sanction is our coming to Jesus singing "Just as I am…", and then remaining just as we were!

THE SPIRIT COMMITTED TO CHANGING US

Now listen to the Apostle talking to the Corinthians: "Do not be deceived; neither the immoral, nor idolaters, nor adulterers, nor sexual perverts, nor thieves, nor the greedy, nor drunkards, nor revilers, nor robbers will inherit the kingdom of God" (1 Corinthians 6:9–10). Then he adds: "And such were some of you" (verse 11a). That's where they had come from. Those were the kinds of people they had been. But all of that changed when the Lord got hold of them and worked in them by the power of the Spirit. So the Apostle adds: "But you were washed, you were sanctified, you were justified in the name of the Lord Jesus Christ *and in the Spirit of our God*" (verse 11b).

This washing, this sanctification, this justification, happens in and through the name of our Lord Jesus Christ *and* in and through the Spirit of our God.

FRUIT

And the major way He does this is through bringing into our lives certain qualities the Apostle calls fruit, which come from the Holy Spirit. Listen to Him: "But the fruit of the Spirit is love, joy, peace, patience, kindness, goodness, faithfulness, gentleness, self-control" (Galatians 5:22–23a). These qualities are not natural to us; they are the fruit of the Holy Spirit within us as we allow His release in our lives. And it gives us a certain spiritual walk or behaviour. Paul urges: "If we live by the Spirit, let us also walk by the Spirit" (Galatians 5:25).

The Spirit will also use certain means to move us forward in this direction, for example, our regular prayers, devotional life, Bible reading, attendance at church, receiving the sacraments, having Christian fellowship with friends in a home group or Bible study, reading Christian books, even listening to Christian messages on CDs or DVDs! By these means we are slowly led by the Spirit into habits of discipline and self-control which finally begin to bring forth the beginnings of the Lord's holiness in us.

Then the Final Discourse also leads us into understanding the Spirit as –

The Spirit of truth

Said our Lord: "I will pray the Father, and he will give you another Counselor, to be with you for ever, even the *Spirit of truth*" (John 14:16–17). Likewise our Lord affirms: "But when the Counselor comes, whom I shall send to you from the Father, even the *Spirit of truth* who proceeds from the Father, he will bear witness to me" (John 15:26). He repeats this again a few moments later: "When the *Spirit of truth* comes he will guide you into all truth; for he will not speak on his own authority, but whatever he hears he will speak, and he will declare to you the things that are to come" (John 16:13).

So then, here we have several dramatic references to the Spirit of truth. First of all, He is going to dwell with us and be in us (14:17). Secondly, He is going to teach us all things (14:26). Thirdly He is going to bear witness to Christ (15:26). Then finally He is going to "guide us into all truth" (16:13).

That's why we can never pretend truth does not matter. We cannot allow any old view of this or that to prevail so long as it is sincerely held. Nor will this "Spirit of truth" sanction people "swerving" from the truth (1 Timothy 1:6; 2 Timothy 2:18) or "twisting the scriptures" (2 Peter 3:16).

TRUTH CONCERNS INSPIRED BY THE SPIRIT

So where people have a deep concern for biblical truth, this is inspired and motivated by the "Spirit of truth". So if sanctification is the Spirit's work, then not surprisingly the Lord prays about all His disciples at any time anywhere: "Sanctify them *in the truth*; your word is *truth*" (John 17:17). And if consecration is something the Spirit leads us into, then unsurprisingly our Lord prays that they/we "may be sanctified *in truth*" (John 17:19), not consecrated in vagueness and in muddled compromises of conflicting positions.

In thinking of the High Priestly Prayer of Jesus following that Final Discourse, it is quite clear that if He refers to the Holy Spirit at least four times in those previous three chapters as "the Spirit of truth", then the disciples could never have missed what He meant or the agency by which it would come about when He prayed for them to be "sanctified in the truth" (17:17).

In like manner Cardinal Leon Joseph Suenens of Belgium could once write: "No generation can claim to have plumbed to the depths of the unfathomable riches of Christ. The Holy Spirit has promised to lead us step by step into the fullness of truth."[5]

The Holy Spirit is also:

THE SPIRIT OF SCRIPTURE

Our Lord affirmed in the Final Discourse that, "When the Spirit of truth comes, he will guide you into all the truth." Knowing, as He obviously did, that some of them would literally write scripture, He must surely have been assuring them that what they would write would be the consequence of having been guided into the truth by the Spirit of truth.

Certainly Peter could affirm that "no prophecy of scripture is a matter of one's own interpretation, because no prophecy ever came by the impulse of man, but men moved by the Holy Spirit spoke from God" (2 Peter 1:20–21). Says the apostle Paul: "All scripture is inspired [Greek *theopneustos:* "breathed out"] by God and is profitable for teaching, reproof, correction, and for training in righteousness" (2 Timothy 3:16). In other words, the Spirit-inspired Scriptures would set forth for our benefit and profit *what we should know* (teaching), *where we should stop* (reproof), *where we should turn* (correction), *and how we should live* (training in righteousness).

Then we find that:

The Holy Spirit is the Spirit of conviction and illumination

Now here's a wonderful truth for pastors, evangelists, and missionaries who spend much time preaching and declaring the gospel as our Lord explains that it is the Holy Spirit who will do the convicting and the convincing. So in the Final Discourse He declares: "if I go, I will send him [the Counsellor] to you. And when he comes, he will convince [or convict] the world concerning sin and righteousness and judgment" (John 16:7–8). In other words, it is not all up to us. It is the work of the Spirit of conviction to take gospel truths home at a deep level into people's hearts. He also convicts us not just of sin, but of sinfulness. The Spirit tells us that we are indeed sinners.

The apostle Paul is telling of the same "spirit of conviction" relating to the truth, when he says: "no one can say 'Jesus is Lord' except by the Holy Spirit" (1 Corinthians 12:3). Every one of us who has ever said a true yes to Jesus Christ as Lord and Saviour has done so with the help of the Holy Spirit. We did not get there on our own. The Reformers called this the Doctrine of Illumination, because it is the Holy Spirit who illumines the mind so that people can respond positively to the gospel. This sovereignty of the Holy Spirit in the conversion of others prevents preachers feeling inflated when they see results or deflated when they don't. We know it is the Spirit's work to bring results in terms of conversions.

THE HOLY SPIRIT AS AGENT IN EVANGELISM

This first came home to me clearly and forcibly in 1962 when I was a student at Fuller Seminary and preparing to go out in our summer vacation to South Africa's city of Pietermaritzburg for our very first citywide, interdenominational evangelistic endeavour. Into my hands had fortuitously come James Packer's wonderful little classic entitled *Evangelism and the Sovereignty of God*. I ate it up, drank it down, and let it find deep rest in my mind and soul.

Thus Packer could write: "In the last analysis there is only one agent of evangelism: namely, the Lord Jesus Christ. It is Christ Himself who through His *Holy Spirit* enables His servants to explain the Gospel truly and apply it powerfully and effectively."[6]

Personal experience

I was to need this truth well embedded in my heart when it came to the beginning of the Maritzburg Mission in August 1962.

As the mission got underway in the thankfully packed out city hall, I was grateful for a fair number of responses on the first couple of nights, maybe forty each night. But then in the middle of the week the responses took a significant dip. The brother who had been assigned the task of training the counsellors came to me after the Thursday night meeting: "Young man, when are you going to produce?"

He said he had these masses of trained counsellors but more than half of them had sat idle for each of the first few nights of the mission. In fact I was shattering his mission expectations! But Packer's book and the truth we are discussing came to my rescue.

"Brother, I can't produce magic rabbits out of a hat," I said to him. "The problem is that you are looking to me to produce. Producing fruit, convictions, and conversions is the work of the Holy Spirit. I can't do that. You have your eyes in the wrong place, brother. So, listen to me, I have a suggestion. Why don't you gather some of your lead counsellors and join me and my team at ten p.m. tonight and we will have a whole night of prayer. We will look to the Lord to move in the power of His Spirit and bring both conviction and conversions."

He looked startled. Then, committed man that he was, he agreed. So a whole group of us met in the local Congregational church. We prayed all night. It was a wonderful time. And certainly everybody's eyes moved off Michael and the

African Enterprise team and onto the Lord and the work of His Spirit.

Looking unto Jesus

Next night, I can assure you, we were all "looking unto Jesus the author and finisher of our faith" (Hebrews 12:2, KJV). And we were asking the Holy Spirit to work. As I arrived at a packed to capacity city hall, possibly the biggest crowd it had ever had, the atmosphere was absolutely charged. The Lord by His Spirit seemed to be electrifyingly present, which it hadn't been in the previous meetings.

After the message the response was so huge that it created a beautiful crisis for the head of the counselling department! In fact, he didn't have enough counsellors to deal with all the people responding. He was certainly a very happy chappy by the end of the evening and right on through the rest of the mission as wonderful results flowed!

Thus was I rescued from being cast to acute evangelistic outer darkness. The fact was that we had all seen the Holy Spirit at work and in the sovereignty of God bringing people to Himself as He convicted them of sin, righteousness, and judgment to come (John 16:8). And then enabled them to say, "Jesus is Lord" (1 Corinthians 12:3).

That is the Spirit's illuminating work.

THE HOLY SPIRIT IS ALSO THE SPIRIT OF NEW BIRTH

Listen to Jesus speaking to Nicodemus in John 3:5–8:

> *Very truly, I tell you, no one can enter the kingdom of God without being born of water and Spirit. What is born of the flesh is flesh, and what is born of the Spirit is spirit. Do not be astonished that I said to you, 'You must be born from above.' The wind blows where it chooses, and you hear the sound of it, but you do not know where it comes from or where it goes. So it is with everyone who is born of the Spirit.*

Nicodemus was apparently baffled and perplexed. But as a Pharisee and professional theologian, he should not have been. Nor should he have been baffled and perplexed by Jesus even mildly rebuking him saying: "Are you a teacher of Israel, [that is, a professional theologian] and yet you do not understand these things?" (verse 10).

Presumably our Lord was saying to him that as an Old Testament scholar he should have known about the prophecy in Ezekiel, for example: "A new heart I will give you, and a new spirit I will put within you; and I will remove from your body the heart of stone and give you a heart of flesh. I will put my spirit within you, and make you follow my statutes and be careful to observe my ordinances" (Ezekiel 36:26–27).

THE LAW WITHIN BY THE SPIRIT

This internalising of the law of God by the Spirit of God (compare Jeremiah 31:33) was what Jesus was referring to when just before His ascension He told the disciples to "wait for the promise of the Father" (Acts 1:4). Then He added: "But you shall receive power when the Holy Spirit has come upon you" (Acts 1:8). Wrote Titus: "he saved us, not because of deeds done by us in righteousness, but in virtue of His own mercy, by the washing of regeneration [new birth] and *renewal in the Holy Spirit*" (Titus 3:5).

THE MATCHLESS EXPERIENCE

The new birth is a matchless experience. Jesus initiates it, but the Holy Spirit is the agent. And in this He works an internal miracle in our hearts with a spiritual birth that is "from above" (Greek: *anothen*). In this new birth our hearts are changed and made spiritually alive in a new way through the Spirit of God *in us* (Romans 8:9–10).

This gives us a sense of being sons and daughters of the living God and of being enabled to speak to Him as "Abba! Father" (Romans 8:15), and we find a deep sense of family.

Says Paul, "It is the Spirit himself bearing witness with our spirit that we are *children* of God" (Romans 8:16).

That sense of newness

And not surprisingly, the new birth in the Holy Spirit makes us feel *new*. The Sunday after my conversion at university I saw the following scripture on the billboard of a church in Cambridge and rejoiced: "Therefore, if anyone is in Christ, he is a new creation; the old has passed away, behold, the new has come" (2 Corinthians 5:17). That was exactly what it felt like. The old had gone. The new had come. Wrote Temple Gairdner, the famous Anglican missionary to Cairo in the early twentieth century as he described his conversion and new birth: "That sense of newness is simply delicious. It makes new the Bible, and friends, and all mankind, and love and spiritual things, and Sunday, and church, and God Himself. So I've found."[7]

So then if we have the Holy Spirit in us through conversion and new birth, we will find a power at work in our lives for witness and service. Paul calls it "the immeasurable greatness of *his power in us* who believe" (Ephesians 1:19).

Unless the Spirit of Jesus is in us ("I in them", John 17:26) by conversion and new birth, that power will elude us.

The Holy Spirit is the Spirit of fullness

This notion, sadly, has become controversial. What is clear is that Scripture does urge this fullness on us. Writes the Apostle in straightforward fashion: "Do not get drunk with wine, for that is debauchery; but be filled with the Spirit" (Ephesians 5:18). Some see this as a mighty eruption, or a tumultuous baptism, or a crisis infilling, maybe with much emotion, and possibly accompanied by the gift of tongues. Some embrace the notion that when we are converted we get a dimension of the Holy Spirit for Christian living, but then we can have a second crisis experience when we are baptised in the Holy

Spirit as an equipment of power for service.

For still others the fullness of the Holy Spirit is something quiet and unspectacular and manifested in our characters in the degree to which we have sold out and surrendered to the Holy Spirit in our hearts. Sadly, there is, in some situations, a great gulf between these two different views.

In my view that should not be the case. The Lord wants us to have the power of the Spirit within and He may bring this about by any one or all of the different experiences and means just mentioned. What we do know is that when the Apostle told us to be filled with the Spirit (Ephesians 5:18), he was using there the continuous imperative in the Greek which means: "Be filled with the Spirit, and *keep on* being filled..." In other words, in fresh acts of obedience and surrender we keep on coming back to the Lord to release His Spirit's fullness within us. Thus was the great American evangelist D. L. Moody once asked: "Mr Moody, have you been filled with the Spirit?" To which Moody replied: "Yes, but I leak!"

I guess that's pretty true of all of us.

OBEDIENCE IS VITAL

To be sure it is worth noting that our Lord does connect the work and presence of the Holy Spirit to obedience. Thus He can say in the Final Discourse: "If you love me, you will keep my commandments" (John 14:15). There we see the moral challenge to obedience. Then He adds: "And I will pray the Father, and he will give you another Counselor to be with you forever, even the Spirit of truth" (John 14:16–17a).

The run of the house

Certainly Scripture does teach us that when we truly believe and receive the salvation of God we are "sealed with the promised Holy Spirit" (Ephesians 1:13). Thus it is that by conversion and new birth we have the Holy Spirit. The question then is – does He have us? But if in fact we allow the Holy Spirit to fill every room and corner of our lives, then we enter into a fullness in the Spirit and receive the power of the Spirit to live in joy, peace, victory, and effectiveness.

THE HOLY SPIRIT IS UNSYSTEMATIC

I myself am not much fussed about the vocabulary on fullness of the Spirit, whether we speak in so-called charismatic or non-charismatic terms, or use evangelical or Pentecostal vocabulary. What I do believe is that the Lord does want us to know His power through the Holy Spirit. He comes to the eager, seeking, and hungry heart.

In reality, as I have written elsewhere:

> intellectual honesty also requires one to record one's own recognition that there are immensely capable scholars, exegetes and men and women of deep piety and spirituality who in full integrity argue for different positions (about the work of the Spirit) very convincingly. Part of the problem comes from the fact that we are also seeking to systematise the work of the Holy Spirit who, because He blows where He wills, is very unsystematic and unpredictable, and therefore the bugbear of systematic theologians.
>
> The fact is that in Acts there are no really tidy theological schemes of Christian initiation. Sometimes reception of the Holy Spirit follows baptism, as in the Pentecostal proclamation of Acts 2:38. Sometimes it precedes baptism, as in the experience of Cornelius and his household (Acts 10:44–48).[8]

Even such a lucid and precise brain as that of Michael Green can affirm: "There is no tidy doctrine of the Spirit found in Acts or for that matter in the whole New Testament."[9]

MY OWN QUEST

Let me now share a word of my own testimony. This I recount in my book *Bursting the Wineskins* where I share at length my own quest in terms of the person and work of the Spirit.

First of all, I can say that when I was converted and experienced the new birth as a student at Cambridge University, I do know I acquired some measure of enabling and empowering to begin trying to live the Christian life. I also found that I was empowered to bring testimony and to witness to my faith that I had never, ever done before. The Lord also empowered me for some very tough years of first undergraduate and then seminary study. Without His indwelling Spirit I don't think I would have made it.

I know also that I was empowered to receive His guidance, sometimes quite dramatically, and from time to time to hear the voice of His Spirit speaking clearly and even forcefully in my own spirit. One blessing and empowerment that I discovered was that of moving from complete paralysis and terror about public speaking to being able to preach in public situations, and even see people, sometimes many of them, come to Christ.

However, I know too that as I pressed on in ministry I found after twelve or fifteen years that I was really yearning for a fresh touch and new empowering of the Spirit in my life. I allowed myself to be prayed for in many different situations to receive a fresh filling of the Spirit, but with little conscious awareness of anything happening. I read books on the subject. I heard lectures and talks on it. I sought the counsel of brothers or sisters who seemed to have entered some fresh experience and who knew much more of the Spirit than I did.

RENEWAL CONFERENCE, MILNER PARK

Finally in a renewal conference in 1977 at Milner Park in Johannesburg, as my earnest quest continued, I experienced during one whole night a fresh infusion, infilling, and release of the Spirit. I rejoiced all night, I sang in my heart all night; I even spoke in a heavenly language. It was awesome. This all happened when I had dealt in a deeper, Calvary way with some personal issues in my life and resolved to die afresh to my own considerable ambitions, dreams and impulses. As I did so, I asked Him to take me over in an altogether new way.

In *Bursting the Wineskins* I put it this way: "Sleep would not come to me. Instead, quite out of the blue, the spirit of praise came upon my soul. All seemed to be release. All seemed to be freedom… He seemed to be bubbling up from within, surrounding from without, ascending from below, and descending from above!"[10]

DETERMINATIVE AND FORMATIVE

Looking back on that experience I can say that it was majorly determinative and formative for me. Have I been filled with the Spirit? Yes, I think so. But, like D. L. Moody, I leak!

Have I been empowered by the Spirit for Christian service? I would like to think so. But I have to come back regularly, almost daily, to be topped up and refuelled! Or is it refilled?!

Let me also add that I have in different ways entered into a new appreciation of the gifts of the Spirit. I don't believe they shut down with the first-century church. They are still with us.

So I am free to affirm that:

THE HOLY SPIRIT IS THE SPIRIT OF GIFTS TO EQUIP FOR MINISTRY

For the church to fulfil its task in the world it needs not only spiritual power, but also spiritual gifting. It needs to be supernaturally equipped to carry out the job. Sometimes people in some sectors of the church resist this promise and assurance of spiritual gifting by saying something like this: "Well, you know, we are not into all that, we are people of love and the important thing is just to love others, and do practical works of kindness and service."

But the apostle Paul does not allow such a facile disposal of the challenge to receive the giftings of God. Thus for example 1 Corinthians 12 is largely concerned with spiritual gifts. Then comes chapter 13 on "the more excellent way" of love. Then chapter 14 is back to gifts again. It is as if there is a sort of sandwich with gifts being the two pieces of bread on the outside and love the filling in-between! Following chapter 12, and after the great hymn of love in chapter 13, the Apostle makes his position more than crystal clear: "Make love your aim, *and* earnestly desire the spiritual gifts, especially that you may prophesy" (1 Corinthians 14:1). There is no either/or here. It is both/and. Love *and* gifts.

People gifts

What then are these gifts? Some speak of people gifts described by the apostle Paul as follows in Ephesians 4:11: "And his gifts were that some should be *apostles*, some *prophets*, some *evangelists*, some *pastors* and *teachers*." These are people whose total and major gifting revolves around one particular aspect of ministry, even if they have other giftings.

But all of these gifts, whether apostles, prophets, evangelists, pastors or teachers, have ultimately one basic and fundamental purpose together and that is "to equip the saints for the work of the ministry, for building up the body of Christ" (Ephesians 4:12). In other words, all the people gifts are meant to combine into one final purpose of "equipping the saints", the ordinary people and members of a given congregation, to carry out the work of Christian ministry. This is not just the pastor's or the minister's job. Ministry is the job of the whole congregation. It speaks about every member involvement. Everyone knowing their gift, having their place, and building up the body of Christ into full maturity and spiritual adulthood.

Service gifts

Then, beyond the people gifts are what one might call *service gifts.*

These would include administration, helps, tongues, healing, prophecy, miracle working, giving, service, leadership, and so on. Some of these are listed for example in 1 Corinthians 12 and 14 as well as in Romans 12.

In thinking of these different gifts that equip the church Jesus prayed for in terms of its needed powers and capacities, it is important not to over-fixate, as some do, on gifts such as tongues, healing, working of miracles and so on, but rather to grasp the fact that also included among the gifts are very practical enablings, such as administration and helps. Every congregation and every para-church agency needs the exceedingly important gift of good administration.

I remember in the early years of African Enterprise praying vigorously that the Lord would send us a top-flight professional administrator with the gift of administration. And in 1974 He sent us Malcolm Graham, a genius of an administrator with just this gift. Malcolm's gifting and genius brought a massively distinguished contribution indeed.

Or else one can think of *the gift of helps.* For example, in every church there are often people, not only women, willing to help on a weekly basis with making tea, or doing flowers for the church, or keeping it clean, or handling the PA or sound systems or whatever. Some may also help a senior leader as a secretary or personal assistant. I know most certainly that I could never have been empowered and enabled to carry out my own work for the Lord over some fifty years had I not had the magnificent help of several amazing secretaries and several class-act personal assistants. Such people empower the church to do its job. They have the charismatic gift of helps.

Another critically important gift is that of *leadership.* No congregations or para-church ministries can thrive or flourish unless at their head is a leader with notable gifts of leadership given by the Holy Spirit, and who will also lead diligently and with zeal (Romans 12:8).

Gift of prophecy

While on the subject of gifts, perhaps it is worth dwelling a moment on the one gift the apostle Paul wants everyone to have. Listen to him again: "Make love your aim, and earnestly desire the spiritual gifts, *especially that you may prophesy*" (1 Corinthians 14:1). This is the one gift above all others that Paul wants everyone to have along with the deep aim and commitment to love ("Make love your aim"). There is also quite a bit of confusion around this particular gift.

I summarised my own conclusions – for what they are worth – on the gift of prophecy in *Bursting the Wineskins*:

> *Drawing the full range of threads together we could perhaps present a summary definition of prophecy in these terms: Prophecy is the exercise of that gift and ministry of the Spirit which takes place when a believer who knows the mind, will and purpose and full righteousness of God declares it, whether to the church or to the world. The knowledge on which this utterance is based is received not only by understanding the Written Word and abiding in the Living Word, but sometimes by supernatural discernment, or by listening and hearing, or even by direct revelation of the Spirit received by faith. The twofold test of prophetic authenticity lies firstly in whether it is consistent with the revealed Word of God, the apostolic deposit, and secondly whether it receives the positive affirmation of the Body of Christ. Especially other prophets.[11]*

All helped to live at the centre of His will

The reason I believe Paul wants everyone to have this gift operative is that if everyone is participating in the process of discerning, understanding, and then sharing with others the mind, will, and purpose of God, then everyone in the body of

Christ is helped to live and remain at the centre of the will of God. And in unity.

This would greatly please our Lord.

Two other very remarkable and important gifts are those referred to by the Apostle in 1 Corinthians 12:8: "To one is given through the Spirit the utterance of *wisdom*, and to another the utterance of *knowledge* according to the same Spirit…"

Wisdom

This gift, I believe, is much more commonly experienced and used than many would realise. Thus I could ask you, my reader – have you not from time to time been in a situation where someone was putting to you a very severe problem they have, or complex situation they are in? They need your counsel and help. Then all of a sudden you seem to know exactly what to say, share, or advise. You almost amaze yourself with the wise counsel you bring forth! I believe that's the operating of the gift of wisdom. And the person hearing you has a deep, deep sense that they are hearing from the Lord through you. And more often than not, they are.

The gift of knowledge

Then the gift of knowledge. This happens when the Spirit enables you to know supernaturally about a person or situation what you could not normally know. And it plays decisively into the situation.

My African Enterprise colleague, David Peters, has operated this gift for years.

Once many years ago, he came to our home to counsel our domestic helper who was getting all caught up in witch doctor mumbo jumbo, sorcery, and consulting the spirits after buying feathers, and bones, and potions, and other paraphernalia from a witch doctor. She was being tormented by spirits at night and was constantly fearful by day. After being asked by David if she had such things, and if so to fetch them, she returned some moments later from her room with a mass of hokey-pokey witch doctor stuff. We all prayed over it with her, as David set it alight and burned it, and our helper called on the Lord in repentance and faith.

Concluding, David asked if she'd brought it all. To which she answered in the affirmative.

Then the Lord gave David the supernatural gift of knowledge.

"No, my dear," David said: "You are *not* speaking truthfully. Let's go to your room, as the Lord has shown me something." So off to her room we all went.

David opened the door and said: "There is more stuff in the bottom right-hand drawer of that wardrobe."

Carol and I were startled. Our house-helper looked terrified.

Then sheepishly and in embarrassment she opened the bottom right-hand drawer. And sure enough, there it all was, another mass of witch doctor paraphernalia.

More prayer. More repentance. More burnings. More tears. And suddenly she was free, never to be thus bothered again.

Another time on one of our missions David was counselling a woman in Cape Town who spoke of a mass of scary, spooky, and paralysing problems in her life and family, and especially related to her mother, then living in Johannesburg. Finally, a perplexed David got a word of knowledge: "Ma'am, has your mother got a statue of Buddha in her sitting room in Johannesburg, because that is what I am seeing? That's the problem."

The startled and electrified woman almost fell over backwards.

"Yes, she does!"

"She must remove that and destroy it," said David.

This was done shortly thereafter. At which point the woman reported back to David: "All the problems in my own life and family which we spoke about have sorted out. And my mother has also come to the Lord. We are rejoicing."

Yes, these gifts of the Holy Spirit – and all the others – are there to empower us for Christian service and enable us to carry it out supernaturally in the world.

*** ***

Conclusion

The Holy Spirit – as the Spirit of Jesus in us ("I–in–them", remember? – John 17:26) is the final and ultimate enabler. Without Him we are helpless and powerless to fulfil the awesome gospel tasks our Lord has committed to us.

No wonder Jesus prayed to the Father asking that the love as between Father and Son should be in them – "*and I in them*" – by the Person and power of the Holy Spirit (John 17:26).

Only that way could the work of world mission get done! Only that way could they love the world as He had loved them.

John Stott once noted: "Before Christ sent the church into the world, He sent the Spirit into the church. The same order must be observed today."[12]

Amen!

Chapter 17

Glory – The Tenth Mark (I)

Its Meaning

"Grace is but glory begun, and glory is but grace perfected."

Jonathan Edwards

"Glory is who God is."

Richard Grey

"Glory is the radiant character of God shining through."

Denzil Tryon

"The public display of the infinite beauty and worth of God is what I mean by Glory."

John Piper

"Father, the hour has come; glorify your Son so that the Son may glorify you… glorify me in your own presence with the glory that I had in your presence before the world existed."

Jesus, John 17:1, 5

Of all the chapters in this book, this curiously enough, is the one – along with its sequel – about which I have felt most daunted. The word "glory" is all over the Bible, featuring in almost every book, and certainly prominent, almost central actually, in this High Priestly Prayer of Jesus. But what really does it mean? What does it signify? How are we to understand its contours, its depths, its seemingly unfathomable dimensions?

After all, we all use the word, or its derivatives, in all sorts of ways. We see a lovely sunset, and say, "It's glorious!" We call a concert of rhapsodic music "Glorious!" We speak of an Olympic athlete not just going for gold but for "glory". We read of two sporting teams in a World Cup final and are reliably informed that every one of their players is seeking cricketing, rugby, or soccer *glory*.

So what are we dealing with here?

The sportsmen or athletes are probably thinking fundamentally of becoming famous, securing big-time name recognition, getting lots of popularity and pats on the back from the public, or else becoming a sporting hero to youngsters and sports aficionados.

However, when we use the word "glory" or "glorious" to describe a majestic scene in nature, an exhilarating cascade of musical sound, or the breathtaking beauty of a rose, we are clearly not talking about fame, pats on the back, name recognition, or any one rose aspiring to be the best in the flower bed!

Something mysterious behind them

No! In these latter examples, wouldn't you say, we are going past the objects of beauty or wondrous admiration to something mysterious behind them, and groping for a category that describes not just the beauty before us, but also the author beyond it. The Himalayas, or the Victoria Falls, or the icebergs of Antarctica do not just touch our aesthetic senses but also our spiritual ones. For me, seeing Antarctica, the Victoria Falls, and the Himalayas were in reality religious experiences, because in them one was sensing an echo of the greater glory behind them. Something spiritual therefore was happening to me as I beheld them. One was not just seeing physical or natural beauty, one was being drawn to the majesty of the creator who created them.

So when we speak of the majestic sights of nature or

the physical universe and we behold glory there, we are not simply commenting objectively or in a detached manner on their beauty, but instead finding our souls meeting the Soul, and our minds the Mind. Thus standing beneath the starry wonders of the night sky we experience the psalmist's affirmation that "the heavens declare the *glory* of God" (Psalm 19:1, KJV). They are telling us something about who He is, about His character and power which constitute that glory.

Deity perceived

So too if we are nature lovers we should more often than not, unless our senses are much dimmed by spiritual blindness, be able to affirm with the apostle Paul that: "Ever since the creation of the world his invisible nature, namely his eternal power and deity, has been clearly perceived in the things that have been made" (Romans 1:20). He is saying that the wonders of nature and of our physical universe alert us to the reality of this invisible and unseen God and to His eternal power and deity behind it all.

My affirmation here is that in reflecting on how we use the words *glory* or *glorious*, we are discovering a key clue to the meaning of the word. We begin to register that many phenomena or beautiful things which we describe as *glorious* and characterised by *glory* are in reality only pointers to the true glory beyond, indeed to the one who is altogether *glorious*, and who is indeed "the King of glory" (Psalm 24:7).

You see, in seeing what we hail as *glorious* and full of *glory*, we are moving from the "pointer" to the "one pointed at", and from the "sign" to the "one signified".

Clues from the church

Taking it as read from Our Lord's prayer that He wants the mark of glory in His church, and seeing He could then affirm that "the glory that you have given me I have given them"

(John 17:22), how or when do people see His glory in the church?

In other words, how would we know what we were looking for if looking for a congregation or individual Christian marked by glory? What would we be hoping to see or experience?

Perhaps this question is easier in the first instance to answer if we think of a congregation rather than an individual. So I ask you if you have ever been in a church or congregation in which you felt you saw or experienced New Testament *glory*. Or about which you would use the adjective "glorious"?

I think I have, although rarely. What did I experience, feel, or see? What was it about that rare congregation or church service which made me want to use the adjective "glorious"? My answer would lie along the following lines.

First of all, there would be a tremendous sense of the presence of God, as if the Spirit of Jesus in the Holy Spirit had showed up in full force. God is felt to be present and inhabiting the praises of His people.

Secondly in some glorious churches I have attended, not only were people full of praise, worship, and adoration for their God, but there was a palpable sense of love and deep Christian fellowship among the people themselves.

Not only that, but new people, strangers, or seekers who had stumbled in looking for something, found themselves loved, warmly welcomed into the fellowship, and genuinely embraced into participation. There would also have been a sense of holiness, purity, and a deep commitment to biblical behaviour among the people. Very high standards of biblical morality and behaviour were set. And sin was taken seriously, quickly confessed, repented of, and forsaken.

What else? One quickly sensed that there were deep commitments to truth and biblical faithfulness. The Bible was powerfully embraced and faithfully expounded.

The church's programmes

More than that, when one heard about the programmes in a church called "glorious", it was clear that the congregation was not only seriously concerned about evangelistic outreach and the winning of people to Christ, but also about socio-political issues, compassionate action, Holy Spirit renewal, as well as discipleship. There were also extensive commitments to prayer, both individual and corporate.

And then, capping it all, there was a sense of fun, laughter, and yes, one might say, obvious joy!

People in need were obviously cared for and prayed about.

Factionalism with in-groups and out-groups were manifestly absent. Problem-solvers outnumbered problem-makers by some way.

One would find their mission programmes revealed a concern not just for themselves, but also for the world beyond and the uttermost parts of the earth.

Beyond that, in some glorious churches I've been in, every group in the church seemed to be lovingly catered for whether they were children or teens, young adults, singles, young married people, parents and families, and not forgetting the oldies.

Mythical, fairyland church

Perhaps by now you think I am describing some mythical, millennial or fairyland church which has never been or ever will be, and which is only a thumbsuck from the momentarily over-fertile imagination of Michael! My friend, you would be wrong. It has been my privilege to minister all across South Africa, the continent of Africa, and around the world. I have seen a lot and had a very wide and privileged exposure to the church of Jesus Christ on every continent.

And my firm – and I hope encouraging – affirmation is

that churches of New Testament glory do indeed exist here and there. In such fellowships – whether that is in congregations or in individual lives – one is encountering the radiant character and moral beauty of God Himself shining through. This, I believe is what Jesus, among other things, was praying for when He prayed that glory should be in His church and among His people. After all, did He not affirm, "The glory that you have given me I have given them" (John 17:22)? And He prayed further for us saying: "Father, I desire that those also, whom you have given me, may be with me where I am, to see my glory, which you have given me" (verse 24). Why should He thus pray? Surely because He wants us to reflect that same glory.

Glory comes when all ten marks Jesus prayed for are present

You see, it was reflections along these lines over many years and in many places that made me finally tumble to the fact that at least in measure *glory is manifested in the church when all ten of the marks Jesus prayed for are present*. Or put differently, we could say that glory is the spontaneous effervescent overflow, manifestation, and consequence of all other nine marks being so consequentially operative that they enable the radiant character of God and His moral beauty, holiness, and love to shine through along with the reality of His unmistakable presence.

Let's summarise these again:

Truth – where the Bible is held in high authority, expounded faithfully, and where truth as coherence with reality is embraced.

Holiness – where there is a commitment to biblical ethics, principles and behaviour and where sin is faced in all its seriousness and dealt with accordingly.

Joy – where Jesus Himself is seen as joy and where deep Calvary obedience to Him is seen as productive of that joy. All other human joys are seen as reflections and pointers to the joy of Jesus Himself.

Protection – where there is the awareness of the real powers of evil supernaturalism and where parishioners have the means through prayer and a sure knowledge of spiritual warfare to combat the Evil One.

Mission – where there is an understanding that Jesus is both the message and the model of mission and believers seriously obey His Great Commission.

Prayerfulness – where there is not only meaningful prayer in the church's services, but regular prayer meetings, special endeavours of prayer and a strong encouragement of individual and personal prayerfulness through ordered devotional lives.

Unity – where there is a commitment for everyone to be at one and in fellowship within the membership, and then experiencing a unity in truth, but not at the expense of it, with other Christian churches/denominations.

Love – where the spirit of love, acceptance of others, forgiveness, compassion, and practical action are pervasive and recognisable qualities and commitments.

Power – where believers are strong on the person and work of the Holy Spirit and where the Holy Spirit is not only the agent in conversion and new birth, but in producing disciples evidencing the fruit of the Spirit and equipped for service with the gifts of the Spirit.

And yes, then glory! This is what shines forth in full measure when all these other marks are operative. Indeed, if all these marks Jesus prayed for are in a church then most surely what we see will be the radiant character and moral beauty of God shining through. And that is glorious!

You see, it's the comprehensiveness and the all-embracing presence of these qualities that is the key and makes for glory. The same principle is true in art or music. Thus if you have a canvas that is a single mass of blue with a red blob in the middle, you will have some colour on the canvas but you won't have glory. Likewise if you have an all-green canvas of rolling hills, with a dusty brown path rolling over them, you might have an interesting, even aesthetic, picture, but you won't have glory. But if you have a Turner masterpiece of a multicoloured and multiflowered English garden, you would have glory.

Or think of the musical analogy. To hear only a single violin or even all the violins of an orchestra playing the main melody of a movement in Beethoven's Eroica Symphony might be pleasant enough. And even if you added the melodic parts of the orchestra's cellos, you would have an improved musical experience. But you would hardly have Beethovian glory! That only comes when all the members of the orchestra – strings and flutes and brass and drums and woodwinds and cellos all combine in great cascades of Beethovian genius. Then you have musical glory.

Thus with the marks Jesus prayed for in the church. If all the marks are there, then there is glory. It's the lopsidedness of so many of our churches, and the incomplete catalogue of qualities and commitments that rob churches of biblical glory and prevents the Lord's radiant character and moral beauty from shining through.

*** ***

However, before we think further of what glory means as a mark of the church Jesus prayed for, we need to go back to the beginning of the prayer and to its most poignant and penetrating petitions where Jesus is in truth praying not for His disciples, but for Himself.

Here He speaks about the Father glorifying the Son that the Son may glorify the Father, and He takes us into the ultimately mysterious depths of the glory He had with the Father "before the world was" (KJV), or as the RSV puts it "before the world was made" (John 17:5).

This means hunting down some understandings of two key words.

The Hebrew word *kabod*

One of the saintliest, deepest, and most loved professors at Fuller Seminary during my time there was Dr Everett Harrison, our Professor of New Testament Theology. When he taught and lectured there was an aura about him, a sense that not only did this man deeply know his subject, but more significantly, he deeply knew His Lord. He was in a curious sense one of those exhibit "A"s of the holy and deep things about which he lectured, a rare man out of whom there quietly shone the glory of the Lord.

In the famous *Baker's Dictionary of Theology*, Everett Harrison writes on the theme of glory in these terms:

> Since kabod derives from kabed, "to be heavy", it lends itself to the idea that the one possessing glory is laden with riches (e.g. Genesis 31:1), power (Isaiah 8:7), position (Genesis 45:13) etc. To the translators of the Septuagint (LXX) it seemed that doxa was the most suitable word for rendering kabod, since it carried the notion of reputation or honour which was present in the use of kabod. But kabod also denoted the manifestation of light by which God often revealed Himself.
>
> But at times kabod had a deeper penetration. When Moses made the request of God, "show me your glory" (Exodus 33:18), he was not speaking of the light-cloud which he had already seen, but he was seeking a special manifestation of God which would leave nothing to be desired (cf. John 14:8)... In reply God emphasised His goodness (Exodus 33:19). The word might be rendered in this instance "moral beauty".[1]

The Greek word *doxa*

Let's consult Harrison again:

> *In general, doxa is used of honour in the sense of recognition or acclaim (Luke 14:10). With reference to God, it denotes His majesty (Romans 1:23) and His perfection, especially in relation to righteousness (Romans 3:23). He is called the Father of Glory (Ephesians 1:17)... Christ is the effulgence of the divine glory (Hebrews 1:3)...*
>
> *The glory of Christ as the image of God, the Son of the Father, was veiled from sinful eyes during the days of His flesh but was apparent to the men of faith who gathered around Him (John 1:14).*[2]

Thank you, Dr Harrison! You were a blessing to me way back then at Fuller Seminary, and you still are today!

With my old professor's insights in our minds let's turn to:

Jesus' petition for Himself in His High Priestly Prayer

Let's listen with deep reverence to our Blessed Lord as He prays:

> *Father, the hour has come; glorify your Son so that the Son may glorify you, since you have given him authority over all people, to give eternal life to all whom you have given him. And this is eternal life, that they may know you, the only true God, and Jesus Christ whom you have sent. I glorified you on earth by finishing the work that you gave me to do. So now, Father, glorify me in your own presence with the glory that I had in your presence before the world existed.*
>
> **John 17:1–5**

See here in the first few petitions of the prayer the notion of glory comes no fewer than five times. This riveting reality sits right at the head of the prayer. What on earth did our Lord mean? And what in heaven did it also mean before the Earth was formed?

What we can say, however, is that what we have here completely transcends any powers of human invention. No trickster, hoaxer, or fabricator could in multiple millennia of moons ever come up with anything like this. We can only here be in the presence of deity.

Obviously the prayer was spoken out loud and so was not only a prayer to the heavenly Father, but a source of monumental comfort to those who overheard it. Our Lord in these five chapters of John's Gospel (13–17) had taught by *action* in chapter 13, by *discourse* in chapters 14–16, and now He is teaching by *prayer* in chapter 17. As He does so He brings forth, as many down the ages have concluded, an utterance that is the simplest in language and the profoundest in meaning in the whole Bible.

As always in these things the Old Testament must be our initial hunting ground for the major clues we need.

In this the experience of Moses is as good a place as any to start.

Moses and glory as God's presence

In Exodus 33 Moses was unequivocally clear in a twofold request to his Jehovah God.

The first was "show me your ways" (verse 13), and the second was "show me your glory" (verse 18). In his heart and mind these probably coalesced into a single burning desire to know who God really was, how He functioned, what He was like.

The Lord's reply is instructive: "My presence will go with you" (verse 14). In other words: "If my presence is with you, it will not only cause you to know me, but lead you into moral behaviour pleasing to me."

"For how shall it be known that I have found favour in your sight, I and your people, unless you go with us? In this way, we shall be distinct, I and your people, from every people on the face of the earth" (Exodus 33:16).

Bearing in mind that Moses' next and intimately related question is about the glory of God, it's clear that the glory of God is going to be deeply connected both to the "presence" of God and to the moral manifestation of His character inspiring us to try and be like Him, thereby making them "distinct", *different* from other peoples. Yes, we are tiptoeing into the experience of divine glory.

Glory as God's goodness

Now Moses is even more forthright: "Show me your glory, I pray" (Exodus 33:18).

The Lord's reply is immediate and unequivocally clear. "I will make my *goodness* pass before you, and will proclaim before you my name" (Exodus 33:19). God equated His glory with His goodness. His glory is not primarily about light, brilliance, dazzling splendour, or overwhelming effulgence (although it could include all that), it is about *character*. About a manifestation of divine goodness. Glory is not physical. It is moral. And the Hebrew word here for "goodness" is *tuwb*, which means good in its widest sense and carries also notions of beauty, gladness, and welfare.

In fact, when Moses asks, "Show me your glory", the Hebrew word that is used is *kabowd*, which speaks of weightiness, honour, and splendour. The truth is that God's glory resides in everything, which in reality makes up who He is, for example His omnipotence, sovereignty, justice, omniscience, and love.

This becomes even more clear when the Lord offers the second part of His answer as Moses requests to be shown His glory. Not only does the Lord say, "I will show You my goodness", but – "I will proclaim my name, the Lord" (Exodus 33:19a, NIV). And then He speaks of His graciousness and mercy (verse 19b). So the glory of God is made manifest where His graciousness, mercy, and goodness are in evidence.

If – or when – churches reach for or even perhaps reach a modest manifestation of these qualities, then glory is on its way.

But God is not finished with Moses and summons him next day to meet with Him on Mount Sinai where God "descended in the cloud and stood with him there, and proclaimed the name of the Lord… and proclaimed: 'The Lord, the Lord, a God merciful and gracious, slow to anger, and abounding in steadfast love and faithfulness, keeping steadfast love for thousands, forgiving iniquity and transgression and sin, but who will by no means clear the guilty'" (Exodus 34:5–7a).

Glory comes when these marks of the divine are present among the people of God.

- **Mercy**: the Hebrew word *rachum* for "mercy" really speaks of compassion. If God's compassionate love is overwhelmingly evident in a church, then hints of glory will be manifest.

- **Graciousness**: Exodus 34:6. The Hebrew *hen* speaks of favour, mercy, kindness.

- **Slowness to anger:** this speaks of God's patience.

- **Steadfast love and faithfulness:** the Hebrew *hesed* is one of the Old Testament's loveliest words speaking of that kind of unwavering love that never lets go.

- **Forgiveness for iniquity and transgression:** to be in a church or fellowship where there is abounding forgiveness on offer – both from God to us, and from us to one another – is to be in the presence of glory.

- **Justice:** as God revealed dimensions of His character and glory, His justice was not omitted. He "by no means clears the guilty" (Exodus 34:7), and if they are unrepentant, visits "the iniquity of the fathers upon the children and the children's children, to the third and fourth generation" (verse 7). God's glory is not sloppily sentimental. It requires Him to burn in holiness against sin.

The great nineteenth-century American evangelist, Charles Finney, commented once on this passage in these terms: "It implies that God considers His goodness, His moral attributes, as making up His essential glory."[3]

Clearly then this message here of our Lord to Moses reveals that God's glory is primarily "moral glory". Indeed, looking at chapters 16–34 of Exodus we see endless references to God's requirements of moral living. As Australian theologian Geoffrey Bingham puts it: "Israel always had God's moral glory before it: never was it absent."[4]

As Moses saw the radiant beauty of God's character, he knew he had seen God's glory. Here was God's glory going public for Moses.

Glory as God's holiness

Isaiah's experience was not dissimilar to that of Moses.

After pronouncing "woes" on others for a few chapters (Isaiah 1–5) – most notably chapter 5 – Isaiah now has his vision of the Lord, "sitting upon a throne, high and lifted up" (Isaiah 6:1). Its dramatic consequence? Isaiah no longer says "Woe is *you*" – but rather "Woe is *me*!" (Isaiah 6:5). As he starts to see God in His glory, so he starts to see himself in all his shabbiness and sin. Seeing God in His glory does that.

How does Isaiah see Him?

Well, He sees Him as sovereign Lord and king enthroned over all creation and all history. This is God in charge. No need for anyone to pray like the little child: "Dear Lord Jesus, please take good care of yourself, because if anything happens to you we are going to be in a terrible mess!" No! Nothing's going to happen to Him. He's fine. He's sovereign.

He's in charge. And with His father He is gloriously on the throne of history.

Then Isaiah sees the heavenly seraphim worshipping God and saying: "Holy, holy, holy, is the Lord of hosts; the whole earth is full of his glory" (verse 3).

Holy! Holy! Holy! It is thrice reiterated. Once is not enough. And because God is everywhere and His holy presence is all-pervasive across the earth, it means, as the heavenly host sang it out, that "the whole earth is full of his *glory*!"

His radiant holiness and perfect goodness are synonymous with, and productive of, His glory. They go together.

No wonder Isaiah was overwhelmed: "Woe is me! I am lost; for I am a man of unclean lips… my eyes have seen the King, the Lord of hosts!" (verse 5).

So if people come into a church where all they see is the radiant character of King Jesus shining forth – in His people, in Word, song and sacrament, then they too see glory and can only cry out, each one – "Woe is me! I am lost! Show me how to be found, forgiven, cleansed, commissioned, by this Holy One, so that I too may reflect and declare His glory. Lord of glory, here am I; send me."

John Piper rightly commented: "I believe the glory of God is the going public of His infinite worth."[5] To glorify God is to show His infinite worth.

Drawing the Old Testament threads together

We are searching out the meaning of glory. The experiences of both Moses and Isaiah give us dramatic Old Testament clues. But the Old Testament and its prophecies leave us panting. We want and need to know more of this God. We are on tiptoes, waiting for a child to be born (Isaiah 9:6) and a Saviour to come (Isaiah 53:4–5).

In fact we are waiting for "the light of the knowledge of the glory of God…" (2 Corinthians 4:6).

Can it be found? Yes it can.

Yes, at last… the glory made flesh

Yes, at last in the fullness of time "God sent forth His Son… to redeem" (Galatians 4:4–5). And the Word which was in the beginning, that Word which was with God, and that Word which *was God* became flesh and dwelt among us (John 1:14a). His name was Jesus. And humans for the first time ever *"**beheld His glory**, glory as of the only begotten of the Father, full of grace and truth"* (John 1:14b, ASV). In that perfection of grace and truth incarnated in that Word, made flesh in Jesus, they saw glory.

More than that, humans now saw and experienced this "God who said, 'Let light shine out of darkness'" so coming to them that they could testify that He "has shone in our hearts to give the *light of the knowledge of **the glory of God** in the face of Jesus Christ*" (2 Corinthians 4:6).

Where is the glory of God? It is in the face of Jesus Christ; in the magnificent and splendid Person, personality, and character of Christ.

And when we are introduced to Him and come to know Him then we find ourselves "seeing the light of *the gospel of the **glory** of Christ,* who is the image of God" (2 Corinthians 4:4).

When we embrace this "good news", this gospel, we embrace "the glory of Christ". We embrace the fullness of "grace and truth". For this is the glory, the glory of Christ. The pantheon of all other prophets, religious leaders, and professed gods must step aside. This is the way and indeed the only way to see God and His glory. There is no other. For "in Him dwells the whole fullness of the Godhead bodily" (Colossians 2:9, NKJV). See that body, and especially that broken body, and you see God. You see glory.

Nor may the glory be seen, found, discovered, or embraced through any other religion or prophet, for in none other than Jesus did "the whole fullness of the Godhead dwell bodily". For "no one who denies the Son has the Father; everyone who confesses the Son has the Father also" (1 John 2:23). And "everyone who… does not abide in the teaching of Christ…

does not have God" (2 John 1:9).

The writer to the Hebrews is equally clear about this Son whom God "appointed heir of all things, through whom also he created the world. *He reflects the glory of God* and bears the very stamp of his nature, upholding the universe by his word of power" (Hebrews 1:3). So Jesus reflects the character of God, including His cosmic power by which He upholds the universe, and reveals it as "fitting that He, for whom and by whom all things exist" (Hebrews 2:10a) should be the one able to bring "many sons to *glory*" (verse 10b).

Astonishing! Remarkable! This king of glory can bring many sons and daughters also into this glory; into this character. But there is only one way. Our Saviour could only do it by pressing through to that "hour".

The Cross as the radiant and radical centre of glory

And so this prayer of all prayers, this chapter of all chapters, opens with this unprecedented petition: "Father, the *hour* has come; *glorify* your Son so that the Son may *glorify* you" (John 17:1).

This was finally the hour, time, and moment for our blessed Saviour to ask the Father to show forth the Son's divine character unmistakably clearly, so that He, the Son, could show forth the Father's character equally unmistakably.

This would call for the Cross.

This would call for the event both planned and destined to be the major fact of history, the salvific fulcrum of the universe.

To be sure even the prophets of old sensed this as they "prophesied of the grace that was to be [ours]", and "searched and inquired about this salvation", enquiring "what person or time was indicated by the Spirit of Christ within them when predicting the sufferings of Christ *and the subsequent glory*" (1 Peter 1:10–11).

They saw and foresaw that the final glory of God would

come through "the sufferings of Christ". Not surprisingly, says Peter, these were "things into which [even] angels long to look" (1 Peter 1:12).

Awesome! Awesome indeed!

And indeed mystery beyond mystery because the Cross, as the glory of God, could never naturally be seen to be so, for its glory was hidden beneath the awful and the sullied.

But there was necessity here.

It had to happen.

Three times in the Gospel of Mark Jesus told them "the Son of man *must* suffer many things and be rejected by the elders and the chief priests and the scribes and be killed, and after three days rise again" (Mark 8:31; compare 9:31). Likewise in Matthew (16:21; 17:22; 20:17–19) as well as Luke (9:27, 44; 17:25).

If they had missed this before the Cross and resurrection, He made it unmistakably clear to the Emmaus disciples post the resurrection: "*Was it not necessary that the Christ should suffer these things and **enter into his glory**"* (Luke 24:26).

The Cross was the prerequisite of His glorification. Neither the Father's glory-filled character nor that of the Son could be adequately displayed without the ultimate expression of forgiving love and fathomless, sacrificial goodness.

As the hour of the Cross approached, He in anticipation tells His bewildered little band of lads and lasses: "Now is the **Son of man** *glorified* and in him **God is** *glorified*" (John 13:31a). In other words, as the Son in ultimate terms reveals His own character and what He is like, so God the Father in ultimate terms shows His own character also and reveals what He is like. And "if God is glorified in Him, God will also glorify him in himself, and glorify him at once" (John 13:32).

This is the heart of the Cross.

It is the principal thing.

That's why Jesus prays "*glorify* your Son so that the Son may *glorify* you" (17:1).

It is God in saving, atoning love showing what He is like. Declaring His glory.

Chapter 18

Glory – The Tenth Mark (II)

Its Meaning For Us

"I have been glorified in them."

Jesus, John 17:10

"Father, I desire that those also, whom you have given me, may be with me where I am, to see my glory, which you have given me because you loved me before the foundation of the world."

Jesus, John 17:24

We ended our last chapter where our Lord prays: "glorify your Son so that the Son may glorify you" (John 17:1). He was setting His face to the Cross, to the place where His divine character would be most fully displayed. And into that path and that display He would soon call us, along with all its implications.

But before we could respond or know what it needed to mean for us, we would have to learn more of what glorifying the Father would involve for Him. Above all we would need to understand that Jesus was now acknowledging to the Father in anticipation of the Cross that He could only fully glorify Him and display His character as He "accomplished the work" the Father had given Him to do (verse 4). More than that, Jesus would, in consequence of His atoning sacrifice, soon have restored to Him what He had temporarily laid aside in His incarnation, namely the full presence and glory of God "that I had in your presence before the world existed" (verse 5).

The late legendary missionary and missiologist Lesslie Newbigin commented helpfully in these terms:

> Jesus has manifested God's glory on earth by a life of total love and obedience to be consummated in the cross (cf. 19:30: "It is accomplished"). In this way He has given honour to the Father. Now, as He approaches the consummation He prays that the Father may honour Him, enabling Him to offer the perfect sacrifice of love and thus to manifest on earth the perfect glory which is the life of heaven – the eternal love of God in whom Father and Son are one in an unceasing life of self-giving. It is by treading the road to the cross in utter faithfulness to the end that Jesus manifests the glory of God and so makes it possible for those whom the Father has given to share in this glory. "It was fitting that He, for whom and by whom all things exist, in bringing many sons to glory, should make the pioneer of their salvation perfect through suffering" (Hebrews 2:10).
>
> And thus those who follow the way of the cross can say: "We all, with unveiled faces, **beholding the glory** of the Lord, are being changed into His likeness from one **degree of glory** to another" (2 Corinthians 3:19). Thus the intention of God "before the world was made" is fulfilled, for all things exist for God's glory.[1]

Part of the response for us as humans would have to be allowing ourselves likewise to be changed by finding our way also to the Cross, and there we too would take on the transforming task of also seeking to glorify God.

The Reformer John Calvin comments on the Cross and its glory in similar terms, noting how it opens to humans the way of salvation as we respond to it by faith: "So whatever ignominy appears in the cross, which could bewilder believers, Christ testifies that the same cross is glorious to Him."[2]

The Cross and God's moral glory

The divine revelation of God's glory is now moving forwards, and what we are edging into is not just the glory of God's character of love and goodness being displayed, but into the radical display of God's moral glory *to which we will have to respond*. Because Jesus' death on the Cross was primarily moral. And at the Cross He is dealing in an atoning way with man's moral sin. Are we able to face that?

After all, what the human race had and has fallen short of is exactly this – the moral glory of God. Writes St Paul: "For all have sinned and come short of the *glory* [the displayed character] of God" (Romans 3:23, KJV). This makes humans guilty before a totally moral and holy God. More than that, in their multiple idolatries, "Claiming to be wise, they became fools, and they **exchanged the** *glory* [the character] of the immortal God for images resembling mortal man or birds or animals or reptiles" (Romans 1:23).

For example, even the most cursory cast of one's eye across life, behaviour, and the religious landscape in India reveals this type of rampant and runaway idolatry that exists in both Hinduism and Buddhism. In the West we are possibly a bit more subtle and instead just put the sexualised human body ("images resembling mortal man") on display for our lustful adoration. Either way, whether we bow at the shrine of the human body or of animals, we are idolaters and are exchanging the moral glory (displayed character) of God for the immoral image of an idol.

So we are sinners. And we need a Saviour. We need someone to rescue us from the just condemnation (John 3:18), "judgment" (John 3:19) and wrath (John 3:36) of Almighty God.

And we have put this God in a divine dilemma. His dilemma is this: how should He reconcile within Himself both the love and justice dimensions of His moral glory, without compromising either.

It could only be done by the justice component of His

moral glory decreeing the penalty for sin ("the wages of sin is death" – Romans 6:23), and the love component of His moral glory ("God is love" – 1 John 4:8, 16), paying the penalty Himself. What God decreed in His justice, He would Himself in Christ pay for in His love. He would accordingly resolve the divine dilemma, as the King James version translates Paul's words, and be both "just, and the justifier of him which believeth in Jesus" (Romans 3:26).

The RSV has St Paul affirming (with that verse 26 in context) that "the redemption which is in Christ Jesus, whom God put forward as an expiation of His blood… was to prove… that he himself is righteous *and* that he justifies him who has faith in Jesus" (Romans 3:24–26).

This was Jesus' errand of glory at Calvary. To show God as both just and the justifier.

When Jesus in the High Priestly Prayer prays pre-Calvary "Father… *glorify* your Son so that the Son may *glorify* you" (John 17:1), He is praying that this character of God as both *just* and *justifier* would come shining through. At the Cross, love and justice would meet.

But it is more than that. He was praying that His "power over all flesh" (John 17:2a), as given Him by the Father, would be evidenced in His right and authority now to give eternal life to "all whom you have given Him" (verse 2b). The glory of the Cross would open to us fallen humans the glory of eternal life, previously lost through sin, but now possible again, and consisting, as Jesus said to the Father, in "that they may know you, the only true God, and Jesus Christ whom you have sent" (verse 3).

All this was made possible because of Jesus "who for a little while was made lower than the angels [that is, there was a loss of glory for our sakes], now crowned with *glory* and honor because of the suffering of death, so that by the grace of God he might taste death for everyone" (Hebrews 2:9).

As this happens, Jesus is ready after He had "emptied Himself" (Philippians 2:7) to pray now to the Father to restore to Him, "the *glory* that I had in your presence before the world existed" (verse 5).

Our Saviour's journey and task is almost complete. There only remains now to weather and bear the agonising Cross, then to reveal fresh divine glory in His matchless resurrection, by which the universe would change gear, and then ascend back to heaven to the glory of the Father.

There is no doubt He would there again say: "I *glorified* you on earth by finishing the work that you gave me to do" (verse 4).

The Saviour is declaring, "Mission accomplished."

Perhaps back in heaven, He would also repeat again "Father, I desire that those also, whom you have given me, may be with me where I am, *to see my glory*, which you have given me because you loved me before the foundation of the world" (17:24).

One thing remains

Jesus said in His High Priestly Prayer: "I am glorified in them" (John 17:10). Somehow now it is our turn from our side to show forth His glory. And find our delight in doing so. It is the one thing that remains. *From our side.*

The point is that we must not waste our lives or this one mysterious opportunity of our lifetime on earth by not seeking above all to display His glory. Says the apostle: "You are not your own; you were bought with a price. So *glorify* God in your body" (1 Corinthians 6:19–20). In other words, let your very being, body, mind, and spirit, radiate the moral excellence and beauty of His character.

This is to be our crystal clear reason for living. For has He not said: "bring my sons from afar and my daughters from the end of the earth, every one who is called by my name, *whom I created for my **glory**"* (Isaiah 43:6–7).

We were created to show forth His glory. Says the apostle Paul even more forcefully: "We... have been destined and appointed to live *for the praise of his **glory**"* (Ephesians 1:12).

That's what life is all about – living so that both we and others will praise Him for His character displayed in us. In fact, says St Paul, this extends to even the most mundane things. "Whether you eat or drink, or whatever you do, *do everything to the **glory** of God*" (1 Corinthians 10:31).

Likewise had Jesus said: "let your light shine before others, so that they may see your good works and *give **glory** to your Father* who is in heaven" (Matthew 5:16).

Don't waste your life – glorify God

The Westminster Larger Catechism of 1647 opens with this question and answer.

> *Q. What is the chief and highest end of man?*
> *A. Man's chief and highest end is to glorify God, and fully to enjoy him forever.*

In his penetrating little volume, *Don't Waste Your Life,* American pastor and theologian John Piper tells of his adventurous quest relating to this truth. Opening his book he says:

> *The Bible says: "You are not your own, for you have been bought with a price. So glorify God in your body" (1 Corinthians 6:20). I have written this book to help you taste these words as sweet instead of bitter or boring.*
>
> *If you are a Christian, you are not your own. Christ has bought you at the price of His own death. You now belong doubly to God: He made you, and He bought you. That means your life is not your own. It is God's. Therefore, the Bible says, "Glorify God in your body." God made you for this. He bought you for this. This is the meaning of your life.*
>
> *If you are not yet a Christian, that is what Jesus Christ offers: doubly belonging to God, and being able to do what you were made for. It was not always plain to me that pursuing God's glory would be virtually the same as pursuing my joy. Now I see that millions of people*

waste their lives because they think these paths are two
and not one.[3]

Piper goes on to share how it became clearer and clearer to him that if he wanted to come to the end of life and not say: "I've wasted it", then he would need to "press all the way in, and all the way up, to the ultimate purpose of God and join him in it." He saw that:

If my life was to have a single, all-satisfying, unifying
passion, it would have to be God's passion. God's
passion was the display of His own glory and the delight
of my heart.

All of my life since that discovery has been spent
experiencing and examining and explaining that truth.
It has become clearer and more certain and more
demanding with every year. It has become clearer that
God being glorified and God being enjoyed are not
separate categories. They relate to each other not like
fruit and animals, but like fruit and apples. Apples are one
kind of fruit. Enjoying God supremely is one way to glorify
Him. Enjoying God makes Him look supremely valuable.[4]

This is lovely. God's desire that His glory and character be manifested through me coincides with my desire to be happy in life and find joy, because as I exalt and glorify Him, and my character grows more like His, so He extends to me His blessings of happiness and joy.

Piper refers to Dan Fuller as his Professor of Hermeneutics at Fuller Seminary. He was also mine. In Dan's lecture entitled "The Unity of the Bible" he hoisted the flag of the glory of God and our delight in Him as the unifying flag over the whole Bible. He said:

God ordained a redemptive history, whose sequence
fully displays His glory so that, at the end, the greatest
possible number of people would have had the historical
antecedents necessary to engender (the most) fervent

*love for God... The one thing God is doing in all of
redemptive history is to show forth His mercy in such a
way that the greatest number of people will throughout
eternity delight in Him with all their heart, strength, and
mind...*[5]

God wants His glory (character), especially of mercy,
displayed in the history of His people. He wants their delight
to be discovered as they share in this venture.

Piper's testimony is that once he saw this he knew, at last,
what a wasted life would look like and how to avoid it. He
concludes: "God created me – and you – to live with a single,
all embracing, all transforming passion – namely, a passion
to glorify God by enjoying and displaying his supreme
excellence in all the spheres of life. Enjoying and displaying
are both crucial."[6]

This is a beautiful, penetrating, and rip-roaring insight
which can tear the covers off our stultified living as we
grasp that in creating us for His glory, "God is creating us
for our highest joy. He is most glorified in us when we are
most satisfied in Him." No wonder then that our Saviour
prayed not only "that they may have my joy [the joy of fully
obeying the Father] fulfilled in themselves" (John 17:13) but
that "those also, whom you have given me, may be with me
where I am, *to see my glory*, which you have given me because
you loved me before the foundation of the world" (verse 24).
Our joy and our beholding and imbibing His glory would be
interconnected, each being by-products of the other.

Glory leading to unity in the body

More than that, this all hooks up to unity in the body of Christ,
so central to this prayer, as our Lord declares:

*The glory that you have given me I have given them [in
other words, I have taken and am putting my radical
character into them] so that they may be one, as we are*

one, I in them and you in me, that they may become
completely one, so that the world may know that you
have sent me and have loved them even as you have
loved me.

John 17:22–23

Obviously, then, in the body of Christ in the church, if all believers in joy and delight are converging on the glory and divine character, imputed or gradually imparted to each believer, the outcome can only be a glorious unity, the likes of which the world has probably not yet seen – but if it did, if it saw God's people "perfectly one", then for sure the world would believe, the credibility gap would be gone, and the world would assuredly know that the Father had indeed sent the Son.

The glory to come

The glory our Saviour has given us, His people now, is of course a temporary and provisional gift which is in anticipation of the full glory we will receive, witness, and experience later on when each of us has shuffled off this mortal coil and when finally we enter and experience "a new heaven and a new earth" (Revelation 21:1) where "the *glory* of the Lord will be revealed, and all mankind together will see it" (Isaiah 40:5, NIV).

For the moment, however "we all, with unveiled face, beholding the *glory* of the Lord, are being changed into his likeness from *one degree of glory to another*; this comes from the Lord who is the Spirit" (2 Corinthians 3:18).

As for any hassles, trials, or tribulations, or "sufferings of this present time, [they] are not worthy to be compared with the *glory* which shall be revealed in us" (Romans 8:18, NKJV).

Yes, we repeat Peter Pan's classic conclusion, "To die will be an awfully big adventure!"[7]

After all, has not the Apostle also told us that, "No eye

has seen, nor ear has heard, no mind conceived what God has prepared for those who love him, but God has revealed it to us by his Spirit" (1 Corinthians 2:9–10, NIV)?

That is absolutely monumental. Completely awesome. And deserving of lifting up some deafening doxologies!

> *So we do not lose heart. Though our outer nature is wasting away, our inner nature is being renewed every day. For this slight momentary affliction is preparing for us **an eternal weight of glory** beyond all comparison, because we look not to the things that are seen but to the things that are unseen; for the things that are seen are transient, but the things that are unseen are eternal.*
>
> **2 Corinthians 4:16–18**

And we heed the apostolic exhortation:

> *If then you have been raised with Christ, seek the things that are above, where Christ is, seated at the right hand of God. Set your minds on things that are above, not on things that are on earth. For you have died, and your life is hid with Christ in God. When Christ who is our life appears, then you also **will appear with Him in glory**.*
>
> **Colossians 3:1–4**

*** ***

Our Lord has prayed for His church. In doing so He uttered the most extraordinary, earth-shattering, and universe-jolting words our planet and cosmos have ever heard. Next to these, all our own words become the babble of babes. Even so, though we march into unimaginable mysteries we can nevertheless glean the headlines of His passionate praying – those qualities we have sought to enumerate. He prayed that His church would be marked by truth, holiness, joy, protection, mission, prayerfulness, unity, love, and power – with glory as the crowning mark, most especially when all the other nine marks are dazzlingly displayed, so that the radiant character and moral beauty of God comes shining through.

Then most surely is He glorified, and His people likewise, and the world stands on tiptoe and reaches forward to be blessed.

*** ***

What remains now but to sing, as we will in glory: "Worthy is the Lamb who was slain, to receive power and wealth and wisdom and might and honour and glory and blessing!" (Revelation 5:12). And yes, as John sees in a vision (Revelation 5:13–14), we will assuredly hear, and most joyfully join "every creature in heaven and on earth and under the earth and in the sea, and all therein, [in] singing, 'To him who sits upon the throne, and to the Lamb be blessing and honour and glory and might forever and ever!'"

And we too will say, "Amen."

And with all the elders will fall down and worship (Revelation 5:14).

Postlude

This Postlude, curiously enough, is penned in the same time (January 2012) and place where the Preface to this volume closed, namely at "Dad's Writing Desk" in Gary and Debbie's Shambala Cottage on the Breede river in South Africa's Western Cape. The Preface, though started thirteen years ago, was lamentably only finally put in place yesterday evening! The book of course by then had been written. Now twenty-four hours later, same time, same place, I pen these lines of postscript! Time can play havoc with our attempts at chronology! But between Preface and Postlude we have, I believe, been flowing in a journey of discovery with time and eternity intersecting in every section of our reflections.

Perhaps then the continuity and flow of a river is a good analogy of linkage from start to finish, because a river meanders and flows into many places in its journey to the sea. But it does have a flow from source to mouth, until finally it is welcomed into the embrace of the ocean.

To be sure, this volume, like the High Priestly Prayer itself – and like the river – catches us in the flow of its embrace and takes us into surprising spiritual places we might not have expected to travel. And perhaps that is exactly what the Lord requires of His church in this prayer, to let itself flow and be led by the Spirit into unexpected truths, realities, and new commitments.

So how does an individual, or a congregation, or a denomination, or a para-church agency process the flow of where we have travelled? How does one absorb what the journey has thrown up, or the assorted ports of call where we periodically anchored?

My suggestion is this. First of all register deeply the ten marks in sequence as stops made from source to mouth. We put into ten harbours. What did we absorb in each? What did we find interesting? Challenging? Arresting? Convicting?

Was one port of call perhaps very familiar, maybe all too familiar? "Been there, done that, on top of that truth. So let's move on."

Or maybe several other ports of call were more challenging. Worth a revisit. Worth going back to work on and master.

If the latter is the case, do please linger with this volume and the prayer, and reflect further on what it has thrown up – how it has challenged you, or could challenge your church, fellowship, or organisation. Maybe even consider going back to study the whole volume all over again in a group, as per suggestions after the Preface at the front of the book.

In any event, the earnest prayer of my heart is that no one will just read this volume – and say – "Well, that's interesting", or whatever. Rather may this most awesome prayer ever uttered in all the history of the universe be allowed to touch us deeply, personally. Perhaps transformatively.

So please act on it. Please pray it home in your own heart, family, and church.

If you do, then heaven will surely record that in your case at least, our Lord did not pray in vain.

More than that, Earth will feel the difference.

God bless you.

Endnotes

CHAPTER 1

1. J. C. Ryle, *Expository Thoughts on the Gospels: St John*, Vol. 3, James Clarke & Co, 1969, p. 192.

2. As quoted in Walter E. Patt, Jr., *Lord, Teach Us To Pray*, Xulon Press, 2003, p. 92.

3. As quoted in A. W. Pink, *Studies in the Scriptures 1926–1927*, Vol. 3, Layafette, IN: Sovereign Grace Publishers, p. 194.

4. John Brown, *An Exposition of Our Lord's Intercessory Prayer*, Edinburgh: William Oliphant and Co., 1866, p. 1.

5. William Temple, *Readings in St. John's Gospel*, London: Macmillan & Co., 1947, p. 307.

6. John Stott, *The Contemporary Christian*, Leicester: InterVarsity Press, 1992, p. 259.

7. P. T. Forsyth, *The Work of Christ*, London: Hodder & Stoughton, 1910, p. 5.

8. Quoted in J. R. H. Moorman, *A History of the Church in England*, London: A & C Black, 1953, pp. 329, 331.

9. Philip Yancey, *Disappointment with God*, Grand Rapids, MI: Zondervan, 1998, p. 161.

10. Dorothy Sayers, quoted in Yancey, *Disappointment with God*, p. 162.

11. John Pollock, *The Cambridge Seven*, Christian Focus Publications, Scotland, reprint ed., 2009.

CHAPTER 2

1. John Stott, I Believe in Preaching, London: Hodder & Stoughton, 1982, pp.228–29

2. Quoted in Thomas M'Crie, *Life of John Knox*, London: Whittaker & Co., 1838, p. 345.

3. William Barclay, *The Gospel of John*, Vol. 2, revised edition, Edinburgh, The Saint Andrew Press, Edinburgh, 1968, p. 214.

4. David Wells, *God in the Wasteland: The Reality of Truth in a World of Fading*

Dreams, Grand Rapids, MI: Eerdmans and Leicester: InterVarsity Press, 1994, p. 39.

5. William Barclay, *The Gospel of John*, Vol. 2, Edinburgh: The Saint Andrew Press, 1968, p. 253.

CHAPTER 4

1. James W. Sire, *The Universe Next Door*, Downers Grove: Il, InterVarsity Press, 1988, p. 17.

2. Sire, *The Universe Next Door*, p. 17.

3. Jean Paul Sartre, quoted in Sire, *The Universe Next Door*, p. 108.

4. William Shakespeare, *Macbeth*, London: Macmillan & Co., 1871, Act V, Scene V, p. 68

5. Carl Sagan, quoted in Sire, *The Universe Next Door*, p. 63.

6. Richard Dawkins, *The Selfish Gene*, Oxford: OUP, 1976, Preface.

7. As quoted in Eleonore Stump and Michael J. Murray, *Philosophy of Religion: The Big Questions*, Oxford: Blackwell Publishing Ltd., 1999, p. 113.

8. David J. Bosch, *Believing in the Future: Toward a Missiology of Western Culture*, Colorado Springs, CO: Trinity Press International, 1995, p. 49.

9. Sire, *The Universe Next Door*, p. 1.

10. Sire, *The Universe Next Door*, p. 19.

11. John MacArthur, *The Glory of Heaven: The Truth about Heaven, Angels and Eternal Life*, Wheaton, IL: Crossway Books, 1996, p. 60.

12. Joni Eareckson Tada, *Heaven: Your Real Home*, Grand Rapids, MI: Zondervan, 1996, p. 67.

13. Eareckson Tada, *Heaven*, p. 53.

14. Christopher J. H. Wright, *The God I Don't Understand*, Grand Rapids, MI: Zondervan, 2008, p. 195.

15. Wright, *The God I Don't Understand*, p. 194.

16. Wright, *The God I Don't Understand*, p. 194.

17. Randy Alcorn, *Heaven*, Vereeniging: Christian Art Distributors, C.C. Edition, 2005, p. 101.

18. Dallas Willard, *The Divine Conspiracy: Rediscovering Our Hidden Life in God*, San Francisco, CA: HarperSanFrancisco, 1998, p. 431.

19. C. S. Lewis, *Letters to Malcolm: Chiefly on Prayer*, New York, NY: Harcourt Brace Jovanovich, 1963, p. 84.

20. A. A. Hodges, *Evangelical Theology: A Course of Popular Lectures*, Edinburgh: Banner of Truth, 1976, pp. 399–402.

21. William Shakespeare, *Hamlet*, Horace Howard Furness (ed.), London: J. B. Lippincott Company, 1877, Act III, Scene I, p. 210.

22. As said by Peter Pan in J. M. Barrie, *Peter Pan, and Other Plays*, New York, NY: AMS Press, 1975, p. 94.

23. See http://fatherhood.org/page.aspx?pid=401; accessed June 2012.

CHAPTER 5

1. Michael Green, *Who is this Jesus?*, Eastbourne: Kingsway Publications, 1992, p. 78.

2. C. S. Lewis, *Mere Christianity*, New York, NY: The MacMillan Company, 1977, p. 55–56.

3. Marcus Rainsford, *Our Lord Prays for His Own: Thoughts on John 17*, Grand Rapids, MI: Kregel Classics, 1985, p. 36.

4. G. K. Chesterton, *The Everlasting Man*, Radford, VA: Wilder Publications LLC, 2008, p. 175.

5. James Montgomery Boice, *The Gospel of John: The Coming of the Light*, Vol. 1, Ada, MI: Baker Books, 1999, p. 1253.

6. Sagan, quoted in Sire, *The Universe Next Door*, p. 63.

7. William Shakespeare, *Macbeth*, London: Macmillan & Co., 1871, Act V, Scene V, p. 68

CHAPTER 6

1. C. S. Lewis, quoted in Jerry L. Walls and Joseph R. Dongell, *Why I Am Not a Calvinist*, Downers Grove, IL: InterVarsity Press, 2004, p. 195.

2. Edward John Carnell, *An Introduction to Christian Apologetics: A Philosophic Defense of the Trinitarian-Theistic Faith*, Grand Rapids, MI: Eerdmans, 1966, p. 46.

3. C. S. Lewis, *The Screwtape Letters*, London: Fontana Books, 1955, p. 11.

4. Carnell, *An Introduction to Christian Apologetics*, p. 46.

5. Dallas Willard, "Truth in the Fire: C. S. Lewis and Pursuit of Truth Today", presented for the C. S. Lewis Centennial, Oxford University, 1998. See http://www.dwillard.org/articles/artview.asp?artID=68

6. C. S. Lewis, *Mere Christianity*, p. 25.

7. Willard, "Truth in the Fire".

8. Willard, "Truth in the Fire".

9. Willard, "Truth in the Fire".

10. Scott R. Burson and Jerry L. Walls, *C. S. Lewis and Francis Schaeffer: Lessons for a New Century from the Most Influential Apologists of Our Time*, Downers Grove, IL: InterVarsity Press, 1998, p. 228.

11. C. S. Lewis quoted by Roger Lancelyn Green and Walter Hooper, *C. S. Lewis: A Biography*, San Diego, CA: Harcourt, Brace, Jovanovich, 1974, p. 282.

12. C. S. Lewis, *Mere Christianity*, p. 39.

13. Francis Schaeffer, "The Practice of Truth" in *One Race, One Gospel, One Task*, World Congress on Evangelism, Berlin, 1966, Official Reference Volumes, Vol. 2, Carl F. H. Henry and W. Stanley Mooneyham (eds.), Minneapolis, MN: World Wide Publications, 1967, p. 453.

14. Schaeffer, "The Practice of Truth", p. 455.

15. David F. Wells, *The Courage to be Protestant: Truth-lovers, Marketers, and Emergents in the Postmodern World*, Grand Rapids, MI: Eerdmans, 2008, p. 80.

16. George Ernest Wright, "God Who Acts: Biblical Theology as Recital", in *Studies in Biblical Theology*, Vol. 8, London: SCM Press, 1962 (reprint), p. 126.

17. As quoted in Michael Cassidy, *Christianity for the Open-Minded*, Downers Grove, IL: InterVarsity Press, 1978, p. 18.

18. John Macquarrie, *Principles of Christian Theology*, London: SCM Press, revised edition, 2003, p. 25.

19. Brooke Foss Wescott, *Lectures on the Apostles' Creed*, New Jersey: Gorgias Press LLC, 2006, p. 26.

20. Kathryn Lindskoog *C. S. Lewis: Mere Christian*, Wheaton, IL: Harold Shaw Publishers, 1987, p. 109.

21. Pierre Marcel, "Our Lord's Use of Scripture", in *Revelation and the Bible*, Carl F. H. Henry (ed.), Grand Rapids, MI: Baker Book House, 1958, p. 133.

22. Geoffrey W. Bromiley, "The Church Doctrine of Inspiration" in *Revelation and the Bible: Contemporary Evangelical Thought*, Carl F. H. Henry, Grand Rapids, MI: Baker Book House, 1958, p. 207.

23. Bromiley, "The Church Doctrine of Inspiration", p. 207.

24. Bromiley, "The Church Doctrine of Inspiration", p. 207.

25. Alister McGrath, *A Passion for Truth*, Leicester: Apollos, 1996, p. 178.

CHAPTER 7

1. Eugene Peterson, *In a Word*, Carlisle: Piquant Editions, 2003, www.piquanteditions.com, p. 14.

2. Malcolm Muggeridge, *Something Beautiful for God*: *Mother Teresa of Calcutta*, Oxford: Lion Hudson, 2008, p. 148.

3. Muggeridge, *Something Beautiful for God*, p. 19.

4. John Pollock, *Billy Graham: Evangelist to the World*, San Francisco: Harper and Row, 1979, p. 148.

5. Pollock, *Billy Graham*, p. 148.

6. Pollock, *Billy Graham*, p. 154.

7. Pollock, *Billy Graham*, p. 156.

8. Pollock, *Billy Graham*, pp. 156–57.

9. Timothy Dudley-Smith, *John Stott: A Global Ministry*, Leicester: InterVarsity Press, 2001, p. 451.

10. Dudley-Smith, *John Stott*, p. 452.

11. Dudley-Smith, *John Stott*, p. 452.

12. Dudley-Smith, *John Stott*, p. 453.

13. C. René Padilla, "Evangelism and the World", delivered at the First International Congress on World Evangelism, Lausanne, 1974, and published in *Let the Earth Hear His Voice*, ed. J. D. Douglas, Minneapolis, MN: World Wide Publications, 1975, p. 130.

14. John Stott, *The Contemporary Christian*, Leicester: InterVarsity Press, 1992, pp. 262–63.

15. Dallas Willard, *The Divine Conspiracy*, San Francisco, CA: HarperSanFrancsico, 1998, pp. 354–55.

CHAPTER 8

1. G. K. Chesterton quoted in David Jeremiah, *Sanctuary: Finding Moments of Refuge in the Presence of God*, Nashville, TN: Thomas Nelson, 2002, p. 237.

2. C. S. Lewis, *Letters to Malcolm: Chiefly on Prayer*, New York, NY: Houghton Mifflin Harcourt, 2002, p. 93.

3. C. S. Lewis, *Till We Have Faces*, quoted in Kath Filmer, *Scepticism and Hope in the Twentieth Century Fantasy Literature*, Bowling Green, OH: Bowling Green State University Press, 1992, p. 41.

4. C. S. Lewis, *Surprised by Joy*, London: Geoffrey Bles, 1955, p. 217.

5. Lewis, *Surprised by Joy*, p. 208.

6. Lewis, *Surprised by Joy*, pp. 223–24.

7. Quoted in Jeremiah, *Sanctuary*, p. 237.

8. D. A. Carson, *The Farewell Discourse and Final Prayer of Jesus*, Grand Rapids, MI: Baker Book House, 1992, p, 100.

9. Carson, *The Farewell Discourse and Final Prayer of Jesus*, p. 100.

10. James Montgomery Boice, *The Gospel of John: The Coming of the Light*, Vol. 1, Ada, MI: Baker Books, 1999, p. 398.

11. Quoted in Joan Oviatt and Joy Robinson, *Of Angels, Dreams and Other Fine Things: Inspirational Gems from Early LDS Publications and Other Unpublished Sources*, Horizon Publishers & Distributers, Inc., 2003, p. 74.

12. Extract from "The Glory of the Garden", in *The Collected Poems of Rudyard Kipling*, The Wordsworth Poetry Library, 1994, p. 762.

13. C. S. Lewis, *The Screwtape Letters*, p. 58.

14. As quoted in George Sayer, *Jack: A life of C. S. Lewis*, Wheaton, IL: Crossway Books, 1994, p. 123.

15. Humphrey Carpenter, *The Inklings*, New York, NY: Ballantine Books, 1978, p. 235.

16. Carpenter, *The Inklings*, p. 252.

17. Lewis, *The Screwtape Letters*, p. 112.

18. Sayer, *Jack*, p. 275.

19. C. S. Lewis, *Prince Caspian: The Return to Narnia*, London: Puffin Books, 1962, p. 165.

20. Sayer, *Jack*, p. 321.

CHAPTER 9

1. C. S. Lewis, *The Screwtape Letters*, New York, NY: HarperCollins Sixtieth Anniversary Edition, 2001, p. ix.

2. Eugene Peterson, *In a Word*, Carlisle: Piquant Editions, 2003, www.piquanteditions.com, p. 22.

3. William Temple, *Readings in St John's Gospel*, New York, NY: The MacMillan Company, 1945, p. 9.

4. William Barclay, *The Gospel of St John*, Vol. 2, Edinburgh: The Saint Andrew Press, 1968, p. 253.

5. Michael Green, *I Believe in Satan's Downfall*, London: Hodder and Stoughton, London, 1981, p. 9.

6. Green, *I Believe in Satan's Downfall*, p. 15.

7. Green, *I Believe in Satan's Downfall*, p. 23.

8. Lewis, *The Screwtape Letters*, p. 9.

9. Green, *I Believe in Satan's Downfall*, p. 26.

CHAPTER 10

1. Christopher J. H. Wright, *The Mission of God's People: A Biblical Theology of the Church's Mission*, Grand Rapids, MI: Zondervan, 2010, p. 23.

2. Quoted in Gordon S. Jackson, *Quotes for the Journey: Wisdom for the Way*, Colorado Springs, CO: NavPress, 2000, p 37.

CHAPTER 11

1. Michael Cassidy, *In Deep In India: A Journal of a Journey of Research and Discovery*, Pietermaritzburg: African Enterprise, 2009, p. 74.

2. Readers wanting to know more about the Indian model could write to us at African Enterprise at PO Box 13140, Cascades, 3202, or email mcassidy@pobox.com to secure a copy of my little book *In Deep In India*.

3. As quoted in Robert Vaughan and B. J. Holdsworth, *The Life and Opinions of John de Wycliffe*, Vol. 2, London: Hatchard & Son, 1828, p. 14.

4. Alexander Whyte quoted in John Stott, *I Believe in Preaching*, London: Hodder and Stoughton, 1982, p. 37.

5. Drawn from Vatican 2 Council on the Decree on the Ministry and Life of Priests, paragraph 4, pp. 539–40.

6. Richard A. Swenson, *The Overload Syndrome: Learning to Live Within Your Limits*, Colorado Springs, CO: NavPress, 1998, p. 15.

7. Swenson., *The Overload Syndrome*, pp. 13–15.

8. Swenson., *The Overload Syndrome*, pp. 180–81.

9. Quote from Pierre Marcel "Our Lord's Use of Scripture", in *Revelation and the Bible*, Carl F. H. Henry (ed.), Grand Rapids, MI: Baker Book House, 1958, p. 239.

CHAPTER 12

1. Robert E. Coleman, *The Mind of the Master*, Old Tappan, NJ: F. H. Revell, Co., 1977, pp. 39–40.

2. Dallas Willard, *The Divine Conspiracy*, San Francisco, CA, HarperSanFrancisco, 1998, p. 269.

3. Willard, *The Divine Conspiracy*, p. 269.

4. Willard, *The Divine Conspiracy*, p. 269.

5. Willard, *The Divine Conspiracy*, p. 268.

6. Willard, *The Divine Conspiracy*, p. 254.

7. Willard, *The Divine Conspiracy*, p. 256–57.

8. E. Stanley Jones, *The Unshakable Kingdom and the Unchanging Person*, McNett Press, 1995, p. 34.

9. Richard Foster, *Prayer: Find the Heart's True Home*, London: Hodder and Stoughton, 1992, p. 181.

10. Foster, *Prayer*, p. 182.

11. Foster, *Prayer*, p. 184.

12. Quoted in Alexander Whyte, *Lord, Teach Us to Pray: Sermons on Prayer*, New York, NY: Harper & Brothers, p. 257.

13. Willard, *The Divine Conspiracy*, p. 265.

14. I have produced a little booklet with my own testimony and procedures for my daily personal prayer life. If you are interested do write to me at: mcassidy@po.box.com or at African Enterprise, Box 13140, Cascades, Pietermaritzburg, 3202, KwaZulu-Natal, South Africa.

15. Coleman, *The Mind of the Master*, p. 40.

CHAPTER 13

1. Marcus Rainsford, *Our Lord Prays for His Own: Thoughts on John 17*, Grand Rapids, MI: Kregel Classics, 1978, p. 385.

2. Michael Ramsay made the same point during the epilogue to his address on "The Church, its Scandal and Glory" during his mission in Oxford University in February 1960. His addresses were published as *Introducing the Christian Faith*, London: SCM, 1970, revised edition, p 76.

3. John Stott, *The Contemporary Christian*, Leicester: InterVarsity Press, 1992, p. 268.

4. Stott, *The Contemporary Christian*, pp. 268–69.

5. Stott, *The Contemporary Christian*, p. 266.

6. William Temple, *Readings in St John's Gospel*, London: Macmillian & Co., 1947, p. 327.

7. Carson, *The Farewell Discourse and Final Prayer of Jesus*, pp. 198–99.

8. Carson, *The Farewell Discourse and Final Prayer of Jesus*, p. 199.

CHAPTER 14

1. Helmut Thielicke, *A Little Exercise for Young Theologians*, Grand Rapids, MI; Eerdmans, 1962, p. xii.

2. John Wesley, *The Works of the Rev John* Wesley, Vol. II, 4th ed., London, John Mason, 1841, p. 367.

3. Hans Küng, *The Church*, New York, NY: Image Books, 1967, p. 13. See also David Watson: *I Believe in the Church*, London: Hodder & Stoughton, 1978, p. 334.

4. Carson, *The Farewell Discourse and Final Prayer of Jesus*, p. 203.

5. Carson, *The Farewell Discourse and Final Prayer of Jesus*, p. 204.

6. Chris Sugden, "'Time Out' on Divisions", Evangelicals Now website, http://www.e-n.org.uk/p-4340-'Time-out-on-divisions.htm, 16 January 2012.

7. Watson, *I Believe in the Church*, p. 333.

8. Karl Barth, *Church Dogmatics*, Volume IV/1, Edinburgh: T & T Clark, 1961, pp. 653–54.

9. Note: Augustine, *City of God, passim: On Baptism*, III. xix. 26 (MPL 43. 152; tr. NPNF IV. 445); Wycliffe, *De ecclesia*, Wycliffe Society edition, p. 37; "*Universitas fidelium praedestinatorum*"; so also Hus, *De ecclesia* 1, ed. S.H. Thomson, pp. 2f., 8; tr. D.S. Schaff, *The Church by John Hus*, pp. 3, 6; J. T. McNeill, "Some Emphases in Wyclif's Teaching", *Journal of Religion* VII (1927), 452 IT.; *Unitive Protestantism*, pp. 25 f. The idea is also familiar to such conciliarists as Dietrich of Niem (see LCC XIV. 150 f.). Luther employs similar language frequently, e.g., in his *Preface to Revelation* (*Sämmtliche Schriften XIV [St. Louis, 1898]; tr.* Works of Martin Luther VI. 488). Other citations from Luther and Zwingli are found in OS V. 12, note 1. Cf. J. Courvoisier, *La notion d'Eglise chez Bucer*, pp. 68 ff.; Wendel, *Calvin*, pp. 225 f.; H. Strohl, *La Pensée de Réforme*, pp. 174–181; McNeill, *Unitive Protestantism*, pp. 39–45; Augsburg Confession, articles vii, viii.

10. John Wesley, *Works*, Vol. VIII, 4th ed., London: John Mason, 1841, p. 309.

11. Wesley, *Works*, Vol. XIII, p. 291.

12. John Stott, *The Living Church: Convictions of a Lifelong Pastor*, Nottingham: InterVarsity Press, 2007, p. 174.

13. John Stott, *The Living Church*, p. 174.

14. S. F. Allison and Henry Chadwick, *The Fullness of Christ: The Church's Growth into Catholicity, Being a Report Presented to the His Grace the Archbishop of Canterbury*, London: SPCK, 1960, pp. 7–8.

15. Ronald Knox quoted in Caroline Chartres, *Why I Am Still an Anglican: Essays and Conversations*, London: Continuum, 2006, p. 14.

16. Francis Schaeffer, *Genesis in Space and Time: The Flow of Biblical History*, Downers Grove, IL: InterVarsity Press, 1972, p. 76. See also Schaeffer on "true truth" in *Escape from Reason*, London: InterVarsity Fellowship, 1968, p. 21 and *The God Who is There*, London: Hodder & Stoughton, 1968, p. 151.

17. Francis Schaeffer, "Form and Freedom in the Church", a paper delivered in the first Lausanne Congress on World Evangelization, and recorded in *Let the Earth Hear His* Voice, Minneapolis, MN: World Wide Publications, p. 365.

CHAPTER 15

1. Francis Schaeffer, *The Mark of the Christian*, Downers Grove, IL: InterVarsity Press, 2006, p. 29.

2. Eugene Peterson, *In a Word*, Carlisle: Piquant Editions, 2003, www.piquanteditions.com, p. 9.

3. First published in *Redemption Hymns*, Text: Charles Wesley, 1747; music: John Zundel, 1870.

4. George Newton, *An Exposition of John 17*, Edinburgh: Banner of Truth Trust, 1995, p. 382.

5. Henry Drummond, *The Greatest Thing in the World: Experience the Enduring Power of Love*, Grand Rapids, MI: Revell, 2011, p. 47.

6. Michael Cassidy, *The Politics of Love*, London: Hodder & Stoughton, 1989, p. 86.

7. This, and variants of it, have been widely circulated as a Quaker saying since at least 1869, and attributed to Stephen Grellet since at least 1893. W. Gurney Benham in *Benham's Book of Quotations, Proverbs and Household Works* (1907) states that though sometimes attributed to others, "there seems to be some authority in favour of Stephen Grellet being the author, but the passage does not appear in any of his printed works".

8. Cassidy, *The Politics of Love*, 1989, pp. 88–89.

9. Joseph Lamb quoted in *The Volta Review*, Vol. 20, Volta Bureau (U.S.), Volta Speech Association for the Deaf, Alexander Graham Bell Association for the Deaf, 1918.

10. Cassidy, *The Politics of Love*,1989, p. 89.

11. Drummond, *The Greatest Thing in the World*, p. 26.

12. Francis of Assisi quoted in Tony Castle, *The Hodder Book of Christian Quotations*, London: Hodder & Stoughton, 1982, p. 50.

13. William Barclay, *The Gospel of Matthew*, Vol. I, Edinburgh: The Saint Andrew Press, 1956, p. 91.

14. Barclay, *The Gospel of Matthew*, p. 92.

15. Cassidy, *The Politics of Love*, pp. 92–93.

16. Quoted in Hannah Ward and Jennifer Wild (eds.), *The Lion Christian Quotation Collection*, Oxford: Lion, 1999 p. 272.

CHAPTER 16

1. John Stott, quoted in Roger Thiessen, *Empowered for Ministry and Mission: Studies in the Book of Acts (Part 1)*, Winnipeg, MB and Hillsboro KS: Kindred Productions, 2001, p. 52.

2. Eugene Peterson, *In a Word*, Carlisle: Piquant Editions, 2003, www.piquanteditions.com, pp. 25 and 49.

3. J. I. Packer, *Keep in Step with the Spirit*, Leicester: InterVarsity Press, 1984, p. 64.

4. Packer, *Keep in Step with the Spirit*, p. 66.

5. Quoted in Martin H. Manser (ed.), *The Westminster Collection of Christian Quotations*, Martin H. Manser, Louiseville, KY: Westminster John Knox Press, 2001, p. 171.

6. J. I. Packer, *Evangelism and the Sovereignty of God*, Chicago, IL: InterVarsity Press, 1961, pp. 85–86.

7. Quoted in Michael Cassidy, *Bursting the Wineskins*, London: Hodder and Stoughton, 1983, p. 20.

8. Michael Cassidy, *Bursting the Wineskins*, London: Hodder and Stoughton, 1983, p. 269.

9. Michael Green, *I Believe in the Holy Spirit*, London: Hodder and Stoughton, London, 1975, p. 120.

10. Cassidy, *Bursting the Wineskins*, p, 122.

11. Cassidy, *Bursting the Wineskins*, pp. 276–77.

12. Stott, quoted in Thiessen, *Empowered for Ministry and Mission*, p. 52.

CHAPTER 17

1. Everett F. Harrison,"Glory", in *Baker's Dictionary of Theology*, (Everett Harrison, Geoffrey Bromiley, Carl F. H. Henry eds.), Grand Rapids, MI: Baker Book House, 1960, p. 236.

2. Harrison, "Glory", pp. 236–37.

3. Charles Finney, "The Revelation of God's Glory", *The Oberlin Evangelist*, 20 December 1843, reprinted in *The Gospel Truth*, copyright © 1999, 2000, Gospel Truth Ministries, www.gospeltruth.net/1843OE/431220_gods_glory.htm, 4/10/04, p. 3.

4. Geoffrey Bingham, *All Cry Glory*, Sydney: New Creation Publications Inc., 1990, p. 16.

5. John Piper, quoted in Philip Graham Ryken, *King Solomon: The Temptations of Money, Sex and Power*, Wheaton, IL: Crossway, 2011, p. 225.

CHAPTER 18

1. Lesslie Newbigin, *The Light Has Come: An Exposition of the Fourth Gospel*, Grand Rapids, MI: Eerdmans, and Edinburgh: The Handsel Press Ltd.,1982, p. 227.

2. Thomas Henry Louis Parker, David W. Torrance (eds.), *Calvin's New Testament Commentaries: The Gospel According to St John 11–21 and the First Epistle of John*, Grand Rapids, MI: Eerdmans, 1994, p. 68.

3. John Piper, *Don't Waste Your Life*, Wheaton, IL: Crossways Books, 2007, pp. 9–10.

4. Piper, *Don't Waste Your Life*, p. 28.

5. Daniel P. Fuller, *The Unity of the Bible: Unfolding God's Plan for Humanity*, Grand Rapids, MI: Zondervan, 1992, pp. 453–54.

6. Piper, *Don't Waste Your Life*, p. 31.

7. Peter Pan in J. M. Barrie, *Peter Pan and Other Plays*, New York, NY: AMS Press, 1975, p. 94.

Index

Acknowledgments

Unless otherwise stated, Scripture quotations are taken from either The Revised Standard Version of the Bible copyright © 1346, 1952 and 1971 by the Division of Christian Education of the National Council of Churches in the USA or The New Revised Standard Version of the Bible copyright © 1989 by the Division of Christian Education of the National Council of Churches in the USA. Used by permission.All Rights Reserved.

Scripture quotations marked ESV are from The Holy Bible, English Standard Version® (ESV®) copyright © 2001 by Crossway, a publishing ministry of Good News Publishers. All rights reserved. Scripture quotations marked GNB are from the Good News Bible published by the Bible Societies and HarperCollins Publishers, © American Bible Society 1994, used with permission. Scripture quotations marked J. B. Phillips reprinted from The New Testament in Modern English, Revised Edition, translated by J.B. Phillips. Published by HarperCollins Publishers Ltd. Scripture excerpts marked NAB are taken from the New American Bible with Revised New Testament, copyright © 1986, 1970 Confraternity of Christian Doctrine, Washington, D.C. and are used by permission of the copyright owner. All rights reserved. No part of the New American Bible may be reproduced in any form without permission in writing from the copyright owner. Scripture quotations marked NCV taken from the New Century Version. Copyright © by Thomas Nelson, Inc. Used by permission. All rights reserved. Scripture quotations marked NIV taken from the Holy Bible, New International Version Anglicised. Copyright © 1979, 1984, 2011 Biblica, formerly International Bible Society. Used by permission of Hodder & Stoughton Ltd, an Hachette UK company. All rights reserved. 'NIV' is a registered trademark of Biblica. UK trademark number 1448790. Extracts marked KJV are from The Authorized (King James) Version. Rights in the Authorized Version are vested in the Crown. Reproduced by permission of the Crown's patentee, Cambridge University Press. Scripture quotations marked NKJV taken from the New King James Version. Copyright © 1982 by Thomas Nelson, Inc. Used by permission. All right reserved. Scripture quotations marked The Message taken from The Message. Copyright © by Eugene H. Peterson 1993, 1994, 1995, 1996, 2000, 2001, 2002. Used by permission of NavPress Publishing Group.

Any italicisation of text within Scripture quotations is the author's own added emphasis.

Excerpts on pages 85 and 145 from *Letters to Malcolm: Chiefly on Prayer* by C. S. Lewis. Copyright © 1963, 1964, 1973 C. S. Lewis Pte Ltd. Reprinted by permission of The C. S. Lewis Company and Houghton Mifflin Harcourt Publishing Company. All rights reserved.

Extracts on pages 91, 108–109, 113 from *Mere Christianity* by C. S. Lewis copyright © C. S. Lewis Pte. Ltd. 1942, 1943, 1944, 1952. Extract reprinted by permission.

Extracts on pages 105, 163, 166, 168, 178 from *The Screwtape Letters* by C. S. Lewis copyright © C. S. Lewis Pte. Ltd. 1942. Extract reprinted by permission.

Extracts on pages 146 and 147 from *Surprised by Joy* by C. S. Lewis copyright © C. S. Lewis Pte. Ltd. 1955. Extract reprinted by permission.

Extract on page 166 from *Prince Caspian* by C. S. Lewis copyright © C. S. Lewis Pte. Ltd. 1951. Extract reprinted by permission.

Images

Page 60, Crosses, walls, vine, bread and wine – Lion Hudson; Pool of Gihon – iStockphoto/Hulton Archive; Jesus in Gethsemane – iStockphoto/Ivan Burmistrov; Bethany – iStockphoto/221A; Jesus sentenced by Pilate – iStockphoto/Duncan Walker; Jesus before Caiaphas – iStockphoto/ZU_09

Page 72 fishbowl – iStockphoto/mehmet torlak (adapted)